ROYAL ROOTS – REPUBLICA

The Survival of the Off

Book-plate bearing the arms of Thomas Pelham Hood. The motto 'Nun
quam despero' (I never despair). *GO, Wilkinson Book-plate Collection.*

Royal Roots – Republican Inheritance
The Survival of the Office of Arms

Susan Hood

The Woodfield Press
in association with
National Library of Ireland

This book was typeset by
Red Barn Publishing, Skeagh, Co. Cork for
THE WOODFIELD PRESS
17 Jamestown Square, Dublin 8
www.woodfield-press.com
e-mail: terri.mcdonnell@ireland.com

Publishing Editor
Helen Harnett

House Editor
Elina Talvitie

© The Woodfield Press and Susan Hood 2002

A catalogue record for this title
is available from the British Library.

ISBN 0-9534293-3-4

Printed in Ireland
by ColourBooks, Dublin

CONTENTS

ACKNOWLEDGMENTS

I wish to acknowledge the following for allowing me to use collections of manuscripts in their custody: the Council of the Trustees of the National Library of Ireland; the Director of the National Archives; the Deputy Keeper of the Public Records, Kew; the College of Arms, London; the Office of Public Works, Dublin; the Deputy Keeper of the Public Records of Northern Ireland; the Representative Church Body Library, Dublin; the Archives Department, University College Dublin; the Irish Architectural Archive; Davison and Associates; Photo European Parliament; *The Irish Times*, and Randal Sadleir, London.

I am greatly indebted to the Chief Herald of Ireland, Brendan O Donoghue, for encouraging me to undertake this work, making available the resources of the GO and NLI, providing invaluable guidance and advice throughout the research, and making useful comments about early drafts. I am also indebted to the staff of the Genealogical Office, Dublin, especially Fergus Gillespie, Deputy Chief Herald of Ireland, who has encouraged me since my student days at the GO. With his co-operation, I was given access to the uncatalogued material in the GO relating to the administration of the Office of Arms, which will not generally be available to readers until cataloguing is completed. I am also indebted to the other staff of the GO, Katy Lumsden, Herald Painter, Della Murphy, Assistant Keeper and Archivist, and Micheál Ó Comáin, Consultant Herald, who have answered endless questions, and given me much assistance throughout.

I am especially grateful to Randal Sadleir, whose vivid memories and enthusiasm were inspiring. The papers of his father, the late Thomas Ulick Sadleir, last Deputy Ulster King of Arms, 1921–43, to which he provided access, were extensively used for research. My special thanks also to Mr Donal Begley, former Chief Herald of Ireland, 1982–95, who gave me a job at the GO as a student during the 1980s, encouraged my interest in the Office, and supplied much useful research material.

My publisher, Terri McDonnell of The Woodfield Press, deserves special thanks for her encouraging advice throughout, and ensuring that I made the final deadline. I am especially grateful for the additional work of my friend, Richard Griffiths, who compiled both the bibliography and the index in record time; of the photographer, David Monahan, who produced outstanding illustrations; and of the cartographer, Sarah Gearty, for the plan of Dublin Castle, all of which have greatly enhanced the book. I am particularly indebted to my friends Siobhán Donovan, Michael Finlay, Sue Hemmens, Andrew Johnstone, Suzanne McLaughlin, Anthea Seager, Elaine White-house, and my Dad, whose excellent comments and criticisms were invaluable in the final stages. Particular thanks also to Bernie Daly for title ideas.

I am indebted to the former researchers, staff, and others connected with the GO, for their willingness to be interviewed, supply information and advice. The collective memory of Eilish Ellis, Inez Fletcher, Steven ffeary-Smyrl, Rosemary ffolliott, Paul Gorry, John Grenham, Máire Mac Conghail, Brian McKenna, Kay Maher, Mary Nowlan, Eileen O'Byrne, Colette O'Flaherty, James O'Shea, and Nora O'Shea, forms the basis of the last chapters of the book. I am also particularly grateful to Myra Maguire, heraldic artist, for her recollections, and access to her scrapbook; and to the family of the late Gerard Slevin, Chief Herald of Ireland, 1954–81, for access to his research papers and press cuttings.

All of the staff of the National Library of Ireland have been of great support, and I would like to thank them collectively for their courteous assistance. Special thanks to Bernard Devaney, for his patient help in organising photographs; and also John Farrell, Joanna Finegan, Dr Noel Kissane, Gerard Long, Gerard Lyne, Sandra McDermott, Gráinne MacLochlainn, Dónall Ó Lunaigh, Sara Smyth and the staff at the National Photographic Archive, for additional assistance.

Archival colleagues have provided invaluable information, and their help is much appreciated, especially the late Dr Philomena Connolly who with characteristic generosity made helpful comments about early drafts, Aideen Ireland, who made available a large volume of material relating to the Office, and Tom Quinlan, all of the National Archives; Robert Yorke, College of Arms; Seamus Helferty and Kate Manning, Archives Department, University College Dublin; Colum O'Riordan, Irish Architectural Archive; John Duffy, Garda Síochána Archives; Dr Michael Goodhall, Public Record Office of Northern Ireland; and the staff of the Royal Irish Academy.

I am grateful to many people who have given me expert advice, and access to material relating to the Office of Arms in their possession, in particular Klaus Unger and his staff at the Office of Public Works, especially Susan Seager; Alf MacLochlainn, former Director of the National Library; Angela O'Donoghue, Dog House Productions; Dr Freddie O'Dwyer, Dúchas; Letitia Pollard, editor, *Ireland of the Welcomes*; and Thomas Woodcock, Norroy and Ulster King of Arms, College of Arms. Thanks also to Gerry Browner, Dúchas; Gerard Crotty, Kerry Houston and the staff of St Patrick's Cathedral, Dublin; Dr Michael Kennedy, Dr Deirdre McMahon, Dáithí Ó Corráin, Dr John M. Regan, Tom Ryan RHA, Jonathan Shackleton and Robert Tobin for additional advice. The work of the Revd Dr Peter Galloway on the Order of St Patrick, with which the Office of Arms was closely linked, has been referred to extensively in this work, and I am grateful also for his advice and assistance.

I appreciate the help of Cecil R. Humphery-Smith, England, Roger Harmignies, Belgium, and Michael Popoff, France, all of the Académie International D'Héraldique, and Dr Whitney Smith, of the Flag Research Center, USA, in tracing information about the design of the European Parliament flag by Gerard Slevin. Thanks also to Sarah Sheil, European Parliament, Dublin, for additional background information about the flag; and Kathlyn O'Brien, Photo Library, European Parliament, and the staff of Pat Cox MEP, President of the European Parliament, for providing photographs.

I would like to thank Dr Raymond Refaussé and my colleagues at the Representative Church Body Library, and Church of Ireland House, Dublin, who have been patient and kind throughout; and also all my friends, young and old, who in many different and diverse ways encouraged me and contributed to this book. Finally, it would not have been written without the support of my family, especially Ted and Vivien Hood, who know all about the Office of Arms now – this is for them.

ABBREVIATIONS

APGI	Association of Professional Genealogists of Ireland
BPW	Board of Public Works
CA	College of Arms, London
CAB	Cabinet
CO	Colonial Office
CSORP	Chief Secretary's Office Registered Papers
DO	Dominions Office
DNB	Dictionary of National Biography
DT	Department of the Taoiseach
FRHS	Fellow Royal Historical Society
GO	Genealogical Office
HMS	His Majesty's Service
HO	Home Office
IFS	Irish Free State
JSAI	Journal of the Royal Society of Antiquaries, Ireland
KC	Knight Companion
MP	Member of Parliament
NAI	National Archives of Ireland
NLI	National Library of Ireland
OPW	Office of Public Works (formerly BPW)
PMDIJ	Preservation of the Memorials of the Dead Ireland Journal
PREM	Prime Minister
PRO (in main body of text)	Public Record Office, Dublin
PRO (in footnotes)	Public Record Office, Kew
PRONI	Public Record Office of Northern Ireland, Belfast
RCBL	Representative Church Body Library, Dublin
RSAI	Royal Society of Antiquaries, Ireland
SC	Sadleir Correspondence, consisting of the personal correspondence and related papers of Thomas Sadleir (1882–1957), Registrar of the Office of Arms and Deputy Ulster King of Arms, 1921–43, concerning his heraldic and genealogical work in general, and for the Office of Arms in particular, 1900–43. Formerly in the custody of his son, Randal Sadleir, London, and deposited in the GO, 2002
T	Treasury
UCD	University College Dublin, Archives Department
Uncat.	Uncatalogued material

For Ted and Vivien Hood,
with love

INTRODUCTION

The Office of Arms was established in 1552 and is Ireland's oldest Office of State. With the exception of the Commonwealth period between 1655 and 1660, its authority derived from the English Crown, which appointed an Ulster King of Arms and Principal Herald of Ireland to oversee all aspects of Irish heraldic practice until 1943. This administrative framework remained in place for some 21 years after the foundation of the State. The final transfer of authority to the Irish Government occurred only after the death of the last appointed Ulster King of Arms, Sir Nevile Wilkinson. On 1 April 1943, the Irish Government changed the Office's title to Genealogical Office, while the Chief Herald of Ireland replaced the King of Arms as the principal officeholder, but its heraldic functions were maintained, in spite of the trappings of royalty and nobility with which the system had been formerly imbued. The Office of Arms thus survived the transition from Crown to Republic.

The delay in the transfer of the Office following Independence in 1922 reflected in part the rather esoteric nature of its business – the design, registration and granting of coats of arms for a relatively small clientele – which did not feature high on the political agenda. It also reflected the constitutional status of the King of Arms, who, by virtue of his royal patent, was empowered to provide heraldic services for all Ireland. His heraldic jurisdiction was unaffected by the division of the island created by the Government of Ireland Act of 1920, and the subsequent Anglo-Irish Treaty of 1921 which brought the Free State into existence. In the context of this political change, the Office of Arms, located at the Bedford Tower in Dublin Castle, carried on its business as it had in the past, and processed heraldic work for clients in Northern Ireland as well as the Free State, including the design of a coat of arms for the new Northern Ireland Government.

This book explores the transition and survival of the oldest Office of State during the most recent phase of its colourful and eventful history – the 150 years since 1853, when Sir J. Bernard Burke became the twenty-first Ulster King of Arms and Principal Herald of all Ireland. At that time the Office was centre-stage in administering the lavish ceremonial events associated with the Victorian Court at Dublin Castle. The Ulster King of Arms played an important role in its related protocol and pageantry, assisted by his staff – an array of heralds, pursuivants, artists and administrative assistants. Gradually, in tandem with changing political circumstances, the ceremonial aspects of the work declined, whilst the demand for expertise in heraldry and genealogical research increased. An important source of this demand came from people of

Irish descent living abroad – at first the descendants of privileged Irish families many of whom sought to embody their roots in Ireland by commissioning ancestral research, and applying for personal coats of arms, as visible marks of their Irishness. By the mid-twentieth century the interest had spread, and people of all social backgrounds with Irish roots were seeking assistance from the Genealogical Office. The book traces this process of gradual evolution through several significant stages from the mid-nineteenth century, culminating in the smooth transition to the authority of the Irish Government in 1943, and the continued success of the Office to the present day.

At the beginning of the third millennium and celebrating 450 years in existence, the Office of Arms provides a range of heraldic services for people of Irish descent, as well as institutions and organisations with Irish connections throughout the world. It thus continues today to carry on a tradition that has been practiced in Ireland since medieval times.

THE ORIGINS OF HERALDRY AND ESTABLISHMENT OF AN IRISH OFFICE OF ARMS

Heraldry originated as a practical form of identification for combatants in medieval warfare, a visual system that has been described as 'Christian, European, graphic, symbolic, territorial and personal'. It was controlled and regulated by kings of arms and heralds, appointed by royal decree, who were usually given a territorial designation by their royal patrons.[1] The Normans introduced the system to Ireland during the late twelfth century. This early influence may still be seen on surviving personal seals and monuments of the leading citizens of the period, and also from contemporary descriptions such as Giraldus Cambrensis's account of the Norman invasion in *Expungatio Hibernica*. Unfortunately, no records of this early heraldic development appear to have survived, and no office was established to register or assign arms.[2] In 1342, the first specific reference to an 'Ireland King of Arms' occurred in Froissart's *Chronicles* of the One Hundred Years' War, when he described John Chandos as 'le roi d'Ireland', but this officeholder never came to Ireland, nor did he have much concern with matters of Irish heraldry.[3] Several of his successors as 'Ireland Kings of Arms' were attached to the College of Arms in London, a body corporate founded by Richard III in 1484 to regulate the heraldic practices of England. None of them however had any direct contact

---

1   Begley, *Manuscript Treasures*.
2   Gillespie, 'Heraldry in Ireland', pp. 7–9.
3   Burke, *General Armory*, p. xxv; Blake Butler, 'Officers of arms of Ireland', pp. 2–3; O'Comáin, *Poolbeg Book of Irish Heraldry*, pp. 21–4.

with Ireland, functioning only as additional servants of the English heraldic establishment. The Gaelic Irish did not take to heraldry at this early period, and the lack of infiltration of heraldic practice may explain the delay in the establishment of an Irish Office of Arms until 1552.[4]

The formal beginning of the Office was allied to the official Tudor policy of bringing order and influence to Ireland. The status of the country was elevated from lordship to kingdom in 1541, when King Henry VIII was declared King of Ireland.[5] To reflect the new kingdom's constitutional position, the arms 'azure a harp or' were formally adopted as the arms of Ireland, replacing the triple-crown motif that had been the symbol of the former lordship. The latter also closely resembled the papal tiara – symbolic of the religious authority rejected by the king. The harp had in fact been recognised as Ireland's symbol in a thirteenth-century roll of arms of various European states,[6] and was thus re-instated as the symbol of the new political order in the sixteenth century, appearing on Irish coinage from the mid-1540s. The use of this heraldic charge required regulation and authorisation, leading to the establishment of an office, and appointment of a local herald, to administer such a development.[7]

The new political regime also wished to make provision for the official registration, design and assignment of arms and titles for the 'new men' to whom it granted lands throughout the kingdom under its plantation scheme of 'surrender and regrant'. These included settlers from England, and also those Gaelic Lords who conformed to the new order, accepting English titles to secure their estates in English law.[8] The early records of the Office include their heraldic achievements and ancestral histories, providing colourful, visual representation of their power, wealth, and influence in the new political order. The surviving records of these achievements include entries of early grants and confirmations dating from 1552; Visitation Books recording the heraldic visitations of the Ulster King of Arms, dating from 1568; a series of Funeral Entries recording the genealogies and armorial bearings of noblemen and their families, commencing in 1588; as well as various rolled family pedigrees recording extensive genealogies.[9]

---

4   Gillespie, 'Heraldry in Ireland', pp. 9–10.
5   Begley, *Manuscript Treasures*.
6   This is the *Armorial Wijnbergen*, preserved in The Hague, see Begley, *Arms of Ireland*.
7   Begley, *Arms of Ireland*; *Manuscript Treasures*.
8   Gillespie, 'Heraldry in Ireland', pp. 13–4.
9   For a comprehensive introduction to the records of the Office, see Grenham, 'The Genealogical Office, Dublin', and Barry 'Guide to records of the Genealogical Office'. Begley's *Manuscript Treasures*, provides a descriptive summary.

The conquest and settlement of the kingdom of Ireland was well advanced under Henry's successor, King Edward VI. It was he who declared on 2 February 1552: 'there was a King of Arms made in Ireland whose name was Ulster and whose province was all Ireland, and he was the fourth king of arms and the first herald of Ireland'.[10] Ulster King of Arms thus became the Principal Herald of all Ireland. In the heraldic order of precedence he was placed behind the three kings of arms associated with the English College of Arms – Garter, the Principal King of Arms; Clarenceux, who had heraldic responsibility for southern and western parts of England; and Norroy, whose jurisdiction comprised the northern parts of England.[11] By royal letters patent dated 1 June 1552, Bartholomew Butler, formerly the York Herald at the College of Arms, was appointed the first Ulster King of Arms, and exclusively appropriated Irish heraldic jurisdiction. His patent of appointment, like those of his successors, was issued under the Great Seal, granting the authority to:

> all rights, profits, commodities and emoluments in that Office … with power … of inspecting, overseeing, correcting, and embodying the arms and ensigns of illustrious persons and of imposing and ordaining differences therein, according to the laws of arms, of granting letters patent of arms to men of rank, and fit persons, and of doing … all things which by right or custom were known to be incumbent of the office of a king of arms.[12]

Butler remained in England until the mid–1550s, but adopted his exclusive Irish remit by relocating to Dublin by November 1558. He publicly proclaimed the accession of Queen Elizabeth I to the throne at this time, the heralding of such official events being another important duty of the King of Arms.[13]

In addition to Ulster King of Arms, a second permanent officer of arms for Ireland was also created by royal letters patent dated 20 June 1552. This officer was styled the Athlone Pursuivant, whose role was to assist Ulster in all heraldic and ceremonial matters. The first Athlone Pursuivant was Philip Butler, Bartholomew's son, who like his father became resident in Ireland, obtaining a 21-year lease on the 'Manor of Eskyr', County Dublin in 1566.[14]

---

10 Quoted in Noble, *College of Arms*, p. 143.
11 *op. cit.*, p. 173.
12 Copy of original patent of appointment of Ulster King of Arms, in GO, MS 388, p. 1.
13 Blake Butler, 'Officers of arms of Ireland', p. 6.
14 *ibid.*

Introduction

This nepotistic appointment was to be the first in a long succession of family
dynasties who controlled the Office until the late nineteenth century. The succession was aptly described in a recent genealogical study of its personnel as
a series of 'nepotists and sinecurists'.[15]

It is unclear why the new officeholder in Ireland was given the name of
the most ancient Irish province of Ulster, but it may perhaps have been
intended to distinguish him from the older title 'Ireland King of Arms', linked
with the College of Arms since the fourteenth century. The title of Ulster King
of Arms did not have any geographic link with the province of Ulster, as successive Kings of Arms and Principal Heralds of Ireland have always been
based in Dublin. However, as the earldom of Ulster was the only part of Ireland formally vested in the Crown, the use of its title for the King of Arms
may have reflected an official desire to symbolise this unique royal association
and symbolise that the heraldic authority was not confined to Dublin.[16] Simi-
larly, there was no apparent territorial significance attached to the title of the
Athlone Pursuivant. Perhaps the intention here was also to signify that the
authority of this second heraldic appointment was not restricted to 'The
Pale'(the area consolidated around Dublin and parts of the Province of Leinster) but extended throughout the island, and included strategically placed
landmarks such as the walled town of Athlone in the midlands.[17]

AN EVOLVING TRADITION

From these specific origins, linked to political developments, the Office of
Arms evolved acquiring additional responsibilities and duties of a ceremonial
nature, including the administration of protocol and precedence at the Irish
Court, as well as supervision of processions and other social events. By virtue
of his royal appointment, the Ulster King of Arms enjoyed a close association
with the official court at Dublin Castle, where power was vested in the Lord
Lieutenant, or viceroy – the Crown representative in Ireland. As early as 1717,
he was placed high in the local precedence, 'next to the person of the Lord
Lieutenant' and before any other officers or dignitaries. By the early nineteenth century, Ulster King of Arms was described as:

> the first and only permanent officer of the Lord Lieutenant's household in
> Ireland, with full responsibility for arranging all the public ceremonies

15 French, 'Nepotists'.
16 Gillespie, 'Heraldry in Ireland', p. 14.
17 Interview with Mícheál O'Comáin, Consultant Herald at the GO.

connected with Government such as the proclamation of a new sovereign, or peace, or war; the reception and inauguration of the Lord Lieutenant; custody of all records respecting such matters and keeping a record of all State proceedings.[18]

Administrative records were created which reflected this role as a state official, including State Ceremonial Books, Vice-Regal Court Books, documents relating to precedence and protocol, official orders, succession lists, and processional details. Many of them still survive in the Office's archives today.[19]

An order of chivalry for Ireland, the Most Illustrious Order of St Patrick, was instituted by royal warrant during the reign of King George III in 1783. The Office of Arms became the registry of the Order, and Ulster King of Arms its Knight Attendant and Registrar. New responsibilities included superintending the ceremonies of investiture and inauguration of new knights; designing and crafting their heraldic banners; taking custody of their insignia and official dress; signing certificates of noblesse; and keeping registers of their achievements and family histories. To assist the King of Arms in this work, an entourage of additional officers was also created by royal warrant, including the Dublin and Cork Heralds, the Genealogist, the Gentleman Usher, and four general pursuivants. Although purely nominal positions, whose presence was usually only required for important ceremonies, these appointments boosted the size of the Irish heraldic establishment considerably, and raised its public profile. They also provided new nepotistic and sinecure opportunities of which several Kings of Arms took full advantage, appointing their sons and friends to a range of positions. The new chivalric duties also resulted in the creation of additional records by the Office, including Registers of Knights, Certificates of Noblesse; Books of Investiture and Inauguration; as well as a range of related correspondence and administrative material.[20]

Among the duties of State exercised by the Office was the keeping of the list of Irish peers, an official document that was updated regularly and known as 'Ulster's Roll'. All those entitled to sit in the Irish House of Lords, whether by creation of a new peerage or by succession, were obliged to inform Ulster's Office before they could be officially introduced to the House. This gave rise to the creation of a series of registers called the Lords Entries in which the names and family details of lords and their coats of arms were registered, and

---

18 'Duties and services preformed by Ulster King of Arms', quoted by Sir William Betham in GO, MS 372, p. 182.
19 Butler, 'Guide to records', pp. 35–6.
20 Galloway, *Most Illustrious Order*, p. 1; French, 'Nepotists', p. 346.

it covers the period 1698–1939. The link with the House of Lords explains why at some point between 1729 and 1790 the Office occupied a suite of rooms in the House of Lords at the Parliament building in College Green. This prestigious link came to an end in 1800, when the Act of Union brought the Irish Parliament to an end. The Parliament building was sold to the Bank of Ireland and for the next 30 years the Office lacked an official address, being accommodated in the private residences of Kings of Arms, and other members of his heraldic staff instead.[21]

In response to a royal warrant issued in 1789, for 'correcting and preventing abuses in the order of baronets', the Office was empowered to make provision for the registration of the arms and pedigrees of baronets. A later warrant of 1795, ordered that changes of name and arms had likewise to be registered in the Office of Arms, giving rise to a series known as 'Royal Warrants for changes of name and licences for changes of name'.[22]

The ability to adapt to political change has been a repetitive theme of the Office's evolution during its long history, and was an important factor in its survival. Since Butler's appointment as the first Ulster King of Arms and Principal Herald of all Ireland in 1552, there has been an unbroken succession of heraldic officers to the present day. Not all of them have been titled Kings of Arms, as the authority under which they operated changed in accordance with an evolving political structure. In the sixteenth century, for example, at the time of the Cromwellian interregnum, the new political regime did not abolish the Office. Instead, the Ulster King of Arms, William Roberts, was simply replaced by a herald, Richard Carney, who in 1655 became 'Principal Herald of Arms for the whole dominion of Ireland'. He was empowered to grant and confirm arms under the authority of the Lord Protector, and in some cases, patents were issued in the name of the 'res publica'.[23] This practice continued until the Restoration in 1660, when the title reverted to Ulster King of Arms, an appointment that was later held by Carney between 1683 and 1692.[24]

Political events after the Jacobite defeat of the Irish in the Williamite Wars in the 1690s, and subsequent Treaty of Limerick, which saw a steady exodus of members of the Gaelic and Old Norman nobility and supporters of the Jacobite regime, also disrupted the Office's business. Among the 'Wild Geese' – being those who followed the defeated King James II into exile to France –

---

21 McCarthy, *Ulster's Office*, pp. 181–2.
22 Grenham, 'The Genealogical Office', p. 6.
23 Gillespie, 'Irish Heraldry', p. 15.
24 French, 'Nepotists', pp. 341–3.

was James Terry, the Athlone Pursuivant, who made off with several of the Office's official books and its seal. He established a rival Office of Arms at the Stuart Court at St Germain-en-Laye, outside Paris. From here he proceeded to issue grants and certificates of arms to his fellow displaced countrymen, on behalf of King James II, issuing them with certificates of nobility, and registering their pedigrees, to provide them with marks of identity. They needed this identity to gain recognition as members of the nobility, to secure employment and property in the countries to which they took flight.[25] After Terry's death in 1725, his records were dispersed, and several ended up in the principal French repositories – the Archives Nationales and Bibliothéque Nationale in Paris. Significantly, after 1725, this continental work reverted to the Irish Office of Arms. Almost half of the pedigrees entered in its books between 1750 and 1800 were registered by émigré families and descendants of the Jacobite émigrés who had left a century before. Their demands for the Office's services during the eighteenth century were to be an early indication of the important business that would be generated by members of the Irish diaspora in the future.[26]

Many of the principal officeholders treated their appointments as sinecures, choosing to make grand appearances at important ceremonial occasions whilst leaving the routine daily administration of the Office's business to their deputies, heraldic artists, and other administrative assistants. However, there have been notable exceptions to this pattern, particularly in the nineteenth century. The most dynamic office holder was probably Sir William Betham – a name familiar to Irish genealogists and family historians because of the many records relating to genealogy that he transcribed. He served as Ulster King of Arms from 1820 until his death in 1853. Originally from England, Betham was appointed Deputy Ulster in 1807, and soon persuaded the then King of Arms, Sir Chichester Fortescue, to give him free reign to run the Office, and reorganise it in return for a fixed income.[27]

Even before his appointment, Betham had been concerned about the poor standards of record keeping he found in Ireland, to which the records of the Office of Arms were no exception. Ireland's turbulent and disrupted history, the inclination of several kings of arms and other officers to regard the records as their own personal property, as well as the absence of a permanent address for the Office, had detrimental consequences for its records. When Betham first became Deputy Ulster in 1807, he found that the Office occupied a room

---

25 Gillespie, 'Heraldry in Ireland', p. 15; Barry, 'Guide to records', p. 17
26 Begley, *Treasures*.
27 Phair, 'Sir William Betham's Manuscripts', pp. 3–7.

in a house in Eustace Street, Dublin, at the home of the book-keeper, Theobald Richard O'Flaherty. Once in command of its administration, Betham sought to make the records more secure, and moved the Office 'from the miserable hole in Eustace Street' to his own home at 7 North Cope Street in October 1809.[28] Several moves to other parts of the city followed, depending on where Betham could get a lease, and make the records most secure. After he became Ulster King of Arms in 1820, he persuaded the Government to provide an annual grant of £140 for the keeping of the Office in 1822, taking a lease for a house in Westland Row.[29] In 1831 this allowance was cut, but a room became vacant in the Record Tower in Dublin Castle, into which Betham reluctantly 'squeezed the Office of Arms' from March of that year.[30] Whilst he complained there was little accommodation for additional records that the Office might acquire in the future, and found its environment 'cold, dark, old and unpainted',[31] at least it had gained a more permanent address.

Betham was a conscientious record-keeper, and submitted a valuable report on the records that had accumulated in the Office to the Irish Records Commission in 1811, which explained their origins and provenance for the first time.[32] Unlike many of his predecessors he attended the Office on a daily basis, and began several new series of records, including Day Books, Letter Books and Official Entries that helped to regularise Office administration. He also helped to bring order to existing records, including miscellaneous documents covering the first three centuries of the Office's existence, which he had found 'bordering on chaos, scattered, neglected and unarranged'. Betham bound this material into a new series of five volumes, which he called 'Chaos', and provided an index for each one.[33] He also revised existing manuscripts and provided transcripts and abstracts of genealogical and heraldic material in other record repositories. His diligence and the value of the transcripts would only be realised later when, as a result of the disastrous destruction of the Public Record Office of Ireland during the Civil War in 1922, they became in effect primary sources.

The move to the Castle precincts also helped to consolidate the position of the Office of Arms. From here it was easier to superintend the great events

---

28 Quoted in *ibid.*, p. 5.
29 Sir William Betham to the Chief Secretary's Office, 13 June 1822, GO, MS 365.
30 Betham to the Board of First Fruits, 21 March 1831, GO, MS 370.
31 Betham to the Board of Public Works, 23 January 1835, *op. cit.*
32 *Reports from the Commissioners Respecting the Public Records of Ireland to the House of Commons, 1-V,* 1811–15; see also Barry, 'Guide to records', pp. 29–43.
33 Chaos volumes, GO, MSS 93–7; index in GO, MS 470.

of the Irish Court, many of which took place in the State Apartments in the Upper Castle Yard. Whilst Betham's role in ceremonial events was relatively low-key, and reserved for major ceremonies such as royal visits and investitures, his successor Sir J. Bernard Burke became more directly involved in a whole range of State occasions.[34] It is at this ceremonial highpoint, at the beginning of Burke's tenure of Office in 1853 that we join the recent history of the Office of Arms.

ROYAL ROOTS – REPUBLICAN INHERITANCE

The complex and colourful evolution of the Office of Arms during the past 150 years is reconstructed in the following chapters. Chapter one introduces the Office and its chief functions at the middle of nineteenth century. The focus at this point was very much on members of the nobility, and the privileged pomp and splendour of ceremonial occasions – prompting a contemporary to observe that 'the grandeur of Ulster [was] complete'. By the time of Sir Bernard Burke's death in 1892, however, there were expressions of concern about the future of the Irish heraldic establishment and its traditional practices. Chapter two demonstrates that during the appointment of Sir Arthur Vicars, 1893–1908, described as an unhappy 'story of bickerings, scandal and neglect', the conflict of interest between the Office's traditional heraldic responsibilities and ceremonial duties emerged. This culminated as a result of the infamous theft of the so-called Irish 'Crown Jewels' from the safe in the Office's public room. The custody of these jewels – the insignia of the Order of St Patrick – had little to do with the daily business of the Office, as Vicars was quick to point out. He had proved himself a conscientious custodian of the traditions of his Office. This was demonstrated by his heraldic expertise, emphasis on keeping accurate information, concern for the welfare of the records by improving the conditions in which they were stored, and his successful relocation of the Office from the Record Tower to the more prestigious Bedford Tower in the Upper Castle Yard in 1903, all of which helped to raise its public profile. These achievements far outweighed any lax attention to the privileged accessories of the Castle Court. Nevertheless, he was unceremoniously dismissed for negligence after they disappeared.

Following Vicars's departure, a sinecurist theme returned to the administration of the Office with the Government's 'safe' appointment of Captain

---

34 Robbins, *Champagne and Silver Buckles. The Viceregal Court at Dublin Castle*, pp. 125–6.

Nevile Wilkinson as Ulster King of Arms in 1908. Whilst a brilliant artist, whose creative skills certainly had a positive impact on the Office's standards of heraldic painting, and led to the foundation of the Heraldic Museum in 1909 – the first of its kind in the world – Wilkinson also enjoyed the high life, and was largely absent from Dublin. However, as chapter three demonstrates the Office was fortunate in having the services of two conscientious and diligent deputies during the course of Wilkinson's long appointment between 1908 and 1940. They were George Dames Burtchaell, who served as Athlone Pursuivant from 1908 until his death in 1921, and Thomas Ulick Sadleir, who, as Registrar and Deputy Ulster from 1921 until 1940, and then after Wilkinson's death in 1940, as Acting King of Arms until the transfer in 1943, ran the Office on a shoestring during the period of political transition. Both Burtchaell and Sadleir were expert genealogists and heralds, who endeavoured to respond to the growing numbers of genealogical enquiries and processing of heraldic commissions – many from outside Ireland – during the early decades of the twentieth century. Their commitment was another important factor in the Office's adaption to change and survival during the changing times of the First World War, 1914–8; the Irish War of Independence, 1919–21, the finally the Civil War, 1922–3, as chapters three and four demonstrate.

In the confusion that followed the transfer of political power to Dublin in 1922, some Irish civil servants assumed that the Office of Arms had, along with all the other offices and buildings in Dublin Castle, passed to Free State control. Chapter four shows that the new Free State Ministry of Home Affairs actually ordered that all its records be transferred to the PRO in Dublin, in April 1922. But for Sadleir's reluctance to comply with this, they might have shared the similar fate of so many other records that were destroyed as a result of the fire and explosion at the Four Courts during the Civil War on 30 June 1922. After the destruction of the PRO, the Office and its records took on a new importance, as in many cases the information contained in its transcripts and genealogical records replaced material that had been lost. Chapter four reveals that a fusion of the Office of Arms with the PRO was even proposed in the aftermath of the disastrous events of 1922, when the PRO was attempting to rebuild itself. This came to nothing, partly because of Wilkinson's determination to hold onto his life appointment as King of Arms, but principally because of the Free State's dominion status and the fact that the Office of Arms remained a Crown office, which had not been transferred.

The Office's anomalous position in the Free State between 1922 and 1943, and the complex constitutional logistics that allowed this to occur, are the subjects of Chapter five. Even after the removal of the King from Irish internal politics as a result of constitutional change in the mid-1930s, the authority from which the Office of Arms derived its power remained unaffected. It continued to issue its patents in the name of King until 1943. Whilst this political anomaly did not go unnoticed in Irish Government circles, the Office's all Ireland jurisdiction was an attractive symbol of unity. By 1938, it had become the last office within in the State to provide services for citizens on both sides of the Irish Border, and on these grounds a decision was taken to maintain the *status quo*. Only after Wilkinson's death in 1940 did the long overdue process to transfer it to Irish control begin, while the intervention of the Second World War delayed events for a further three years.

The personal involvement of the then Taoiseach, Éamon de Valera, in bringing the anomalous position of the Office of Arms to a satisfactory conclusion was significant, and helped to ensure its continuity under Irish Government authority. As Chapter six demonstrates, de Valera attended the transfer ceremony on 1 April 1943, when the Office was formally assigned to the supervision of the National Library of Ireland, and showed a keen interest in its work. The theme of this chapter is the Office's continuity as Ireland's heraldic authority. Although the style and the title of King of Arms was changed to Chief Herald of Ireland, and the format of the patents issued was altered to reflect its new authority, the Office of Arms continued to provide the heraldic and genealogical services of the old regime.

In spite of the negative predictions made by some that it could not succeed without royal authority, the Office was to flourish in the decades after the transfer. Chapter seven explores its success under the new political regime. By the early 1950s, ancestral research was no longer a pursuit reserved for the wealthy and privileged. With the onset of global communication made possible by cheaper air travel, the world at large began to discover 'roots' and a new genealogical research mania took off. Reflecting the global 'roots' phenomenon, the Office became the first point of contact in Ireland for many seeking guidance about their ancestral research, and thus genealogy became the main focus of its work.

In spite of the emphasis on genealogy – which seemed to justify the Office's new working title as Genealogical Office – its heraldic remit was also maintained, and several new innovations were introduced by the first Chief Herald of Ireland, Dr Edward MacLysaght, aimed at promoting Gaelic heraldry. In the context of global tourism, the Heraldic Museum became an attractive tourist landmark, and was described as one of the showplaces in Dublin Castle by the mid 1950s. The Office also conducted a number of high-profile heraldic commissions, including the design of arms for President John F. Kennedy in the early 1960s, which enhanced its international status. Chapter seven also reveals that the design concept for a new Council of Europe flag was the work of Ireland's longest-serving Chief Herald, Gerard Slevin. Today the emblem of 12 stars on a blue background has become Europe's symbol *par excellence*. Back in the 1950s when it was designed, its impact could hardly have been predicted. The central involvement of a former Chief Herald of Ireland in the process powerfully symbolises the international significance and recognition of Irish heraldic authority.

Finally, chapter eight brings the story up to date, and covers the Office's relocation from Dublin Castle to Kildare Street in 1986. Changing circumstances over the last 20 years have brought about a gradual reduction of its genealogical research remit, and a return to more specialist heraldic functions. In this context, the time may now be appropriate to abolish the confusing and redundant title of 'Genealogical Office', and replace it with the traditional and historically more accurate title of 'Office of Arms' – arguably a fitting development after four and a half centuries in existence.

Lower Castle Yard, Dublin Castle, c. 1890, showing the Record Tower, home of the Office of Arms 1831-1903, and the archway leading to the Upper Castle Yard, where the Office was re-located in 1903. *NLI, Lawrence Collection, R. 378.*

ONE

'The triumph of Ulster complete'

Ceremonial reaches a high point under Sir Bernard Burke, 1853–92

THE PASSING OF ULSTER'S CROWN

The legendary Sir William Betham died unexpectedly on 26 October 1853, having suffered a heart attack the previous night. He had worked to the end, attending the Office of Arms and writing several letters from the Castle on 25 October.[1] His sudden passing upset the course of Office business considerably, and was compounded by the fact that no clerk was employed at this time. This left his two sons, Molyneux, the Athlone Pursuivant and Cork Herald of the Order of St Patrick, and Sheffield, the Dublin Herald of the Order, as well as Robert Smith, pursuivant and herald painter, to operate as best they could. In addition to their own work they acquired many of the daily responsibilities for the Office that had previously been supervised by Betham, including the ordering of coal for heating the Record Tower. Thus we find Smith writing to the Board of Public Works 'in the place of Sir William, who had charge of this Office' to requisition 'a ton of coal, as our stock is entirely out', in November 1853.[2]

There were also delays in completing work that Sir William had been overseeing. One client received an explanation as to why his letter had gone unanswered for over two weeks: Molyneux Betham pleaded that 'due to the sudden death of my father. . .[you will] make allowances for the state of confusion and uncertainly into which we have been thrown by that melancholy event'. However, he also anticipated, somewhat hopefully, that his brother Sheffield would soon succeed their father as Ulster King of Arms and Principal Herald of Ireland. The former had already applied to the Lord Lieutenant, Sir Edward Granville Eliot, third Earl of St Germans, to succeed. 'Should he succeed in obtaining it', Molyneux continued, Sheffield would 'be most happy

---

1   GO, MS 378.
2   Robert Smith, Ulster's Office, to H. Toler, Dublin Castle, 1 November 1853, GO, MS 378.

to contemplate your business which my father left unfinished'. They expected 'daily to hear His Excellency's decision'.[3]

The vice-regal decision was not, however, to be directed in Sheffield Betham's favour. The profile of the Office of Arms had been raised considerably during their father's lifetime, and as far as the Government was concerned, a more significant individual was required to follow Betham. By letters patent dated 18 November 1853, less than a month after Betham's death, (John) Bernard Burke was appointed Ulster King of Arms and Knight Attendant of the Order of St Patrick. His initial salary was 40 marks (£200), together with the right to recover the traditional fees of the said Office. In accordance with tradition, Burke was empowered to examine, view, correct and ratify the arms and ensigns of eminent men, also to correct any mistakes 'according to the law of arms', and to 'execute all other things' by custom associated with his Office. These duties were to be carried out by him in person, or when 'specially permitted' by a deputy or deputies appointed by him.[4]

Burke's family name had long been associated with the compilation of detailed pedigrees of the nobility of the United Kingdom and Ireland. He was a son of John Burke, founder of the genealogical printing house that had produced the red and gold volumes known as *Burke's Peerage* (which first appeared in 1826) and *Burke's Commoners*, later *Burke's Landed Gentry* (which first appeared in 1837), both of which were updated and re-published annually. Following an education in Chelsea and Normandy, Burke had been called to the English bar in 1839, and developed a good practice in peerage and genealogical cases.[5] Indeed, he continued to practise in some high-profile inheritance cases after his appointment to the Irish heraldic authority. Since his father's death in 1846, Burke had re-edited both the *Peerage* and *Landed Gentry* on an annual basis. He also published revised editions of the *Extinct and Dormant Peerage* (in 1883), the *General Armory of England, Scotland and Ireland* (in 1878 and 1883), in addition to an impressive original list of publications of his own.[6]

Given his family's reputation in the fields of genealogy and heraldry, and his own experience as an inheritance lawyer and author of genealogical texts,

---

3 Molyneux Betham to John Gibbs, 7 November 1853, *op. cit.*

4 Royal warrant of appointment, 18 November 1853, GO, MS 152, pp. 190–3.

5 'Portrait of Sir Bernard Burke', in *Dublin University Magazine,* July 1876, pp. 16–24.

6 The most widely read of these included: *The Romance of the Aristocracy*; *The Rise of Great Families; Vicissitudes of Families; The Book of Precedence.*

Sir Bernard Burke, Ulster King of Arms, 1853–92. *Dublin University Magazine,* 1876.

Sir Bernard Burke registered his own knighthood, which included his coat of arms, 22 February 1854. *GO, MS 101.*

Burke was considered a suitable successor to Sir William Betham. However, he would later be accused of being an unreliable genealogist by other professionals, many of his published pedigrees allegedly containing spurious accounts of the early generations of prominent families.[7] Indeed, during a debate in the House of Commons about the future of his Office, one speaker remarked that Sir Bernard would, 'for a fee', and providing they were distinguished, give anyone a pedigree from the Norman Conquest onwards'.[8] The inaccuracies in his published works did later tarnish his reputation as a genealogist.

In spite of these shortcomings, he remained a respected authority on heraldry, and his *General Armory* continues to be used as a standard work of reference. Burke also made a significant contribution to the administration of the Office of Arms during his long tenure of office, and in particular the standards of record-keeping and their preservation.

In anticipation of the services that he would provide, Burke was honoured with a knighthood on 22 February 1854. He recorded the event himself in the

7   French, 'Nepotists', p. 349.
8   *Hansard*, 13 September 1886, 309, 272.

Register of Knights, his crest motto, 'One King, One Faith, One Law' capturing a loyal spirit.[9] He was further honoured with membership of the Royal Irish Academy in the same year; appointed Keeper of the State Papers at Dublin Castle, for which he received the additional income of £500 from 1866; and became a Governor of the National Gallery, in 1874.[10]

RECORD KEEPING

The principal themes of Burke's administration of the Office of Arms were efficiency and attention to detail, demonstrated by his creation of new records for the registration of heraldic and genealogical business. He opened several new series of registers to facilitate administration. The most important of these were the five volumes of Official Entries and Letters commenced in January 1854. These volumes contain copies of official outgoing correspondence signed by Burke, some original incoming letters, memorandums, requisitions for furniture and supplies for the Record Tower, and occasional minutes. These provide a rich insight to the nature of daily Office business, although a drawback is that they concern Burke's dealings only,

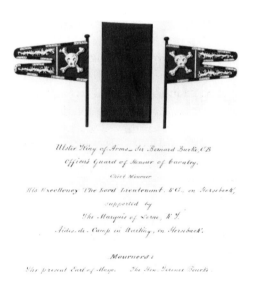

Funeral entry recording guard of honour and chief mourners, led by Sir Bernard Burke, at the funeral of the Most Revd John Beresford, Church of Ireland Archbishop of Armagh, who died in 1862. *GO, MS 77.*

---

9   Register of Knights, 4, GO, MS 101, p. 13.
10   *DNB*, p. 338; Boase, *Modern English Biography*, p. 545.

and do not provide much enlightenment about the work of other members of staff.[11]

A further record addition was a new volume of Funeral Entries, opened in 1862, for the occasion of the State funeral of the Most Revd John Beresford, Church of Ireland Archbishop of Armagh and Primate of all Ireland. This revived the practice of formally recording the funerals of prominent people, last registered in 1787.[12] The entries made during Burke's tenure were particularly colourful, reproducing the arms of the deceased person in full colour, together with the shields and flags of the chief mourners. A new Register of Knights was also opened, including the entry for Burke's knighthood.[13] Burke produced an elaborate index to the changes of name and other formal events registered in Office records and published in the *Dublin Gazette* making their records more accessible.[14]

His tenure also resulted in the creation of several Ceremonial Books recording the affairs of the Irish Court at Dublin Castle. These in particular, capture his mastery of the privileges, ceremonies and precedence regulations connected with the Lord Lieutenant's household, and the careful attention that Burke devoted to his courtly duties and official proceedings.

Burke was also concerned about improving the manuscript holdings of the Office, thus contributing to a better understanding of its history and tradition. Indeed, one of his first tasks as King of Arms was to secure many of the late Sir William Betham's private genealogical and heraldic papers when they came up for sale in 1854 and again in 1860. Burke lamented that Betham's sons, who were also his executors, had sold their father's personal library, thus denying Ireland of access to the valuable information it contained. Burke warned the Irish Administration of the folly of allowing such material to be lost: 'whilst England is rich in records elucidating family history, Ireland is lamentably deficient in such sources of information'. He emphasised that if the genealogical and personal matters included in the wills, administrations, marriage licences and other family evidences, as collected by Betham, were deposited in his Office, it 'would be of the greatest public utility, and also contribute to raising its profile'.[15]

Whilst only a fraction of the 21,000 items constituting this private collection actually ended up at the Office of Arms, those secured by Burke

---

11 Official Entries and Letters, 1854–92, GO, MSS 323–6.
12 Funeral Entries, 1862–98, GO, MS 77.
13 Register of Knights, 1853–92, GO, MS 101.
14 GO, MS 202.
15 Burke to Lieut. Col. Larcom, 13 May 1854, GO, MS 322, pp. 3–5.

included some of Betham's most important compilations. As Keeper of the State Papers, Betham had spent much time collecting, transcribing and editing the wills and administrations of the Prerogative Court of the Church of Ireland Archbishop of Armagh. The Court was located at Henrietta Street in Dublin from 1816 until its abolition in 1857. The wills and other records created during the course of its work were stored there until their final transfer to the PRO in 1867. Betham abstracted genealogical information from this material, which he entered into some 240 notebooks. The notebooks went elsewhere after his death in 1853, although the PRO later purchased them at auction in 1935.

As a result of negotiating directly with Betham's sons, Burke managed to secure not only several collections of pedigrees based on these wills but also several other sources for the Office of Arms. This included 37 volumes of Irish pedigrees, the *Collectanea Genealogica*, reconstructing the connections of every family whose wills were recorded in the Prerogative Court.[16] He also secured Betham's indexes to all the marriage alliances recorded in the wills,[17] other sketch pedigrees based on the same data,[18] and pedigrees based on other sources, including four volumes of *Ancient Anglo-Irish Families*; three volumes of *Milesian Families*; and 23 volumes of miscellaneous pedigrees.[19] Some 17 volumes of Betham's Letter Books, containing copies of his correspondence with the nobility and gentry, chiefly on genealogical matters, were also purchased,[20] along with a variety of extracts from Plea and Patent rolls.[21] Finally, Betham's transcript of *Linea Antiqua* was secured. This was a collation of earlier genealogies compiled by Roger O'Ferrall in 1709, which remains the Office's most extensive source for Gaelic genealogy, and the arms associated with Gaelic families.[22]

At Burke's insistence, each of these items was purchased by the Government for just £1,500 – considerably less than the £10,000 originally asked for, and most of them had been safely transferred to the Record Tower for permanent safe-keeping by August 1854.[23] Burke was confident that the deposits

---

16 Pedigree Sketches based on wills, pre-1700, GO, MSS 223–6; 1700–1800, GO, MSS 227–54. Each of these volumes is indexed.
17 GO, MSS 255–6.
18 GO, MSS 203–14.
19 GO, MSS 215–9; MSS 220–2; MSS 261–76; 292–8. All of these are indexed in GO, MS 470.
20 GO, MSS 355; 362–78.
21 GO, MSS 189–93.
22 GO, MSS 145–7
23 Burke to Larcom, August 1854, GO, MS 322, p. 109.

would 'materially assist . . . in the grand object of [his] ambition – the restoration to perfect efficiency of the ancient and important Office which [he] had the honour to hold'.[24] Little could he have predicted just how invaluable the material would later become. With the destruction of the PRO in the Four Courts in 1922, all of the original manuscripts on which Betham's abstracts and pedigrees were based were destroyed. Secure in the Office of Arms, the laboriously compiled copies have been widely consulted by genealogists and other researchers since 1922.

FINANCIAL SECURITY

Burke's other major impact on Office administration was to make it financially more secure. To this end, he was rigorous in enforcing the scale of fees he had inherited from his predecessor, informing one enquirer in 1856 that a fixed scale of fees was in operation in the Office, 'from which I never deviate'.[25] Detailed memorandums in the entry books provide an insight to the rate of the heraldic business conducted by the Office for the ten-year period between 1859 and 1868.

A typical year was 1862, when seven new grants and 14 confirmations were processed, realising a total of £367.10. In addition, four exemplifications (copy illustrations) of existing arms were painted for clients, realising a total of £95.11, while four changes of name (a procedure that required a royal warrant) were processed and registered, including the publication of the details in the *Dublin Gazette*, realising £63. The arms of a knight were also registered and certified, for which £15 was charged. A frequent heraldic service provided by the Office was the grant of supporters – the figures bearing the shield on an existing coat of arms. In 1862, the cost for adding supporters to an existing coat was £52.10. However, only two supporter grants were processed and registered between 1863 and 1868.

The breakdown of charges for the various services provided by the Office in the mid-nineteenth century was as follows: £31.10 for a grant of new arms, £10.10 for a confirmation of arms already in use, £38.15 for a change of name (or £94.3.7 if it included the design and registration of a new coat of arms), £15 for the registration of a knighthood under seal, including posting a notice of same in the *Dublin Gazette*, £52.10 for a grant of supporters, and £23.17.9 for an exemplification or illustrated reproduction of an existing coat of arms. In contrast to the latter, which was a full-colour

---

24 Burke to Larcom, 13 May 1854, *op. cit.*, p. 5.
25 Burke to the Revd R.O. Dawson Duffield, 22 March 1856, *op. cit.*, p. 53.

reproduction, clients could pay 15 shillings for a sketch or written descrip-tion of a coat of arms instead.

In addition to these heraldic services, Burke also enforced charges for conducting searches through the Office records. Five shillings was the charge for conducting a search for a coat of arms or other specific items of informa-tion from various internal records, while £2.2 was charged for a certificate of such information, as authenticated and signed by the Ulster King of Arms him-self. He also introduced a charge of five shillings for a direct search in the reg-istered pedigrees in 1865 and later increased to ten shillings in 1871, while an additional charge of five shillings per generation was demanded for each pedi-gree copied. Reflecting a growing demand for purely genealogical informa-tion, Burke distinguished between general searches and specific searches, introducing a new fee of £3 for a general search in cases where records might not necessarily exist. This charge was increased to £5 in 1879. The re-intro-duction of the process registration of a funeral entry at the Office of Arms was intended to reap further income, £3 per entry being charged to the family of the deceased. However, only 12 such registrations were actually made during Burke's term of office.[26]

In addition to collecting these official fees, which, in accordance with the terms of his patent, Burke was obliged to return to the Treasury, he could also charge fees of honour to supplement his income. He claimed these fees every time a new dignitary was created. Thus, whenever a new knight of the Order of St Patrick was appointed, Ulster would contact the new knight to claim a fee of £50 from him – the most lucrative creation fee. Likewise, the creation of a new duke realised £32.17.2, while a marquess realised £26.0.5, an earl £19.13.10, a viscount £14.15.5, a baron £11.16.04, an archbishop £10.13.04, a bishop £4.18.06, and an ordinary knight (not connected to the Order) £3.03.04. However, relatively few honours were being created during the late Victorian period, and Ulster's income varied accordingly. In 1866, Burke informed the paymasters that it was difficult to guarantee a steady income from these fees:

> To accomplish all [his business] and to pay all the salaries of his clerks which amount to £312 a year, Ulster is allowed £200 a year only as King of Arms . . . and whatever else is derived from fees which are fluctuat-ing and uncertain.[27]

26 Scale of fees for Ulster's Office for approval of the Treasury Board, drawn up by Burke, 20 December 1871, GO, MS 324, pp. 161–2.
27 Burke to Lord Kimberly, HM Treasury, London, 25 April 1866, GO, MS 323, p. 241.

Burke provided comparative figures to demonstrate just how much fluctuation there was. In 1860 and 1861, for example, only £3.3.4 was received in fees following the creation of just one knight in each of those years. In contrast, a total of £107.1.11 was recouped in 1868, because no less than eight knights, a duke, marquess, and baron had been created. However, 1868 proved to be an exceptional year on account of the visit of Prince Albert to Ireland, which resulted in a special royal installation ceremony, held at St Patrick's Cathedral, Dublin. A more typical year was 1863, when one archbishop, one baron and one knight resulted in fees of £21.9.[28] With such variation, the fees were simply not meeting the costs of covering the salaries of other members of staff which, again under the terms of his patent of appointment, Burke was obliged to pay.

Following the death of William Crawford, his Athlone Pursuivant, in November 1865, Burke began to push for a fixed salary to pay his successor. On Burke's recommendation Captain Robert Smith, who would be a faithful employee of the Office for the next 27 years, was appointed Athlone Pursuivant and Deputy King of Arms in December 1865. Rather than paying Smith's salary himself, as had been the tradition in the past, Burke argued Treasury that a fixed salary scheme would be more appropriate, and might allow him to secure suitably qualified officers in the future:

> Without a public office of this nature in Ireland, innumerable questions which constantly arise involving the descent of honours, the evidences of pedigrees and the preservation of inheritances would be in the utmost confusion. Scarcely a day goes by that its archives are not rendered of avail in questions of descent and property.[29]

Although not successful on this occasion, Burke maintained the pressure for the next four years. He sent various memorandums and letters to men of influence, reminding them of the 'national importance' of his Office, which he described as 'the chief repository for the preservation and perpetuation of family evidences in this country'. Without the security of a fixed salary scheme, the Office might, he insisted, be in jeopardy.[30]

Eventually the politicking paid off. Burke secured a lucrative deal with the Treasury whereby he renounced his right to claim all the fees of honour, plus his original salary of £200, in return for an annual salary of £750. A similar arrangement was made for his Deputy – Smith received a fixed annual salary of £190

28 Table of the fees recouped by Ulster's Office, 1859–68, *op. cit.*, pp. 19–32.
29 Burke to Lord Kimberly, Treasury, London, 25 April 1866, *op. cit.*, pp. 239–42.
30 Burke to James Stansfield Esq, MP, Treasury Chambers, 4 January 1870, *op. cit.*, pp. 17–8.

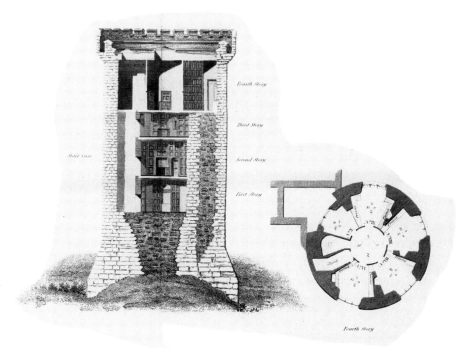

Section of the Record Tower, with detail of the fourth floor, occupied in part by the Office of Arms. *Third Report From Commissioners Respecting the Parliamentary Records of Ireland to the House of Commons*, 1813.

thereafter. Annual salaries were also secured for the messenger at £45 and for the cleaner £20, together with a joint allowance of £24.12 for clothing.[31]

The new financial arrangement was a significant triumph for Burke personally. In addition to his increased salary, he was also entitled to retain his private genealogical practice.[32] More significantly, and a factor which would have important repercussions for the Office following Irish independence, Burke insisted that he should be allowed to keep his royal appointment. The Treasury wanted to revoke the royal letters patent, thereby allowing its officials to control future appointments, which seemed logical given that it was paying for the Office's upkeep. Burke, however, refused to surrender the royal links, which he argued threatened to 'alter the whole constitution of the ancient Office ... and would endanger to a great extent its dignity, legality and authority'.

---

31 Copy of Treasury minute, dated 24 February 1872, GO, MS 324, pp. 191–2, royal warrant authorising discontinuance of the fees of honour and establishment of fixed salaries for Ulster's Office, 27 June 1872, GO, MS 153, pp. 78–9.
32 Declaration of Sir John Bernard Burke, 17 May 1872, GO, MS 324, p. 191.

The royal patent was retained, and the Crown remained the power from which Ireland's Office of Arms derived its heraldic authority.[33]

A related royal warrant to the Treasury arrangement, issued on 14 July 1871, concerned the regulation of the Order of St Patrick. The most significant aspect of this warrant, as far as the Office of Arms was concerned, was that it reduced its staff. Several of the traditional officers of the Order were abolished following the death or retirement of the existing office holders. These included the offices of the Genealogist, Prelate, Cork Herald, Dublin Herald and the offices of Junior Pursuivants. One by one, as these officers died, beginning in 1885, with Sir William Lesson, the Genealogist, and ending with the last of the pursuivants, George Frith Barry, in 1891, the size of Burke's heraldic court at Dublin Castle began to shrink. After Lesson's death, however, Burke decided that a Genealogist was needed to research the family pedigrees of new knights, and he appointed his eldest son Henry Farnham Burke (Somerset Herald at the College of Arms) to that position in 1889.[34]

In connection with his financial reforms Burke ensured that under the general head of 'Miscellaneous Expenses' he would in future be repaid directly 'when out of pocket' for any expenses incurred during the normal course of Office business. This included payments for vellums and patents, inks and equipment used in the execution of grants and confirmations of arms.

Furthermore, in 1879 he also secured that the costs for the Order of St Patrick would be met from a separate vote of expenses for the Lord Lieutenant's household, thereby divorcing ceremonial costs from the general expenses incurred by the Office in its heraldic and genealogical work.[35] In addition, the Treasury agreed to give a grant of £63 to cover the costs of emblazoning arms and towards the provision of the insignia of the Order of St Patrick, in 1880. In 1891, the Office was also paid for supplying the services of a 'part-time reporter', to account for the affairs of the Court during the Castle Season – when the Lord Lieutenant was in residence at Dublin Castle – usually between the first week of February and mid-March. This generated an additional payment of £30.[36]

In the context of these new financial structures we find Burke making regular returns to the Treasury from 1872 onwards. He carefully accounted for the fees and emoluments, losing no opportunity to remind his superiors of the

---

33 Burke, Record Tower, to Mr Murray, Treasury, 13 November 1871, GO, MS 323, pp. 158–9.
34 Galloway, *Most Illustrious Order*, p. 69.
35 Treasury memorandum, PRO, T 15880.
36 Estimates for 1891–2, GO, MS 325, pp. 314–14a.

considerable national value that it provided. In 1887, for example, he reported that 'the fees received annually by Government from this Office exceed considerably the salary for which I committed'. His boastful language was supported with financial evidence. Between 1872 and 1879 receipts of income were well in excess of the predicted estimates, representing an annual average excess of £419.4.2. Over the seven-year period these figures amounted to an accumulated total of some £2,934. Thus, Burke could proclaim that 'the difference between the estimated amount of office fees . . . and the amount realised . . . is due to more official business than calculated'.[37]

ADMINISTRATIVE REFORMS

In addition to his heraldic, genealogical and ceremonial duties, Burke's appointment as the Keeper of the State Papers in 1866 complemented his role as Ulster King of Arms and also resulted in improvements for the Office itself. He was the custodian for all the records in both the Bermingham Tower, the principal repository for Irish records, and the Record Tower, where more recent State Papers and records of the Office of Arms were kept. He contributed significantly to the transformation of standards of record-keeping in both locations and to the passage of the Record Act of 1866, which led to the establishment of the PRO of Ireland in 1867. Whilst the entire contents of the Bermingham Tower and significant quantities of State Papers from the Record Tower were transferred to the new Records Office as a result of this legislation, Burke's influence ensured that the records of the Office of Arms remained *in situ*. The Act specifically excluded those records located in the Record Tower 'appertaining to the Office of Ulster King of Arms', and State Papers under 50 years old, including those from the Chief Secretary's Office. Thus, the new archive legislation strengthened the integrity of the Office of Arms, by making specific provision for the preservation of its records as a distinct archival collection.[38]

In preparation for his involvement in the development of the new Records Office, the Government commissioned Burke to visit Paris to inspect the French record system in September 1866. The resulting detailed report that had an influential impact on the official policy towards record keeping and preservation. The original draft of this report is contained among the Official Entries, and provides an insight to Burke's meticulous attention to detail and

---

37 Estimates and receipts, Ulster's Office, 1872–79, GO, MS 324, pp. 26–30, and memorandum dated 20 July 1882, *op. cit.,* p. 194.
38 *An Act For Keeping Safely the Public Records,* 1867, section 4.

vision for the future. In it he advised that Ireland should 'borrow from the French some of their improvements'.[39]

Based on his French visit, he undertook a thorough examination of all of the records in the Record Tower including the records of the Office of Arms, and ordered that they be cleaned, restored, properly classified, and securely shelved to facilitate retrieval. In 1872 we find him requisitioning 300 cartons from the Board of Public Works for the storage of the State Papers.[40] In 1875, 100 yards of gut web tape, cut into straps of 30 inches with buckle attached were ordered 'for the ongoing management of the State Papers and other records carried on year by year in this department'.[41] Many of the registers of pedigrees and grants were rebound at this time, and labelled 'Ulster's Office' to distinguish them from other materials remaining in the Tower.

Between 1867 and 1868 the process of transferring many of the Public Records in the Tower to the new PRO at the Four Courts freed up space for the papers of the Office of Arms, which remained *in situ*. The transfer of the Plea, Pipe and other Rolls, records of the Irish Houses of Parliament to 1801, and papers of the Record Commissioners, for example, vacated several rooms in the Tower, and Burke appears to have designated at least one of these specifically for the use of his Office. Later plans of the Tower show that a small room on the ground floor had been acquired as a waiting room, presumably for visitors to inspect State Papers, or to consult with Burke concerning material in the collections of Ulster's Office, while on the fourth floor, where the Office had been located since 1831, he fitted out a room for himself, with an additional room beside it to serve as the clerk's office.[42] Burke also requisitioned new furniture for these areas, including storage presses and shelves for arranging the records, and had a fender installed to heat his own 'private office', as he referred to it, for which a new carpet was also provided.[43]

Although the Office of Arms was not officially open to the public at this time, it was possible for researchers to request the staff to undertake searches on their behalf, or to make an appointment with Burke for a consultation. He appears to have advertised this fact. In 1867, for example, he explained to one enquirer:

39 Sir J. Bernard Burke, 'Report on the French records', in GO, MS 322, pp. 253–279. Other copies of the report are available at NLI, MS 11219.2. See also Ó Dúill, 'Gilbert and the PRO', in Clark et al, *Gilbert*, p. 35.
40 Burke to Mr Hornsby, Board of Public Works, Dublin Castle, 1 August 1872, GO, MS 323, p.197.
41 Requisition for straps, 3 May 1875, *op. cit.*, p. 217.
42 Plan of Office of Ulster King of Arms, Dublin Castle, *c.* 1900, OPW, A6/14/7/48.
43 Requisition for furniture, 12 August 1873, GO, MS 323, p. 218.

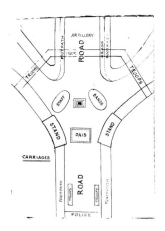

ORDER OF PROCEEDING

AT

THE DEPARTURE

OF

HIS GRACE, JOHN WINSTON, DUKE OF MARLBOROUGH, K.G.,

Lord Lieutenant-General & General Governor of Ireland,

28th APRIL, 1880.

Plan for dais and stands, with order of proceeding at the state departure of the Duke of Marlborough, Lord Lieutenant of Ireland, 1876–80. *GO, MS 337.*

> Ulster's Office [the Office of Arms] is in fact the depository of the heraldic and genealogical records of Ireland . . . it is not open to the public. I have however since my appointment, supplied information when it has been required for historical or literary purposes.[44]

His room was clearly frequented by customers, by 1874 Burke ordered that the four chairs in it needed repair and recovering.[45] Increasing business also necessitated increasing quantities of drawing paper during the 1870s, when

---

44 Burke to William Law Esq., 14 November 1867, GO, MS 322, p. 97.
45 Requisition for furniture, 12 August 1875, GO, MS 323, p. 256.

Burke reported that the paper was 'constantly in use . . . for pedigrees, draw-ings, genealogical reports, armorial bearings, etc'.[46] The steady income from fees recouped by the Office bears out this daily activity. Between 1859 and 1868, for example, an annual income of £40 was recovered for conducting general searches (at five shillings a search) and other more detailed searches (at £3 a search).[47]

Later memorandums reveal the self-importance that Burke attached to his heraldic and genealogical work. There are innumerable occasions when he reminded the Lord Lieutenant, Under-Secretary and other Castle dignitaries about the 'numerous and important' duties of his Office – thus making him-self appear more indispensable every time he wrote.[48] By the 1880s, Burke had identified seven principal duties for which he was responsible requiring 'his constant attendance at the Office'. His outline of these provides a useful insight to the nature of the business of the Office of Arms by the latter half of the nineteenth century.

Firstly, he arranged, investigated, and registered the pedigrees 'of the families of Ireland', thus providing 'evidence of essential, sometimes vital, use in the descent of title and property'. In relation to this particular task, as King of Arms and Principal Herald of Ireland he acted as a referee on behalf of the Crown, in relation to all matters relating to descent and property for both the Government and members of the public. Secondly, he had absolute control in Ireland of the right to armorial bearings. This required him to process applications to authenticate if applicants were entitled to bear arms, to oversee the design of new coats of arms, and to administer the process of registering them in the official registers for the permanent record. Thirdly, he investigated and reported on applications for royal licences (usually to change a surname and bear different arms) and registered such changes. Fourthly, he protected the rights and inheritances of the Irish peers and baronets. Fifthly, he registered all knighthoods conferred by the Lord Lieutenant. Sixthly, he acted as the executive officer of the Order of St Patrick, keeping its registry and records, conducting its correspondence, and administering its investi-tures, installations and other ceremonies. Finally, and of particular pride to Burke, was his ceremonial role:

---

46   Burke to the Office of Under Secretary, Dublin Castle, 22 August 1874, GO, MS 324, p. 257.

47   Table of fees, Ulster's Office, GO, MS 323, pp. 19–22.

48   Memorandum transmitted to the Chief Secretary's Office, outlining the functions of Ulster King of Arms, 11 August 1887, GO, MS 325, p. 209, with additional notes p. 129.

Ulster directs also all State ceremonies and regulates the proceedings of the vice-regal court. He has the custody of the Crown Jewels [the Order's insignia] during the absence of the Lord Lieutenant, and also the Sword of State and other insignia of the vice-royalty.[49]

CEREMONIAL DUTIES

Having devoted the first two decades of his appointment to the re-ordering and classification of its records, securing of its financial position, and introduction of administrative reforms, it was his ceremonial duties to which Burke devoted most of his energies from the mid-1870s onwards. To this end, he became a prominent and indispensable figure at the Victorian Court in Dublin Castle, where he was widely respected for his knowledge on matters of precedence and court procedure, both nationally and internationally.[50] Indeed, Burke became quite a celebrity, unlike any of his predecessors. One contemporary observed the dutiful manner in which he conducted his business:

> How familiar was his little chirruping, cock-sparrow figure, his bright, round face, and with what reverence used he to call out the sacred words, "Their Excellencies"! I believe he looked upon the Lords Lieutenant as something supernatural. A good-natured soul, [he was] always ready with some little service, capable of grand display – fluttering in his tabard or the blue mantle of St Patrick.[51]

Burke established an international reputation as an expert on aspects of precedence, which brought renown to his Office in Dublin. Just some of the examples revealed in his Official Entries are letters seeking his advice on matters as diverse as 'the position of Roman Catholic prelates and other precedence issues in Canada', for the Colonial Office, in 1884; the precedence of the judges of the County Court in Ireland, in 1885; and a private request about where to seat the Russian ambassador at a dinner party in London, in 1890.[52]

Burke also provided precedence advice for the various churches in Ireland. For the Church of Ireland, for example, he decreed in 1876 that the Bishop of Meath had long 'been *primus inter pares* among Irish bishops', and thus enjoyed first place among the Church of Ireland bishops, behind the arch-

---

49 *op. cit.*
50 Robins, *Champagne and Silver Buckles*, p. 126.
51 Fitzgerald, *Recollections of Dublin Castle*, p. 30.
52 GO, MS 325, pp. 9, 107, 303.

bishops. Unlike the other bishops, who were styled the Right Reverend, Meath like the archbishops was styled as the Most Reverend.[53] For the bishops of the Roman Catholic Church and the Moderator of the Presbyterian Church in Ireland, Burke devised the correct form of address for formal occasions, in 1880 and 1886 respectively.[54] The fact that Burke himself was a Catholic allowed him to quietly encourage the clergy of that Church to attend at Court, although they seldom accepted. In an undated memorandum on the subject, for example, Burke commented that there was no reason why 'the clergy dress regulations . . . registered here should not apply to Roman Catholic as well as Protestant divines'.[55]

The frequent and detailed memorandums drawn up by Burke in the process of administering Court events vividly demonstrate his attention to detail. As a permanent officer of the Lord Lieutenant's household, Burke and his staff provided guidance and advice for successive administrations about the traditions, rights, privileges and ceremonies of the Court:

> Ulster King of Arms takes cognisance of, and decides all matters relating to precedence, and conducts all State ceremonies. His official lists guide the household in the regulations of the levées and drawing rooms.[56]

At the commencement of the viceroyalty of John Winston Spencer Churchill, seventh Duke of Marlborough, in 1876, Burke began a new series of Court Books, in which he set out the rules and regulations for administering every aspect of business connected with the household.[57] These volumes included the precedence lists for attendance at various official functions; the code of dress to be observed; the standing orders to be followed by the official household staff, and official lists of suitable guests. The precedence lists also underlined Ulster's own prominent place at the Irish Court. This had been established at the institution of the Office in 1552, and re-affirmed at various times after that;

---

53 'Opinion on the Precedence of the Bishop of Meath', 18 December 1876, RCBL, MS 209. Burke's original draft of this document is found at GO, MS 323, pp. 304–12.

54 Address forms for the prelates of the Roman Catholic Church, GO, MS 324, p. 64. Form of address for the Moderator of the Presbyterian Church in Ireland, 1886, GO, MS 325, p. 80.

55 Comments on the attendance of Catholic prelates at Castle functions, GO, MS 323, p. 44.

56 Draft memorandum on the functions of Ulster King of Arms, undated, GO, MS 337, p. 14.

57 GO, MSS 348–50.

but Burke used every opportunity to emphasise that the place assigned to him was ahead 'of the officers of State, and next to the person of the viceroy'.[58]

Burke's efficiency on State ceremonies held outside the Castle was also observed from the contents of these books. Some of the exacting directions reveal attention bordering on military precision. Burke even sketched detailed plans of processions, numbering carriages, and anticipating where the crowds would gather to view the Lord Lieutenant and other dignitaries making their customary speeches. A case in point is the detailed planning given to the departure of the Duke of Marlborough, the outgoing Lord Lieutenant, in April 1880. Burke (being a Tory like Marlborough) ensured that he went out in style. Under Burke's direction, bands played along the route between the Castle and Kingstown, where a special steamer awaited to convey his party to Holyhead. The streets were lined with military and boys from the Hibernian School in uniform, while guards of honour were arranged to salute the outgoing viceroy in the Upper Castle Yard, again at Westland Row, and finally at the pier at Kingstown.[59]

Another State occasion that had prophetic consequences for the Office of Arms, was the ceremonial organised by Burke for the laying of the first stone of the Museum of Science and Art and of the National Library of Ireland by the Prince of Wales in April 1885. Less than 60 years later, the Office of Arms would be taken over by this institution and renamed the Genealogical Office in 1943, while in 1981 it would be relocated from its nineteenth century base in Dublin Castle to Kildare Street. This was close to the spot where the National Library's foundation stone had been laid in the presence of the Lord Lieutenant and the Earl and Countess Spencer, the first Trustees, together with hundreds of onlookers in 1885.[60]

Similar attention to detail is found in Burke's Funeral Entries. For example, he included much detail in the entry concerning the State reception and funeral of the sixth Earl of Mayo, the Honourable Richard Southwell, formerly the Viceroy of India, which was held in St Patrick's Cathedral, Dublin, in April 1872. Burke included robustly drawn colour plans of the banners and flags of the bishops and other dignitaries as they had made up the funeral cortege. The result is a particularly beautiful heraldic display.[61]

---

58 Burke, *General Armory*, p. xxvii.
59 Plans of the order of procession of staff and troops for the departure of Marlborough, April 1880, GO, MS 337, pp. 260, 273–4.
60 Form of ceremonial to be observed at the laying of the first stone of the Museum of Science and Art and of the National Library of Ireland, 10 April 1885, GO, MS 348.
61 GO, MS 77, pp. 3–5, 15–22.

Copy.

37.

CEREMONIAL

at the

LAYING OF THE FIRST STONE

of

THE MUSEUM OF SCIENCE AND ART, AND OF THE

NATIONAL LIBRARY OF IRELAND,

by

HIS ROYAL HIGHNESS THE PRINCE OF WALES,

on Friday, the 10th. of April, 1885, at a quarter to 4 o'clock.

— · — · — · — · — · — · — · — · — · —

A flourish of Trumpets will announce the arrival at the Entrance in Merrion Square of their Royal Highnesses the Prince and Princess of Wales, and their Excellencies the Lord Lieutenant and the Countess Spencer.

A Guard of Honour will mount at the Entrance.

The Band will play the National Anthem.

On their Royal Highnesses alighting from their carriage at Leinster House, East Entrance, they will be received by the Visitors of the Museum, the Trustees of the National Library, and the Commissioners of Public Works. The Director of the Science and Art Museum, Professor V. Ball, F.R.S., will be presented to the Prince.

Their Royal Highnesses will then be conducted through Leinster House, the National Anthem being played by the Second Band, during which a Bouquet will be offered to Her Royal Highness by Students of the Metropolitan School of Art.

On reaching the dais their Royal Highnesses and their Excellencies will be conducted to their seats.

Ceremonial instructions for the laying of the first stone of the Museum of Science and Art and of the National Library of Ireland, by the Prince of Wales, as issued by Sir Bernard Burke, Ulster King of Arms, 10 April 1885. *GO, MS 348.*

Burke also flourished in the ceremonial duties connected with the Order of St Patrick. Perhaps the highpoint of his public career was the royal visit to Ireland by Prince Albert in April 1868, during which the prince was invested as a knight of the Order in St Patrick's Hall at the Castle on 18 April, followed by installation to the stall assigned to him in St Patrick's Cathedral, on 20 April 1868. On an earlier occasion Burke had bemoaned the fact that royal visits to Ireland were 'like the angels, few and far between',[62] so when the opportunity arose to supervise and direct a royal spectacle in Dublin, he threw himself into event with enthusiasm.

Significantly, not one business entry was recorded in the Official Entries and Letters during 1868, indicating that Burke's time was completely devoted to superintending the royal visit that year. No installation service had in fact been held since 1821, unceremonious dispensations being granted instead. For the royal visit in 1868, Burke surpassed all expectations. The spectacle was reported to be magnificent, and the 'triumph of Ulster complete!'[63]

Burke led the royal procession into the cathedral followed by dean, clergy, members of the official household, and the Knights of the Order, to a flourish of trumpets. Following the system devised by Betham for the installation ceremony held in 1821, a colour code system was used to facilitate the entry of guests into the cathedral from a number of entry points, depending on the colour of their tickets. Details of the arrangements were published in advance in several newspapers. Four temporary artists were employed to paint the new banners and stall plates in the quire, whilst local builders, supervised by Burke, constructed extra seating galleries. Life at the cathedral was completely disrupted in Burke's favour:

> St. Patrick's Cathedral has been virtually closed for some time back during the process of altering and decorating it for the installation of the Prince. Divine service has been intermittent. . . . No one, however, grumbles at the Dean of St. Patrick's for abdicating his functions temporarily in favour of Sir Bernard Burke. The latter gentleman is eminently popular, and Dublin is too low church in its religious proclivities to make a fuss about the Ulster King of Arms reigning for the nonce over St. Patrick's.[64]

---

62   Burke to Mr Hanby, 24 July 1862, GO, MS 322, p. 190. Previous visits during the nineteenth century were made by King George IV in September 1821 and Queen Victoria in August 1849; 1853 and 1861.

63   *Dublin Evening Mail*, 17 April 1868.

64   From Galloway, *Most Illustrious Order*, pp. 62–6, quoted in *Clerical Journal, xxii*, 16 April 1868.

The Survival of the Office of Arms

Burke's excessive attention to detail, and rather pompous displays, were not, however, favoured by everyone. The pro-Liberal *Daily News* published a report to the effect that he had become something of a figure of fun, his bowing and floating about in his tabard allegedly provoking 'titters from spectators' at an installation ceremony held in Dublin Castle in August 1871.[65]

Following the general election in 1885, when the Liberals were returned to power with a reduced majority, the Irish Parliamentary Party (IPP), led by Charles Parnell, increased its political clout, winning 86 seats. This enabled the Nationalists to secure Liberal support for Home Rule. With the IPP effectively holding the balance of power, several aspects of Irish administration were examined in greater detail, including the cost of the upkeep of the Lord Lieutenant's household and related expenses.

During some of the debates on this issue in 1886 and again in 1888, the Office of Arms was specifically discussed, when several MPs enquired what use it had for the general population. Mr John Joseph Clancy, Nationalist MP for Dublin North, for example, speculated that it 'was surely as good a specimen of medieval mummery as is to be found in the civilized world'! Apart from presenting coats of arms and mottos to people that 'had not got them', he believed that it had 'no use at all'. His colleague, Mr Patrick O'Hea, MP for Donegal West, believed it was 'one of those ornamental offices, the expenditure on which [was] considerable, but the utility of which [was] only fanciful'.[66]

In contrast, other Irish speakers emphasised the history and tradition associated with the Office. John O'Connor, the Nationalist MP for South Tipperary, expressing more traditional views, suggested that the Ulster King of Arms represented a 'relic of old decency' that should be retained for as long as Ireland had a Lord Lieutenant. Government policy was firmly in favour of the continuance of the Office at this time, especially as it was making a profit. The Chief Secretary for Ireland, Sir Michael Hicks-Beach, summed up the majority feeling, that as the Office of Arms had functioned continuously since 1552 and was thus over 300 years old, it could not be abolished. It was 'of ancient estate and dignity', in charge of matters related to the history of Ireland, and the history of individual families. Whilst some honorable members, he argued, 'might not attach much importance to these things', the Office should continue, especially as it was not costing the State anything. During the previous five years, some £6,000 had been paid in fees

---

65 *The Daily News*, 17 August 1871.
66 *Hansard*, 10 September 1886, 307, 270–1.

to the Treasury, with the result that 'the country was the gainer, and not the loser by the bargain'.[67]

Similar arguments were debated in 1888, but when figures were presented to show that the Office was paying for itself, there was relatively little opposition. Again O'Connor argued that the Irish people were 'somewhat partial to State and legal forms', and the motion for its abolition was defeated by a large majority.[68]

Indeed, a few years later, when ill-health prevented Burke's attendance at ceremonial events, critics were not slow to inform the Lord Lieutenant about laxities in the formalities. The Marquiss of Drogheda, for example, reported after an investiture ceremony not attended by Burke that he believed 'the duties of the heraldic department [were] carried on in an increasingly careless and irregular manner'.[69]

The complaint forced Burke to apologise for his own absence and the shortcomings of his colleagues, but he pleaded that it was 'his health so shattered of late' that had prevented his 'personal attendance'. In addition, Sheffield Betham, the Dublin Herald, was ill (and died later in the year). His senior clerk and pursuivant George Barry, on whom Burke relied for much administrative assistance, was also ill.[70]

Following the nepotistic practices of his predecessors, Burke had provided appointments for his sons. Bernard Louis was appointed Athlone Pursuivant in 1883, while Henry Farnham Burke served as Genealogist for the Order and Deputy Ulster from 1889 until his death in 1930. His youngest brother, John Edward, succeeded Bernard Louis as Athlone Pursuivant following his early death in July 1892. These were honorary rather than salaried appointments, and as a result their attendance at the Office was less than regular. Henry, for example, was also serving an appointment in the College of Arms in London and made only periodic visits to Dublin. This may explain the administrative shortcomings.

Burke's health continued to deteriorate. He had long suffered from rheumatism, complaining as early as 1872 that his hand was 'so cupped' that he could 'scarcely hold the pen'.[71] The deteriorating scribble makes many of his later memorandums and draft letters difficult to decipher. Scanty entries

---

67 *op. cit.*, pp. 272–3.
68 *Hansard*, 3 December 1888, 331, 858–74.
69 Copy of letter from the Marquess of Drogheda to the Marquess of Zetland, Lord Lieutenant, 28 February 1890, GO, MS 325, p. 277.
70 Burke to Zetland, 4 March 1890, *op. cit.*, p. 328.
71 Burke, Dublin Castle, to John Ribton Garstin, 9 February 1872, RCBL, MS 14/8.

and letters in the official records from this period onwards indicate that he was frequently absent, and on occasions when he did appear, he overworked himself 'endeavouring to make up for lost time'.[72]

The death of his eldest son, the Athlone Pursuivant in July 1892 at the age of only 31, probably hastened Burke's own death, in December of the same year, aged 71.[73] Whilst it might have been predicted that the Burke dynasty would continue – inherited by one of his sons perhaps – there were other heraldic and genealogical experts waiting in the wings, who were not only anxious to secure an appointment at the Office of Arms, but also keen to develop the Irish heraldic authority in a more dynamic way.

---

72 Burke to D.C. Lloyd Owen Esq., 28 September 1891, GO, MS 326, p. 19.
73 Galloway, *Most Illustrious Order*, p. 72.

TWO

'A story of bickerings, scandal and neglect'

The rise and fall of Sir Arthur Vicars, 1893–1908

THE END OF THE BURKE DYNASTY

Arthur Vicars was born in England in July 1864, but had close connections with Ireland through his mother, Jane Gun-Cunninghame, who had first married Pierce K. O'Mahony of Kilmorna, County Kerry in 1839, producing two sons, George and Pierce. Following O'Mahony's death in 1856, her second marriage to Colonel William Henry Vicars of Leamington, Warwickshire in 1857, produced four more children, the youngest of whom was Arthur. Both Arthur's parents died before he reached the age of ten, and his older Irish half-brothers played a significant role in his early life, helping to foster a romantic attachment to Ireland. The Mahonys claimed to trace their roots to the third century, and it was this long ancestral tradition that prompted Vicars's early interest in genealogy.[1] He spent his school holidays in Ireland at Grange Con in County Wicklow and Kilmorna in County Kerry – his half-brothers' respective seats – and once his education was completed, he moved to Ireland permanently.[2] Initially his intention was to train as a barrister, but this was abandoned in favour of full-time genealogical and heraldic pursuits.[3]

By the 1880s Vicars had an established reputation in the fields of genealogy and heraldry. The editors of the *Irish Builder* credited him as 'one of the very highest authorities in this country on heraldic matters'. This compliment had first appeared as their preface to Vicars's 'Heraldic notes on the monuments in St Audoen's Church, Dublin', published in 1887, when, in advance of his appointment to the Office of Arms, he used evidence from the Funeral Entries there to verify monument inscriptions.[4] His heraldic expertise again came to the fore in his study of the mummifying properties of the vaults in St Michan's

---

1 GO, MSS 77, pp. 24–5; Gaughan, *Listowel*, pp. 322–3.
2 Galloway, *Most Illustrious Order*, p. 73.
3 Bankes, *Vicious Circle*, p. 7.
4 Pre-text to Vicars, 'Heraldic notes' in *Irish Builder*, xxix, (1887), p. 205.

Guard of honour in Upper Yard, Dublin Castle, during Queen Victoria's visit to Ireland, April 1900. The balcony of the Bedford Tower, home of the Office of Arms 1903–81, is full of onlookers. *R. Livingstone Collection, Irish Picture Library. Courtesy, Davison and Associates.*

Church, Dublin, when he was able to establish the identity of several individuals buried there, by deciphering the arms on their vaults.[5] Vicars was also a founder member of the County Kildare Archaeological Society, and served as an Honorary Secretary from its foundation in 1891 until his death in 1921, publishing regularly in its journal, and in several other antiquarian publications.

Even before the end of Burke's reign there was evidence that the transition between the Burke and Vicars dynasties would not be smooth. Arthur Vicars had a high opinion of his own ability as a herald and genealogist, but he was also genuinely concerned about the integrity of the Irish heraldic authority. He had previously tried unsuccessfully to secure a post in the Office following Sheffield Betham's death in 1890,[6] but Burke was reluctant to employ him. The post of Dublin Herald had not been advertised, because it had been scheduled for abolition in accordance with the reforms which Burke had issued for the Order of St Patrick, in 1871. Vicars, however, saw the vacancy as an opportunity, confidently declaring:

> The duties of the Office are such as I believe I am competent to discharge, requiring as they do, a knowledge of heraldry and the usages of state ceremonials. To this branch of study I have applied myself for several years and believe I am the only person in Ireland who – not being an official – has steadily and almost exclusively given his attention to the study of heraldry and cognate studies.[7]

The official reply from the Castle authorities at this time was in keeping with the decision made in 1871. It remained firm that there 'were no grounds for recommending the reestablishment of any other of the offices of the Order of St Patrick'.[8]

Clearly Vicars was experienced and well respected in the fields of genealogy and heraldry, because among his general referees he included Dr David Digges La Touche, Deputy Keeper of the Public Records of Ireland, several prominent members of the Royal Irish Academy, and even Burke himself. The Duke of Norfolk, as Earl Marshal, had also placed Vicars's name on the list for preferment in the Herald's College in London, and 'could speak highly of [his] qualifications'. But Vicars wanted to work for the Irish heraldic authority, and persisting with his plans, he applied to the

---

5   Vicars, *Account of Antiseptic Vaults* (Dublin, 1888), p. 5.
6   Galloway, *Most Illustrious Order*, p. 72.
7   Arthur Vicars, Clyde Road, Dublin, to the Rt. Hon. Arthur Balfour, Chief Secretary for Ireland, 12 July 1890, NAI, CSORP 1890/11178.
8   Mulhall to Vicars, 23 July 1890, *op. cit.*

Lord Lieutenant to fill the post of Dublin Herald. He offered to serve 'without any emolument', so anxious was he 'to be connected officially with a department' to which he believed he could 'be of some use'.[9] Again, Vicars was rejected, as Burke was adamant that the office of junior pursuivant was superfluous. It was, the latter declared:

> abolished and rightly so. It was perfectly useless and very troublesome. No duties were attached and there was no connection whatever between it and the heraldic staff in Ireland . . . it had nothing to do with heraldry and genealogy.[10]

Not easily deterred, Vicars's persistence continued. When George Frith Barry, the last surviving pursuivant and Burke's clerk, died in March 1891, Vicars offered to fill this position, again without emolument. Concerned that the Irish heraldic authority should not be diminished, he compared it with the other two heraldic authorities of the United Kingdom:

> The heraldic establishment of Ireland only consists of Ulster King of Arms and Athlone Pursuivant. There are no heralds, whereas the Herald's Office in Scotland has a staff of a King of Arms, four heralds and six pursuivants, besides other officials, all with salaries attached to their offices. In like manner the Herald's College in London is a very considerable body, larger again than that of Scotland.

He suggested that Burke's revival of the post of Genealogist for the Order of St Patrick, given to his son Henry Farnham Burke in 1889, had set a precedent for the revival of other positions in the Office. Such revival, he continued, 'should be maintained to encourage those studying a rare branch of knowledge such as heraldry and genealogy', and that the State had a duty to uphold it. He reiterated his own qualifications: 'I may add that I am the only professional herald in Ireland not officially connected with Ulster's Office'.[11] These views put him at odds with the Burke establishment, and a few weeks later he informed the Chief Secretary that he had:

> reason to believe that Sir Bernard Burke is somewhat antagonistic to my getting any heraldic appointment in Ireland, tho' he doubtless assigns

---

9   Vicars to John Mulhall, Private Secretary to the Lord Lieutenant, 21 July 1890, *op. cit.*

10 Bernard Burke to John Mulhall, Lord Lieutenant's Private Secretary, 5 March 1891, *op. cit.*

11 Vicars to Marquess of Zetland, Lord Lieutenant of Ireland, 17 March 1891, *op. cit.*

Sir Arthur Vicars, Ulster King of Arms, Registrar and Knight Attendant of the Order of St Patrick, 1893–1908, in full ceremonial dress, including the tabard of royal arms, his knighthood badge, the collar of the Registrar of the Order of St Patrick, and the collar of 'Ss' bearing the badge of the Ulster King of Arms. He also holds his baton, which features the cross of St Patrick. In the top left corner may be seen Vicars's arms, impaled with those of the Office of Arms. *GO Collection.*

other official reasons. It may be that he thinks that my entry into office would trench upon his monopoly.[12]

Vicars assumed that Burke did not want him, even though he had agreed to act as one of his referees. In fact, Vicars' application to replace Barry as Burke's clerk was turned down by Burke on the grounds that Vicars' qualifications were 'so extraordinarily high'. Perhaps Vicars simply knew too much for Burke's comfort. Vicars, however, remained convinced that he was the right person to act as Burke's assistant, and to uphold the Irish heraldic establishment. He wondered why 'should not the Government look favourably on my application?'[13]

ULSTER'S CROWN FOR VICARS

Vicars's applications for employment remained on the Government file, together with supporting testimonials from such prominent political figures of the day as the Earl of Mayo and Lord Rayleigh. Given the administrative laxities that had marred the latter years of Burke's tenure, combined with Vicars's influential connections, to say nothing of his dogged determination to reform the Office, the Government's decision to appoint him just two months after Burke's death was hardly surprising. On 27 February 1893, Lord Houghton, the Lord Lieutenant, appointed Mr Arthur Vicars, then a comparatively unknown man, aged just 29 years, to succeed Burke as Ulster King of Arms and Principal Herald of Ireland, Registrar and Knight Attendant of the Order of St Patrick.[14]

His patent of appointment stated that he would hold the said 'office at the King's pleasure'. As had been the case for Burke, this empowered him to appoint a deputy or deputies to act on his behalf. In a separate arrangement with the Treasury, it was agreed that Vicars would receive an annual salary of £500, and that his appointment would 'not interfere with his right to engage in the private practice of his profession'.[15] Vicars received £250 less than Burke (and he would later protest about this), but the reduction took into account that the additional post of Keeper of the State Papers, held by Burke since 1867, had reverted on his death in 1892 to the Deputy Keeper of the Public Record Office. Thus, Vicars was entrusted solely with the administration of the Office of Arms.[16]

---

12 Vicars to Sir West Ridgway, 26 March 1891, *op. cit.*
13 *ibid.*
14 Patent of appointment, 27 February 1893, GO, MS 154, pp. 117–9.
15 NAI, CSORP 1913/18119.
16 McDowell, *Irish Administration*, p. 278.

'A story of bickerings, scandal and neglect'

Although a diligent researcher and scholarly writer of dozens of papers, Vicars was not so attentive to more mundane administrative matters. Lord Walter Fitzgerald, who became the second Honorary Secretary of the Kildare Archaeological Society in 1894, complained about Vicars's laxity in sending out notices for meetings, and other clerical failings. One exasperated exchange of correspondence during 1896 (preserved in the papers of Thomas Ulick Sadleir, who became a member of the Society in 1907, and was a prominent member of the Office of Arms staff from 1913), reveals that Fitzgerald even suggested to Vicars that he should resign as Secretary of the Society, because he could not undertake his duties properly. Vicars did not resign but on future occasions Fitzgerald issued the notices instead, adding his co-secretary's name for, as he put it, 'ornament only!'[17]

Sir Henry Robinson, a contemporary who worked in the Castle Administration for the duration of Vicars's appointment, remembered him as a 'notoriously forgetful, casual sort of creature, nearly always late for his engagements.[18] Others became even more critical in the light of his premature departure from office in January 1908, when he was dismissed for negligence. This followed the infamous theft of the 'Crown Jewels' or the insignia of the Order of St Patrick worn by the Lord Lieutenant in his capacity as Grand Master of the Order, which had been in the safe in the public room at the Office.[19] In the aftermath of this theft it seems there were some who would have had entirely written Vicars out of the history books. For example, one harsh and, it transpires, inaccurate Government memorandum, summed up his contribution thus:

> Sir A. Vicars was a persistent applicant for benefits, including £1000 a year, a residence at Dublin Castle and pension rights . . . however he left Office in 1908, preceded by certain Crown jewels.[20]

Another Treasury official, when asked about official attitudes towards the Office of Arms in the early 1920s, commented that whilst it had 'fulfilled a

---

17 Lord Walter Fitzgerald, Kilkea Castle, Kildare, to Vicars, 29 January 1896, and two undated letters of same, SC.

18 Robinson, *Memories: Wise and Otherwise*, p. 221.

19 Crown Jewels (Ireland) Commission, *Report of the Vice-Regal Commission, Appointed to Investigate the Circumstances of the Loss of the Regalia of the Order of Saint Patrick and to Inquire if Sir Arthur Vicars Exercised Due Vigilance and Proper Care as the Custodian Thereof, Presented to Both Houses of Parliament* (London, HMSO, 1908), hereafter *Crown Jewels Commission*.

20 Treasury minute, PRO/T/62/709.

useful and chivalrous purpose', its record since 1893 had been 'a story of bick-erings, scandal and neglect'.[21]

Contrary to these anecdotal comments, Vicars's administration of the Office of Arms demonstrates anything but a casual or lax attention to detail. Indeed, his heraldic expertise, combined with an informed awareness of the importance of keeping accurate historical records and his knowledge about their care and custody, shows that Vicars was meticulous in the attention to the duties and tradition of his Office. He was not the offhand, disorganised, casual person portrayed by his critics. This belies the story presented by those in power, who were anxious to portray him in a different light.

REFORMS

Vicars's got off to a flying start during his early days at the Office of Arms. He brought a scholarly air to the Castle, and his world-famous collection of book-plates attracted many visiting antiquaries.[22] In 1897, he developed the work of Sir William Betham, and, using Betham's abstracts, published a comprehen-sive *Index to the Prerogative Wills of Ireland 1536–1810*. This accounted for, and listed alphabetically, the testator of every will proved in the Prerogative Court between those dates. On the destruction of the Public Records Office in 1922, Vicars's publication became the only readily available source of the information that the wills had contained. It remains a valuable tool for genealogical researchers and is Vicars's best-known work.[23]

Sir Arthur Vicars (as he became in 1896) encouraged aspiring researchers in the fields of heraldry and genealogy. In 1901, he invited Thomas Sadleir, then a young trainee barrister and genealogical enthusiast, to dine with him, introducing him to his collection of books and other material. He explained 'most of my interesting things are at the Castle' where he was 'always glad to encourage anyone interested in heraldry'.[24]

Vicars's most significant contribution to the development of the Office of Arms was his commitment to building up its archival collections and pre-serving them in a suitable environment. Early on, he was surprised to find that there were barely 200 volumes of manuscripts in the custody of the Office, dating 'chiefly from before Betham's time'. He set out about increasing its

---

21 Treasury memorandum, *c.*1924, *op. cit.*
22 French, 'Nepotists', p. 350.
23 Arthur Vicars, *Index to the Prerogative Wills of Ireland 1536–1810* (Dublin, 1897).
24 Vicars, 44 Wellington Road, to Thomas Ulick Sadleir, 18 December 1901, SC.

Book-plate of Sir Arthur Vicars, bearing his arms and badges of office, 1896. *GO, Vicars Book-plate Collection.*

Book-plate of William Chamney, 1905. *GO, Vicars Book-plate Collection.*

holdings, persuading the Stationery Office to give an annual allowance of £50 for the purchase of further manuscripts, and encouraging private gifts to buy printed genealogies of individual families.[25] By the time of his premature departure in 1908, the manuscript collections in the Office had grown to over 400 items, in addition to a fine collection of printed genealogies and other secondary works.[26]

Vicars successfully blocked the incoming Keeper of the State Papers, Dr Digges La Touche (who took on this position in addition to being Deputy Keeper of the Public Records following Burke's death in 1893) claiming records that rightfully belonged to 'Ulster'. La Touche made a bid to keep one particular volume known as 'Lodge's Manuscripts', which had been compiled during the eighteenth century by John Lodge, the author of the *Irish Peerage*.[27] This contained miscellaneous memorials and extracts taken by Lodge from rolls and other sources, and had been transferred to the PRO in 1893. Vicars insisted that as the volume bore the label of 'Ulster's Office', it should be excluded from transfer to the PRO, in accordance with the terms of the Public

25 Vicars, Grange Con, to James Fuller, FSA, 26 June 1909, NLI, P.4944.
26 Correspondence relating to archival collections of the Office of Arms, February –March 1908, NAI, CSORP 1913/18119.
27 Lodge, *Peerage of Ireland*, 4 vols. (Dublin, 1754).

Records Act of 1867.[28] His protestations were successful, and it remained in the Office of Arms.[29]

With both the SPO and Office of Arms occupying the Tower, Vicars appears to have taken a keen interest in the records of the former, examining incoming collections of papers, to satisfy his own scholarly curiosity. In 1902, following the deposit of the Farnham Papers, he borrowed three books from the collection. He requisitioned these 'catalogues of various pictures etc.', which were awaiting examination in the store room, for his own use, and returned them some weeks later.[30]

Unfortunately other documentation that had belonged to the Office of Arms before 1893, was lost to Ireland because of 'bickering' with Burke's son, Sir Henry Farnham Burke, who might have expected to succeed his father, or at least to retain the position of Deputy Ulster. After his appointment as King of Arms Vicars, perhaps aware of Burke's regular absences and his work for the College of Arms, demoted him from the post of Deputy Ulster – it being the right of the incoming King of Arms to appoint his own deputy.

Once in power, Vicars endeavoured to rebuild the Office of Arms from the decline that, in his opinion, it had suffered towards the end of the Burke regime. In July 1893 he invited George Dames Burtchaell, a barrister in the Bankruptcy Court, who had previously worked as a part-time and unpaid secretary for Sir Bernard Burke, to became 'Assistant to Ulster King of Arms and Principal Herald of All Ireland'. The following month he appointed Henry Claude Blake, a young solicitor, as another 'Assistant'.[31]

Thus, Sir Henry Burke retained only the relatively nominal position of Genealogist of the Order of St Patrick. He was so disgruntled by this demotion that he operated almost exclusively from London thereafter, taking several of his father's manuscripts with him, to the detriment of the Office of Arms in Dublin. He also 'declined to part with Ulster's fees' for 1892, amounting to £750.[32] Burke remained at the College of Arms, eventually serving as Garter King of Arms until his death in 1930. It was here that some 33 volumes entitled 'Irish Pedigrees', compiled by Burke senior during his tenure as Ulster King of Arms, and a further 39 volumes of his miscellaneous genealogical collections, were lodged and catalogued. They remain there to this day.[33]

---

28 Vicars to J.J. Digges La Touche, 13 March 1893, GO, Official Correspondence.
29 GO, MS 22.
30 NAI, SPO Search Book, vol. 3, p. 216.
31 Appointments of Burtchaell and Blake, 1893, GO, MS 154, pp. 133–4.
32 Treasury minute, PRO, T 62/709.
33 Wagner, *Records and Collections of the College of Arms*, pp. 30–1, 52.

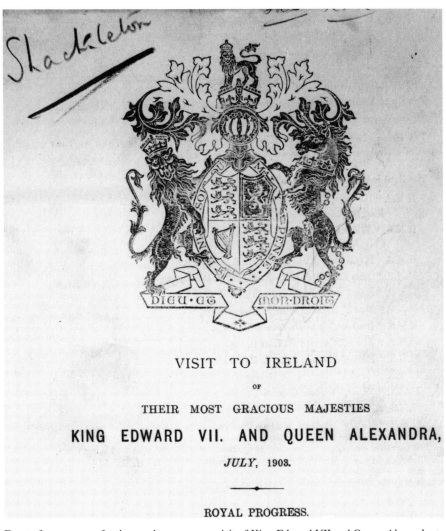

VISIT TO IRELAND

OF

THEIR MOST GRACIOUS MAJESTIES

KING EDWARD VII. AND QUEEN ALEXANDRA,

JULY, 1903.

ROYAL PROGRESS.

Front of programme for the royal progress on visit of King Edward VII and Queen Alexandra to Ireland, July 1903, marked 'Shackleton', in Vicars's hand. *GO, Material Relating to Royal Visits.*

As well as the loss of Burke's private manuscripts, the Treasury files covering this period record that the year 1893 was also 'much concerned' with a related 'insignia squabble'. This arose when Sir Henry Burke claimed the tabard, gold chain and solid silver collar (the latter valued at £300), which were presented in 1831 to Sir William Betham by King William IV on his coronation. These had passed to Sir Bernard Burke following his succession in 1853, who 'received, but never wore them'. Instead they were carefully stored in 'Messrs

West and Son', the well-known jewellers in College Green, along with the insignia of the Order of St Patrick, also presented by William IV in 1831. Again, as part of the Office's heritage, they should rightly have passed to Arthur Vicars. Instead, with Burke Junior's intervention, Betham's tabard, crown and collar, like Burke's private manuscripts, ended up in London.[34] This would not be the last squabble about insignia to trouble Vicars – the next one cost him his job and his reputation.

Breaking with the tradition of storing the 'Crown Jewels' outside the Castle, Vicars was provided on his arrival in 1893 with a safe for their storage in the Record Tower. This facilitated the organisation of State occasions, when, as Registrar and Knight Attendant of the Order of St Patrick, he was entrusted with conveying them to the State Apartments for 'dressing' the Lord Lieutenant. After each function was over, Vicars was further responsible for returning them to the safe, sometimes in the small hours of the morning.[35] The 'jewels' consisted of a jewelled star made with 394 stones, a jewelled badge, formerly owned by King George IV, and a partly jewelled gold and enamelled badge, set with emeralds and rubies. Their estimated value *c.* 1900 ranged between £30,000 and £50,000.[36]

When Vicars later had to defend himself in the light of the mysterious theft of the jewels, he protested that he had always taken 'the greatest precaution with keys'. There were two keys of the safe. He kept one on his key ring, except on full dress-nights (when the insignia were in use), on which occasions he wore the key around his neck. The duplicate key was 'concealed at his house'. Whilst the custody of the insignia of the Order was only secondary to the daily administration of the Office and its growing heraldic and genealogical output, Vicars's confidence in the security arrangements was confirmed by the fact that he 'entrusted [his] own family jewels to the same repository'.[37]

Mindful of his responsibility for the insignia, and because of his concern for the safety of the Office's documents, Vicars showed punctilious care when appointing new members of staff. He was scrupulous about obtaining references for potential employees, to ensure that they were capable, versatile, and above all trustworthy. When Burtchaell and Blake were appointed, for example, both men had to sign a declaration 'agreeable to the rules of

---

34 Treasury minute, PRO T62/709.
35 'Larceny of the State Jewels', report of Superintendent John Lowe, 9 July 1907, NAI, CSORP 1913/18119.
36 Galloway, *Most Illustrious Order*, pp. 80–1.
37 Vicars to Sir George Holmes, Office of Works, 13 July 1907, PRO, BS 22/7.

Ulster's Office'. In this they undertook not to enter any information in the records of the Office, or entrust any manuscripts, records or books to another party, without obtaining permission directly from 'Ulster or persons appointed by him'.[38]

He was also careful when recruiting clerical staff. His typist, Miss Mary Gibbon, appointed in 1897, was reliable and loyal, and continued to work for him after his dismissal in January 1908.[39] His concern for the safety of the records and for preserving the confidential nature of some of the Office's work was also evident when he advertised for a new messenger and porter in 1900. He insisted that the holder of this position had to be 'both trustworthy and fit', given that he would be 'entrusted with the custody of much valuable property and confidential records'. The number of stairs in the Record Tower also made it 'necessary that a young and active man should be appointed'.[40] When the post fell vacant in November 1900 on the retirement of the previous incumbent, Vicars took time to get the right person, commissioning a search in the records of the SPO to ascertain the terms and conditions of employment established by Burke in 1873.[41] Indeed, it was April 1901 before William Stivey, a Naval Pensioner, took up the duties. Stivey was subject to the same rigorous code of practice in relation to the care of its documents and other materials.[42]

In contrast to the relaxed manner in which, on account of illness, Sir Bernard Burke had allowed the Office to operate towards the end of his reign, Vicars ran a tight ship. He sacked the last remaining member of the Burke dynasty – Sir Bernard's youngest son – as Athlone Pursuivant, when he failed, without offering an explanation, to turn up at the investiture of Lord Lucan, on 2 March 1899. Vicars recommended to the Lord Lieutenant, Lord Cadogon, that Burke be dismissed on the grounds that he could not 'be relied upon to efficiently discharge duties in the future'.[43] In his place, Vicars elevated Henry Claude Blake, already serving as his assistant, to the position of Athlone Pursuivant, on 19 May 1899.[44] Burke's departure also presented him with the opportunity in October of the same year, to bring in his friend Francis Richard

38 GO, MS 154, pp. 133–4.
39 Vicars, Grange Con, County Wicklow, to James Fuller, 6 July 1909, NLI, P.4944.
40 Vicars to the Secretary, Treasury, 22 November 1900, GO, Official Correspondence, uncat.
41 NAI, SPO Search Book, vol. 3, p. 91.
42 Declaration of William Stivey, messenger, 14 May 1901, GO, MS 154, p. 381.
43 Earl Cadogon to Sir Matthew White Ridley, 28 April 1899, PRO, HO 45/9860/B2823, quoted in Galloway, *Most Illustrious Order*, p.74.
44 GO, MS 154, p. 315.

Upper Castle Yard, showing the Bedford Tower or 'Clock Tower' building, flanked by the gates, and positioned directly opposite the State Apartments, c. 1900. *NLI, Lawrence Collection, IMP 9.*

Shackleton, an officer in the Royal Irish Fusiliers, and the brother of the Polar explorer Ernest, as an unpaid assistant.[45]

There has been much speculation about the precise nature of the personal relationship that existed between Vicars and Shackleton. Subsequent writings have inferred that it may have been homosexual.[46] Shackleton was known to be homosexual, and later had several clandestine affairs with prominent gentlemen, including Lord Ronald Gower, uncle of the Duke of Argyll. The latter, with whom Shackleton was also acquainted, had royal connections through his marriage to Princess Louise, the sister of King Edward VII.[47] After his appointment in 1899, Shackleton was called up to serve with his battalion in the Boer War, but was invalided home again in August 1901. Thereafter he pursued private investment interests from a house on Park Lane, London, and made regular visits to Dublin, to attend ceremonial events. For the King's visit in 1903, Vicars arranged for Shackleton to participate in the proceedings as a Gold Staff Officer,[48] and a programme of events marked 'Shackleton' in Vicars's hand, is still found in the uncatalogued material in the Office – attesting perhaps to favoured treatment on the part of his senior colleague.[49] By 1905 the two men became co-tenants of a house in Clonskeagh, County Dublin, Vicars having previously lived nearer the city centre in Clyde Road, Donnybrook. Shackleton also helped Vicars to carpet and furnish the new residence,[50] and they had various joint financial dealings, Vicars guaranteeing bills for Shackleton, and vice versa. One subsequent letter from Vicars to Shakleton reveals that their accounts had become 'so mixed' that Vicars confessed he was unsure 'where matters stand between us regarding expenses', for their house and household.[51]

Notwithstanding their personal relationship, intimate or otherwise, Shackleton was subject to the same strict code of office practice as his other colleagues. Again his signed declaration found in the Register of Warrants, he promised to uphold the rules of the Office, and in particular, 'not knowingly

---

45 *op. cit.*, p. 321.
46 Even the title of Bamford and Bankes's book, *Vicious Circle*, implies Vicars's central involvement in such a scandal, see pp. 7, 10–11. In a fictionalised, but nonetheless widely publicised account of the story, there is much homosexual innuendo created by Robert Perrin, *Jewels* (London, 1977).
47 Bamford and Bankes, *Vicious Circle*, p. 63.
48 *ibid.*, p. 10.
49 Programme for Royal Visit, 1903, GO, uncat.
50 H.C. Blake to Sir James Dougherty, 17 December 1907, PRO, CO 904/221.
51 Vicars to Shackleton, 7 August 1907, reproduced in *Crown Jewels Commission*, p. 6.

enter into the books any pedigree or insert any other information until duly approved by Ulster', or 'entrust any manuscripts, books or other records to the custody of any person', except with Ulster's permission.[52]

IRISH HERALDIC JURISDICTION

In addition to protecting the records and other collections belonging to the Office of Arms, and regulating the conduct of its staff, another aspect of Vicars's term in office was his contribution to defining the extent of Irish heraldic jurisdiction. He endeavoured to prevent encroachment from the other heraldic authorities in London and Edinburgh. Perhaps aware of the views expressed by some MPs in the House of Commons who had questioned the usefulness of the Office of Ulster King of Arms during the mid-1880s, he defended its exclusive right to conduct the heraldic business for people of Irish descent. In one early, reflective memorandum on the subject, he argued that, unlike the English College of Arms, the Irish Office of Arms was not subject to the jurisdiction of the Earl Marshal. The Ulster King of Arms:

> held heraldic jurisdiction by the terms of his patent . . . over all Ireland and over Irishmen by descent, resident outside Ireland, as well as those persons not of Irish birth who have taken up their residence permanently in this authority. [53]

Vicars's sentiments reflected a general process of review to which the three heraldic authorities of the United Kingdoms of England and Wales, Scotland and Ireland were subjected from the late 1890s. This culminated in an 'Opinion on Heraldic Jurisdiction' being issued by the Law Officers of the Crown on 1 April 1906, and subsequent opinions were delivered in 1908 and 1912. Having taken evidence from each of the Kings of Arms, including Vicars, the 'Opinion' of 1906 affirmed, in relation to Ulster, that the authority of the Principal Herald of Ireland was derived directly from the Crown, and not subject to the Earl Marshal. Vicars must have been gratified: Irish armorial matters, including changes of name and arms (which required the royal warrant), concerning people of Irish descent or domiciled in Ireland, had to pass through the Office of Arms in Dublin.[54]

---

52 GO, MS 154, p. 321.
53 Arthur Vicars, Memorandum about heraldic jurisdiction, c. 1898, GO, Official Correspondence, p. 252, uncat.
54 Printed opinion, 1 April 1906, GO, Material Relating to Heraldic Jurisdiction, uncat.

Vicars's term in office saw a steady increase in the rate of the Office's heraldic business, which had dwindled somewhat towards the end of Burke's time. There were just seven heraldic patents issued during Burke's last year as Ulster (1892) and only six during Vicars's first year of business (1893). Significantly, his first commission, in March 1893, was to confirm arms to his brother, Captain William Henry Vicars, who, although residing in Yorkshire, was entitled to register in Dublin by virtue of their mother's Irish ancestry.[55] Output increased thereafter – to 11 patents in 1894, 17 in 1895, and 22 in 1896. Indeed, during the 11-year period between 1897 and Vicars's premature departure from the Office in 1908, an average of 21 patents was issued per year.[56]

Some of these patents included early examples of Gaelic mottoes. The Earl of Dunraven, for example, replaced his family's traditional Latin motto with an Irish one, 'Ceann Natharah Abú' ('A Snake's Head to Victory'). This was registered by Vicars in June 1907. Vicars's very last heraldic commission, processed just ten days before he left office, was for his half brother, George Philip Gun Mahony, later 'The O'Mahony', and also included an Irish motto, 'Iarair Rómain Abuadr' ('A Torch in Front of Us, To Victory'), registered on 20 January 1908.[57]

Vicars's reforms and general impact on Office administration appear to have met with the approval of the Tory Government Administration, which came to power in 1895 and continued until 1905. In particular, Vicars was on good terms with the incoming Lord Lieutenant, the sixth Earl Cadogon, who served between 1895 and 1902. Cadogon personally knighted him, at a private ceremony held in the Vice-Regal Lodge in August 1896.[58] Whilst the Conservative Government embarked on a policy of 'killing Home Rule with kindness', Sir Arthur Vicars was on hand to superintend the last great ceremonial events in Dublin, aimed at encouraging the loyalty of the general populace. On 18 August 1897, Prince George, the Duke of York, arrived for a three-week state visit that included his investiture as a Knight of St Patrick at a sparkling ceremony, reported to be as 'impressive as ever'.[59] In 1900, Queen Victoria returned to Dublin for the first time in 39 years, less than a year before her death, and was impressed by the warmth of her reception at public events, including reviews of the troops and salutes of loyalty.[60] In honour of his role during this trip, Vicars was created a Knight Companion of the Victorian Order. Following

---

55 GO, MS 111J, p. 236.
56 GO, MSS 110 & 111J.
57 GO, MS 111J, pp. 197, 209. I am grateful to Máire Mac Conghail for translations.
58 GO, MS 102, p. 35.
59 Galloway, *Most Illustrious Order*, pp. 74–5.
60 See Murphy, *Abject Loyalty*, pp. 284–9.

the Queen's death and the succession of Edward VII to the throne in January 1901, the new King made the first of three visits to Ireland in July 1903. On that occasion, Sir Arthur Vicars was promoted to Commander of the Order at a ceremony on board the royal yacht, docked at Kingstown.[61]

It was Earl Cadogon who first introduced the idea of revising and updating the regulations governing the Order of St Patrick.[62] As far as the Government was concerned, revival of the Order was aimed at raising the profile of the Crown in Irish political life, but it provided Sir Arthur with an opportunity to fulfil his pre-appointment ambitious strategy of boosting the size of his heraldic court.

As a scholar, Vicars cared less for the ceremonial trappings of office in comparison to its heraldic and genealogical research, especially, it would appear, in relation to his obligations to the Order of St Patrick. He was easily fussed by the burden of responsibility and demands on his time. On one occasion – prior to the investiture of the Earl of Mayo in February 1905 – he admitted to a correspondent that 'one little realis[ed] what trouble such a ceremony involved' to insure its smooth-running, and that his hands were 'pretty full' with administrative work.[63]

Vicars was particularly anxious to secure more staff, and following Cadogon's retirement in August 1902, continued to put pressure on Cadogon's successor, Lord Dudley, the Lord Lieutenant until 1905, to implement the proposed reforms. Vicars consulted Sir Albert Woods, Garter Principal King of Arms since 1869, who had an unrivalled knowledge of ceremonial matters, and who appears to have done most of the revision before his death in 1903.[64] As far as the Office of Arms was concerned, the most important aspect of the Revised Statutes was that they resuscitated the offices of the Dublin and Cork Heralds.[65] This enabled Vicars to appoint his nephew, Pierce Gun Mahony as Cork Herald, and to elevate Francis Shackleton to the post of Dublin Herald. Both were sworn into office on 5 September 1905, within two months of the Statutes being published.[66]

---

61 O'Mahony, *Viceroys of Ireland*, pp. 309–14; 318–22; *Who's Who, 1916*, Galloway, *Most Illustrious Order* p. 81.
62 *ibid.*, pp. 76–7.
63 Vicars to Mr Byrne, Home Office, 21 December 1904, PRO, HO 45/109512/3.
64 Galloway, *Most Illustrious Order*, p. 77.
65 The Statutes were published on 29 July 1905, GO, MS 150, pp. 526–8; Galloway, *Most Illustrious Order*, p. 79.
66 GO, MS 154, pp. 528–8.

RELOCATION TO THE BEDFORD TOWER

Sir Arthur's greatest single achievement for the Office of Arms was securing its relocation to the Bedford Tower in Upper Castle Yard, in 1903. This became the Office's base from November of that year, until its eventual transfer to Kildare Street, in November 1981. During this 78-year period, the unique functions and integrity of the Office of Arms were enhanced by its being the sole occupant of this prestigious building.

Anticipating the growth of his heraldic department, Vicars had been pleading for additional accommodation since his appointment. As early as September 1894, he informed the authorities that the records of his Office were 'of a special and valuable kind', requiring careful storage and 'to be readily accessible for constant reference'.[67] At this early stage, he also asked for his own residential quarters within the Castle complex – pointing out that Sir Bernard Burke had lived in the Castle prior to marrying in 1856. It would, he argued, be easier to 'live in', as it was 'inconvenient to be at a distance [and] keep a carriage', and yet be in 'constant and daily attendance all year round', especially because he enjoyed 'only half the salary' of his predecessor.[68] Later, in November 1900, he informed the Board of Works that 'we are becoming so seriously overcrowded here that our Office work is much hampered'. Whilst keen for residential quarters for himself, the safety of the records, and in particular provision of a fireproof room for their safe storage, nonetheless remained his primary concern.[69]

It was his ally Earl Cadogon who first recommended relocating the Office of Arms in March 1901. Initially Cadogon instructed that the Under Secretary's House be:

> fitted up for the purposes of a Public Office in connection with the Office and duties of Ulster King of Arms, and for the safe custody of the insignia of the Order of St Patrick.

He further instructed that residential quarters might also be provided and 'placed at the disposal of Ulster' during his pleasure.[70]

---

67 Vicars, to Lord Houghton, Lord Lieutenant, 10 September 1894; Vicars to Mr Stevenson, BPW, 28 March 1901, GO, Official Correspondence.
68 Vicars, to Lord Houghton, Lord Lieutenant, 10 September 1894, *op. cit.*
69 Vicars to Secretary, BPW, 21 November 1900, *op. cit.*
70 Public Works of Ireland memorandum relating to office accommodation for various departments including Ulster King of Arms, 13 March 1901, OPW, A6/14/7/48. I am most grateful to Dr Freddie O'Dwyer for access to this file.

The Survival of the Office of Arms

Location and ground floor plan

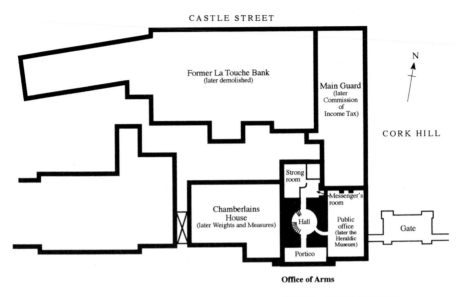

CASTLE STREET

Former La Touche Bank
(later demolished)

Main Guard
(later
Commission
of
Income Tax)

N

CORK HILL

Strong
room

Messenger's
room

Chamberlains
House
(later Weights and Measures)

Hall

Public
office
(later the
Heraldic
Museum)

Gate

Portico

Office of Arms

UPPER CASTLE YARD

Second floor plan   ## First floor plan

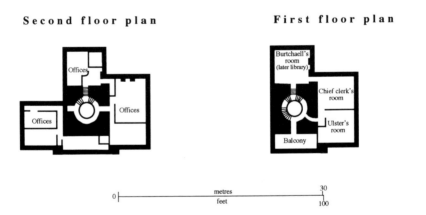

Offices

Offices

Offices

Burtchaell's
room
(later library)

Chief clerk's
room

Ulster's
room

Balcony

metres   30

0   feet   100

Location and layout of the Office of Arms in the Bedford Tower, Dublin Castle, as fitted out to the specifications of Sir Arthur Vicars in 1903. *Map by Sarah Gearty, based on plan in OPW, A6/14/7/48.*

This plan did not come to fruition, however, because of security problems. The house was connected to other buildings on the north side of the Upper Castle Yard, and was found unsafe for the storage of valuable documents and the insignia. By June 1902, clearly concerned about protecting the valuable contents of the Office, Cadogon had concluded that 'it was not desirable that Ulster's offices should be approached by a common door and staircase'. The Under Secretary's House was therefore given up, and instructions were given for a house to be designated specifically for the Office of Arms.[71]

The Inspectors of Fisheries occupied the Bedford Tower building in the Upper Castle Yard, but as part of a general re-arrangement of Government Departments in August 1902, they were to be relocated to the Department of Agricultural and Technical Instruction in Merrion Street. Having consulted with Vicars, Cadogon deemed that this building would be secure.[72]

The Bedford Tower was a striking symbol of grandeur and austerity. Located on the north side of Upper Yard, directly opposite the State Apartments, it had been completed in 1761. Designed by Arthur Jones Nevill,[73] it was named after the fourth Duke of Bedford, Lord Lieutenant 1757–61. Originally it functioned as the residence for the Dean of the Chapel Royal, but during the nineteenth century, was occupied by a succession of Government offices, and by 1900 had become the 'Fisheries' headquarters. An attic floor had been added during the early nineteenth century, detracting somewhat from its external appearance but providing additional space, and on this floor there was a connecting entrance into the Guard House. The Guard House, where the main Castle Guard were stationed, was situated behind the Bedford Tower, at the main Castle entrance from Cork Hill.

The 'clock-tower' building, as the Bedford Tower also became known, stood out from surrounding buildings, rather like a grand wedding-cake. A portico supported a balcony to the first floor – the latter providing vantage overlooking the Yard while two striking stone portal gates, constructed in the early 1750s, flanked the building. The east gate provided the State entrance into the Yard, while the gate on the west side was a dummy – its purpose being to balance the building as a whole. Both gates were surmounted by Van Nost's leaden statutes of 'Fortitude' and 'Justice', and the latter gave rise to the well-known Dublin saying: 'Statue of Justice, mark well her station, her face to the Castle, her back to the Nation!'[74]

---

71 Sir David Harell, BPW, to Mr Holmes, 3 June 1902, *op. cit.*
72 BPW minute, June 1902, *op. cit.*
73 Nevill was Surveyor General of Ireland. See McParland, *Public Architecture in Ireland*, p. 105.
74 T. U. Sadleir, 'The romance of Dublin Castle', p. 58.

With its Corinthian columns, handsome archways and spacious internal rooms, the Bedford Tower provided a striking contrast to the 'dark and dismal' Record Tower.[75] Internally, its rooms were well proportioned, while a fine, cantilevered stone staircase, carved out of the thick supporting walls beneath the tower, spiralled upwards from the entrance hall to the floors above giving access to the roof. Here the faces of the clock were lit during the Castle Season.

In the early plans for the conversion of the building for the use of the Office of Arms, Earl Cadogon insisted that the existing link with the Guard House 'be locked up'. All other rooms lately occupied by the 'Fisheries' were to be converted and 'used for the purposes of Ulster' only. The occupation of the building by different departments at different times meant that at some point during the nineteenth century the internal west side of it became completely partitioned off from the rest of the building. By 1902 this area was occupied by the Chamberlain's Office, and was entered through a separate external door. There was no internal access between the Chamberlain's Office and the Office of Arms. Again, in the basement shared by all three departments (Arms, Chamberlain's and the Guard) connecting doors were also closed off. As the building was much smaller than the Under Secretary's premises, there was no possibility of a residence for Vicars.[76]

Although not large enough to provide a residence, the new building almost trebled the space that had been available in the Record Tower. Two existing rooms on the ground floor were converted into one larger room for use as a public office, where the substantial and growing collection of secondary works could be consulted, and in which visitors to the Office could be attended to by staff.[77] Two existing closets and part of a messenger's room, also on the ground floor, were converted to a purpose-built strong room for the records of the Office, while a closet was added to the basement. A smaller messenger's room was fitted out beside the strong room on the ground floor. There were three rooms on the first floor. One that adjoined the balcony, overlooking the Yard, was designated 'Ulster's room', while a larger room beside it was assigned for the use of his 'chief clerk' – presumably Blake. The third room (located at the rear of the building) was specifically allocated to Burtchaell, while two smaller rooms on the attic floor were respectively allocated to Shackleton and the typist. A third and smaller room in the attic where

---

75 Bayly, *Historical Sketch and Description of Dublin Castle*, pp. 29–31.
76 Public Works minute, 20 July 1902, OPW, A6/14/7/48.
77 Evidence of G. D. Burtchaell, *Crown Jewels Commission*, p. 6.

Changing of the Castle Guard at the State entrance to the Upper Castle Yard, alongside the Guard House and Office of Arms, c. 1890. The three rectangular windows on the ground floor nearest the gate belonged to the public office of the Office of Arms, where the safe was stored in 1907. *NLI, Lawrence Collection, R. 6809.*

a number of the manuscript volumes were subsequently re-bound, was used to accommodate a bookbinder, and also provided storage space for 'those papers, vellums and books' at present lying on the stairs and elsewhere in the Record Tower'. Access to the basement of the building from the Office of Arms was gained through a door off the hallway, near the strong room.[78]

A STRONG ROOM FOR THE RECORDS AND OTHER SPECIFICATIONS

In fitting out the new building, Vicars's top priority was to secure a strong room for the records. This had been his consistent position, informing the Board of Public Works back in 1901, for example, that 'a fireproof room was the first consideration and should be the first work executed'.[79] Having been designated the Bedford Tower by 1902, he insisted that the new strong room constructed for it must 'be made absolutely fireproof', warning that 'if the records here were burned it would be a national loss'.[80] Under Vicars instruction, orders were given for the new room to be built 'with 14-inch brick walls, supplied with a Milner's door, steel sash and iron shutters on the external window', and thus reduce the risk of fire. Provision was also made for the shelving of manuscripts.[81]

When Vicars later requested that an additional inner lining wall be added using fire bricks to increase the protection of the room, the Board declined, advising him that the work was too far advanced, and unnecessary because 'all precautions to make the room fireproof' had been taken. Having been assured that the room was fireproof, Vicars again demonstrated his concern for the records by specifying that the shelves in the strong room be made from wood rather than sheet iron 'because it would cause less injury' to bindings and be less prone to condensation. The Board agreed to this amendment.[82]

When work on the strong room was completed in December 1902, Vicars was under considerable pressure to relocate from the Record Tower immediately, but he refused. Poor weather and the absence of sunlight meant that the walls of the new strong room had not dried out, and he was concerned to find

---

78 Designation of rooms, as specified by Vicars, June 1902, OPW, A6/14/7/48.
79 W.M. Paton, BPW, to J. Mellor, Chairman, BPW, Dublin Castle, 27 March 1901, *op. cit.*
80 Vicars, Office of Arms, Dublin Castle, to the Secretary, BPW, 1 October 1902, *op. cit.*
81 BPW memorandum, June 1902, *op. cit.*
82 Vicars to the Secretary, BPW, 21 October 1902; BPW minute, 24 October 1902, *op. cit.*

that they were 'shedding a sort of fungus' by February 1903.[83] He insisted that fires be lit throughout the building, and a brazier brought into the strong room to speed up the drying process, conscientiously informing the chief engineer: 'I dare not transfer valuable illuminated manuscripts until I am sure of the place being dry'.[84]

The internal specifications for the building, as drawn up by Vicars, again emphasise his attention to detail. Finding 'the place so very dark', on account of its north-facing location, and that it was over-shadowed by the buildings behind it – including the former La Touche Bank in Castle Street – he determined to maximise the amount of natural light in the building. Thus, several doors were fitted with clear glass, while reflectors were fitted outside windows on the ground floor to throw more daylight into the rooms. To facilitate reading by daylight, Vicars also requested ledges 'for consulting books in the window'.[85] These requests appear to have been sanctioned by the Board of Works.

As well as requisitioning various articles of furniture for each of the rooms in the new building, Vicars also ensured that fire-guards, fenders, irons and coal boxes were provided – making provision for their safety, as well as their heat. He was most perturbed to find that gas was used to light the building, and urged that this should be converted to electricity. Indeed he was particularly anxious about the gas supply for the clock tower. When the clock was lighted during the Season, the 'lighting man' (employed by the Board of Works) opened a stop-cock in the Upper Yard, and while he ascended the tower via the internal stairs (carrying a lighted taper) gas escaped into the tower until he arrived with his torch. The practice was, Vicars advised, both 'dangerous and antiquated' and he urged it should cease, to protect the building and its valuable contents.[86]

Whilst agreeing to many of Vicars's early demands in relation to the strong room, the Board was increasingly reluctant to accede to his additional requests. One engineer formed the view that Vicars's requisitions amounted 'practically to having the offices newly furnished'. His hopes for a knee-hole writing table and a leather-covered armchair for his own room had to be given up, and more seriously, the conversion from gas to electricity was also refused, because it would cost '£50 or £60, or possibly considerably more'.[87] Gas continued to light the building until 1908.

---

83   Vicars to Mr Pentland, BPW, 23 February 1903, *op. cit.*
84   Vicars to Pentland, 15 April 1903, *op. cit.*
85   Vicars to the Secretary, BPW, 16 February 1903, *op. cit.*
86   Vicars to do. 22 December 1902, *op. cit.*
87   BPW memorandum, December 1902, *op. cit.*

The walls of the strong room finally dried out during the summer 1903, but internal work remained unfinished, and Vicars again refused to move until it was complete. This included the fitting of storage presses in the public office; repairing the lift to convey manuscripts to the first floor; connecting internal telephones; putting linoleum on the floors of the public room and strong room; and providing enamel letters 'A-J' for marking up strong room shelves for corresponding volumes. By August 1903, he was exasperated by the delays, especially as he had been promised that 'all would be fixed' after the royal visit in July. It seemed to him that 'more and more obstacles appeared at every turn', and he wondered if he would get into the new premises before 1904.[88]

The tone of the correspondence between the King of Arms and the Board of Public Works became increasingly antagonistic towards the end of 1903. Vicars remained punctilious about the nature of fittings that he required for the storage of manuscripts and books, while Board officials were unable to appreciate his specialist requirements. For example, Vicars had insisted that spring-locks be fitted to the presses in the public room, where the books were to be stored, but the Board decided he could make do with dead-shut locks instead. Vicars was having none of this, insisting such locks would not 'be tamper free', and if someone 'desired to commit a burglary . . . [they] would not create much defence'. Adamant that the locks be changed, he resorted to paying for them himself, and recouped the expense from the Treasury. Reflecting increasing frustration, he asked Blake to write to the Board on his behalf, expressing dismay that 'a dozen locks costing 3/6 each' should cause such difficulties. Blake informed the Board, in no uncertain terms, that 'Sir Arthur imagines that he is the best judge as to his requirements for the safety of his records!'[89]

Another more serious shortcoming of the fitting out process concerned the storage of the 'Crown Jewels'. When work on the strong room was almost finished, and the opening for a grille door had been put in place, Vicars discovered that the safe that had been provided for them back in 1893 would not fit through the space. This was in spite of his pointing out 'all along that I wanted the safe placed inside'. The Board, in contrast, protested that Sir Arthur had not informed them of the need for the safe to be in the strong room, until four months after it was completed (April 1903). They may also have been confused by the fact that a locked cabinet was provided and successfully

---

88 Vicars to Secretary, BPW, 15 and 16 August 1903, *op. cit.*
89 H. C. Blake, to do., 28 September 1903, *op. cit.*

fitted into the strong room for the storage of the State Swords and Maces – an additional responsibility designated to Ulster King of Arms at this time. The cabinet was in place by December 1902. For the insignia, Vicars had in mind that there would be a similar arrangement, and was insistent that the expenses for this should be borne from the Lord Lieutenant's allowance, rather than those of his heraldic department. In May 1903 he wrote:

> I do not like the idea of the safe being in the public office, for various reasons, besides it would be inconvenient for me. . . you say the money is nearly consumed, but this is strictly a matter personal to the Lord Lieutenant, and not rightly chargeable to this Office.[90]

Discussions followed, and suggestions were made about taking down part of the wall, or removing the bars and shutters that had been placed over the window of the strong room, to get the safe through that way. Vicars even requisitioned a new safe that would be small enough to fit through the door, at a cost of only £23.[91]

The Board was apparently reluctant to devote any more public expense to either of these options. At a conference held later to discuss the problem, it was agreed that given the Office's location beside the Guard House, where there was 'a sentry night and day on duty outside', the public room should be secure for its custody. According to the Board's memorandum on the matter, Vicars was, by this stage, more concerned to get a trolley 'to prevent damage to books and manuscripts' than about the safe. Thus, 'the item for a new safe was cancelled and the trolley allowed', pending replacement of the safe at some later stage.[92]

Vicars's long-awaited relocation to the Bedford Tower finally took place on 9 November 1903. Whilst the move did not generate any apparent press interest, Mr D.A. Chart of the SPO made the following entry in the Search Book for the Record Tower: 'All the books, furniture etc. belonging to Ulster were this day removed by him from here to his new offices'.[93] We have no details about the move itself, because the relevant internal correspondence

---

90 Extracts of Vicars's letters to H. Coghlan, BPW, 19 May and 4 June, produced for minutes of evidence, PRO, BS 22/7.
91 BPW minute concerning conference with Sir Arthur Vicars about the matter of the safe, 22 December 1903, *Crown Jewels Commission*, p. 3.
92 Copy of minute of Chairman of Board of Works on Estimate of Schedules, 1903, *ibid.*
93 NAI, SPO Search Book, vol. 3, p. 280. I am most grateful to the late Dr Phil Connolly for finding this entry.

book for this period is missing, and no passing references have come to light. However, we may suppose that Stivey and other Castle porters were enlisted to carry down the registers and files of records from the upper floor of the Tower. They were probably loaded onto the back of a cart and conveyed through the archway into the Upper Castle Yard, where no doubt Sir Arthur was on hand to instruct exactly where they should go.

We may presume too that the notorious safe was hauled onto a cart, and unceremoniously conveyed to its new resting place in the front room of the Bedford Tower. The temporary arrangement enforced by the reluctance of the Board to purchase a smaller one became permanent after the relocation in 1903. The safe remained in this position, even after the publication of the Revised Statutes of the Order of St Patrick in 1905, which included the specific clause that the insignia were to be 'deposited for safe keeping in a steel safe in the strong room . . . of the Office of Arms'.[94] In this location, it appears to have become something of an Office novelty, around which Vicars and his colleagues would consult materials in the storage presses, and initially meet members of the public. Occasionally favoured visitors – usually antiquarians and others whom Vicars or Burtchaell knew personally – would be given a privileged glimpse at the jewels.[95]

One final aspect of the relocation process, which helped to cement the presence of the Office in its new home, was the fitting of a large brass plate to the front door of the building, previously requisitioned by Vicars. This bore the words 'Office of Arms', announcing to passers-by that his little heraldic department had moved up in the world, and was established at the heart of the Castle Court.[96]

DISASTER: THE DISAPPEARANCE OF THE 'CROWN JEWELS'

Having secured and successfully relocated to the Bedford Tower by 1903, augmented his staff by 1905, and introduced a series of reforms that tightened up procedures and practices within it during the first 15 years of his appointment, Sir Arthur Vicars might have enjoyed a long and flourishing career. His

---

94 Revised Statutes of the Order, published 25 July 1905, quoted in Galloway, *Most Illustrious Order*, p. 282.
95 For example, Mr J. C. Hodgson, an antiquary who visited the Office, was shown them on 11 June 1907, while in March of that year Burtchaell showed them to his cousins from Kilkenny, Mrs Tarleton and her daughter; and on another occasion, 'to a lady friend'. Statement of Sir Arthur Vicars, 12 July 1907, PRO, BS 22/4.
96 Requisition for fittings to the Bedford Tower, June 1903, OPW, A6/14/7/48.

dismissal for negligence under a cloud of controversy by January 1908 was not the anticipated outcome.

The story of the missing 'Crown Jewels' has been the subject of much speculation and innuendo over the years, giving rise to several publications – some based on research, others purely fictional accounts seeking to sensationalise the event.[97] The known basic facts are these. On 6 July 1907, just four days before the arrival of King Edward VII for his third visit to Ireland – to include the Irish International Exhibition, and investiture of Lord Castletown as a Knight of St Patrick – Vicars and Stivey discovered that the insignia of the Order of St Patrick were not in the safe. Missing with them were the collars of five knights and another badge deposited for safekeeping, together with a box containing Vicars's mother's jewels, placed in the safe by Vicars himself. Indeed all that was left were the empty cases, his patent of appointment, and his and his brother's wills.[98]

The police were informed, and it soon transpired that no force had been used, the safe having been found unlocked. It was further reported that on the morning on which the theft had been discovered, the Office cleaner had found the outer door of the strong room ajar with two keys hanging in the grille.[99] These findings emphasised that access to both safe and strong room had been

---

97 These range from J. Christian Bay, *The Mystery of the Irish Crown Jewels* (Private printing, Iowa, 1944), which was rather dismissive of the role of the Office of Arms. The next study, Francis Bamford and Viola Bankes, *Vicious Circle* (London, 1965), provides the most comprehensive and reliable account, having been based on substantial archival research, although a drawback to the work is the absence of references. Gaughan's *Listowel* (Naas, 1973), pp. 322–8; 337–42, provides a useful local history account of Vicars's life and misfortune. Galloway's recent work on the Order of St Patrick provides a valuable contextual study, *Most Illustrious Order*, pp. 80–95. Audrey Bateman's *The Magpie Tendency* (Canterbury, 1999) speculates that the record of the Athlone Pursuivant, Bennett-Goldney, was far from perfect, while the most recent and very readable account by John Cafferky and Kevin Hannafin, *Scandal and Betrayal: Shackleton and the Irish Crown Jewels* (Dublin, 2002), makes the dramatic claim that the theft was a failed Unionist plot to undermine the pro-Home Rule Liberal Administration. To cover their tracks, suggest the authors, the conspirators may have returned the jewels to the Crown. Perin's novel *Jewels* is pure fiction. Several press articles and even television documentaries have followed in recent years. The story will again be examined on television in the near future in a new documentary by Dog House Productions Ltd.

98 Statement of Sir Arthur Vicars to police, 6 July 1907, PRO, BS 22/4; Vicars to John Crawford Hodgson, 6 July 1907, GO, MS 507.

99 *Crown Jewels Commission*, p. vii.

possible for the cunning intruder. Furthermore, the ribbon attached to the star, and tissue paper lining the case, were carefully replaced after the items were removed, indicating that the thief did not act in haste. Although a police reward of £1,000 was offered for information leading to the recovery of the jewels or the perpetrators of the crime, and an extensive investigation of 'every crack, crevice, basement cellar' in the building carried out, neither the jewels nor thieves were located. The whole episode remained an 'official mystery', but it soon became an open secret that the safe and strong room had been opened in a 'regular manner'.[100] The first police report on the incident concluded that the theft 'had been committed by some person familiar with the place, who had ordinary means of access', and that either the safe had been left open, or there had been 'surreptitious access to Sir Arthur's keys'.[101]

Considerable press interest soon focused on the Office. Bulmer Hobson, the journalist and Nationalist commentator, would recall later that most people in Ireland did not know of the existence of the 'jewels' until they had been stolen.[102] Within days, there were few people throughout Ireland or United Kingdom who did not know about the either the 'jewels' or the Office of Arms. Posters and billboards advertised the sensation in Dublin.[103] On 8 July 1907, the *Irish Times* carried the simple but striking headline: 'Burglary in Dublin Castle. Disappearance of the State Jewels',[104] and next day confirmed the Bedford Tower, 'now the Office of Arms', as the scene of the crime.[105]

The London *Times* drew attention to lax security at the centre of British administration in Ireland, commenting that 'the Office of Arms where the jewels were kept' was surrounded by Government Departments, and patrolled by soldiers and policemen night and day. There was 'no spot in Dublin, or possibly the United Kingdom', the paper concluded, that was 'more constantly and systematically occupied by soldiers and policemen'.[106]

Sir Arthur's dismay was palpable. To one confidant he wrote on the day of the discovery: 'this is awful for me, but what more can [a] mortal do when a safe is picked as appears to be the case'.[107] In his first police statement, he

---

100 *The Irish Times,* 8 January 1908.
101 'Larceny of the State Jewels', report of Superintendent John Lowe, 9 July 1907, NAI, CSORP 1913/18119.
102 Hobson, *Ireland Yesterday and Tomorrow*, p. 85.
103 Reports of witnesses, PRO, BS 22/7.
104 *The Irish Times*, 8 July 1907.
105 *The Irish Times*, 9 July 1907.
106 *The Times*, 9 July 1907.
107 Vicars to John Crawford Hodgson, 6 July 1907, GO, MS 507.

magnanimously defended his staff, none of whom, in his view, could have had any thing to do with it. He refused to entertain the idea that the actual key of the safe had been utilised by the thieves presuming that someone must have obtained a wax impression of it.[108] Mortified by the discovery, he consoled himself that the whole episode might be some terrible prank, informing Detective Officer Kerr of the Dublin Metropolitan Police that 'he would not be surprised if they were returned by parcel post'.[109]

At an early stage, a press report sympathetic to Vicars's plight, published in the *Dublin Express*, drew attention to the heavy responsibility that custody for such valuable jewels had placed upon his shoulders, in addition to his heraldic and genealogical work. In spite of his requests for a new safe to fit in the strong room, the cost of buying it had been refused. It further commented that the safe appeared completely secure in a room 'backed against the Guard Room' – the latter occupied by soldiers, who also paced on sentry duty outside the windows. The report begged the question of how the intruder had passed the sentry guard without arousing suspicions.[110] However, all the policemen and sentries who had been on duty during the previous 24 hours before the theft was reported, declared to investigating police, to a man, that they 'saw no suspicious persons enter or leave the Castle . . . during the tour of duty'.[111]

Whilst Vicars was shattered by disbelief, the Irish Administration was embarrassed that, on the eve of the King's visit, valuable symbols of the imperial presence in Ireland had disappeared. The King was furious, his official biographer later reporting that he was 'unimpressed by the feeble efforts to elucidate the mystery', viewing the Irish Government and Lord Aberdeen as dilatory.[112] The whole episode certainly detracted from his visit, the press reporting that Lord Castletown's investiture had been cancelled on the day that the King arrived.[113] Before the end of his trip, he made it clear to Lord Aberdeen that whoever had been careless in the custody of the jewels should be punished.[114]

Behind the headlines, many speculated that the authorities soon uncovered exactly who had committed the crime, but for fear of a scandal would not press

---

108 Statement of Sir Arthur Vicars, 9 July 1907, PRO, BS 22/7.
109 Evidence of Detective Officer Kerr, who stated Sir Arthur told him this on 8 July 1907, *op. cit.*
110 *Dublin Express*, 15 July 1907.
111 Evidence given by the bugler, foot soldiers and sergeant on the main Castle Guard, PRO, BS 22/7.
112 Lee, *King Edward VII*, ii, p. 473.
113 *The Irish Times*, 11 July 1907.
114 Lee, *Edward*, pp. 473–4.

charges. In a series of articles published by Bulmer Hobson in the *Gaelic American* newspaper, from July 1908, the blame was put on Shackleton. Hobson speculated that he and an accomplice (whom Hobson later identified as Captain Richard Gorges, a musketry instructor responsible for training soldiers at the Castle at the time) had masterminded the whole thing.[115] Hobson's theories were printed anonymously in the United States because he could not get anyone to publish them in Ireland on account of their salacious content. One of his banner headlines had read 'Abominations of Dublin Castle Exposed', and reported various late-night drinking parties at the Office of Arms and other locations within the Castle, involving Shackleton and prominent Castle officials.[116]

Based on information confided in him by Pierce O'Mahony, Vicars's half-brother, Hobson revealed the manner in which the crime had been committed. Sir Arthur regularly entertained members of staff and indeed other Castle officials to drinks in the Office of Arms. On one such occasion, the two accomplices had succeeded in getting Vicars drunk. They then took the key of the safe for duplication, replacing it later, and when Shackleton was out of the country, Gorges passed without suspicion through the sentries on the gate. He got into the building via the basement of the adjoining Guard House, and under cover of darkness, abstracted the contents of the safe. Hobson also claimed that Scotland Yard detectives who came to Dublin to conduct an investigation soon uncovered the involvement of Shackleton and Gorges. However, the charges against Shackleton were not pursued on account of his alleged sexual associations with high-profile political figures, which it was feared would be uncovered, thereby embarrassing the Government.

It was later speculated that the King was terrified of a homosexual scandal, as had occurred at the German Court just a few months before, when several high-profile members had been relieved of their posts, accused of homosexual activities, much to the Kaiser's embarrassment.[117] According to Vicars, having become a suspect, Shackleton himself worked up the scandal 'for all he was worth', blackening his own moral character in the process, by 'threatening to produce a social scandal and involve high persons', none of whom, Vicars was at pains to point out, he 'even knew'.[118] One of these individuals may have been the King's brother-in-law, the Duke of Argyll, and other leading officials at Dublin Castle.

---

115 Hobson, *Ireland Yesterday and Tomorrow*, pp. 85–90.
116 *Gaelic American*, 4 July 1908; see Bamford and Bankes, *Vicious Circle*, p. 114.
117 Bamford and Bankes, *Vicious Circle*, p. 94; Gaughan, *Listowel*, p. 338.
118 Vicars, Grange Con, County Wicklow, to James Fuller, recounting events, 16 June 1909, NLI, P. 4955.

Whilst his prior close associations with Shackleton did not help his own reputation, Vicars himself came to an early conclusion that his Dublin Herald and 'co-tenant' was in fact the culprit. Having initially defended all his staff, on 3 August 1907 he hinted to police 'that he suspected Mr F. Shackleton and a person with whom he was associated' had perpetrated the crime. Then on 20 September he informed Detective Kerr: 'It was my guest . . . while staying at my house he treacherously took an impression of my key while I was in my bath', and added that his accomplice had got into the building from the basement.[119]

Instead of pursuing Vicars's theory, however, the authorities chose to take action in a different direction. On 12 October, the unfortunate messenger, Stivey, was dismissed, although he was in no way held responsible for what had occurred. Following a meeting of senior Castle officials with the Commissioner of the Police, Sir John Ross of Bladensburg, on 14 October, it was decided that Vicars and his other colleagues would also have to go. Vicars stood his ground, determined not to give up the appointment he had worked so hard to secure for himself, and the department that had developed so impressively during his 15 years of service. He demanded an official judicial inquiry to investigate in public the circumstances surrounding the disappearance.[120]

There were many prepared to rally to his support, including 15 of the 21 knights of the Order of St Patrick, who petitioned the King that he had discharged his duties for the Order faithfully throughout this period, in addition to his heraldic responsibilities, and deserved a fair trial.[121] His half-brother Pierce O'Mahony (who championed a campaign both to clear Sir Arthur from any responsibility for the loss of the jewels, and to end the damaging and inaccurate gossip that began to circulate in the months after the theft), was also vocal in demanding a judicial hearing for him. In contrast, however, the sentiments of others reveal that Vicars had his enemies, who, perhaps because of unsettled scores from the past, remained unsympathetic.

His old critic Lord Walter Fitzgerald, who had become editor of the *Journal of the Association for the Preservation of the Memorials of the Dead* in Ireland, had long regarded Vicars as overly protective of the records in his custody, to the detriment of general scholarly research. Fitzgerald had attempted to reproduce the contents of the Funeral Entries preserved in the

---

119 Statements of Superintendent Lowe and Detective Officer Kerr, 20 September 1907, PRO, BS 22/7.
120 Bamford and Bankes, *Vicious Circle*, pp. 99–110.
121 Galloway, *Most Illustrious Order*, pp. 85–6.

Office of Arms in the *Journal*, but Vicars refused permission, thus preventing 'the means of putting on lasting record valuable information' that might, in Fitzgerald's opinion, 'be liable to destruction'. In the first *Journal* published in the light of the theft, Fitzgerald used the opportunity to remind readers that 'the recent burglary of the insignia . . . from the Office of Arms, Dublin Castle' proved 'nothing [was] safe from loss or destruction, no matter what precautions [were] taken against thieves or fire'.[122] After Vicars was dismissed, a review of the *Journal* published in the *Freeman's Journal* hoped that 'the new regime in the Office of Arms [might] be less conservative', and grant permission to have the documents in its custody reproduced.[123]

Underlining tensions in Office administration were subsequently revealed by the contents of a letter of Henry Blake, Vicars's former assistant and the Athlone Pursuivant, to Sir James Dougherty, Under Secretary for Ireland, now preserved in the Home Office files at the PRO. The letter reveals that Blake had resigned his position to pursue his legal career in Canada in December 1906, as the atmosphere in the Office of Arms had disillusioned him. Blake disliked the manner in which Vicars stamped his authority. In Blake's opinion, he had used the Office to develop his own private research and genealogical interests, tending 'to run it as a private hobby'. Blake reported that he had often remonstrated with Vicars for allowing his private business to interfere with official work, to be reminded that he was only a clerk.[124]

Vicars's patent of appointment, however, had specifically made provision to allow him to continue his private genealogical practice; but perhaps he devoted too much attention to this. Later submissions made on Vicars's behalf by his solicitors indicate that their client had firmly been of the view that the Office of Arms was principally a place of registration, where information previously 'gathered by means of genealogical and heraldic research' would be entered in its books. He was entitled to undertake 'the preliminary steps' leading to official registration in a private capacity.[125] Aside from Sir Arthur's private business interests, and returning to Blake's revealing letter (which may remain on the Government file because it is damaging to Vicars) it was further intimated that the King of Arms' personal interests were affecting business. Blake was anxious to emphasise that he 'always had [his] friends outside the

122 *PMDIJ, vii,* 1907, p. 1.
123 *Freeman's Journal,* 4 August 1908.
124 Blake to Sir James Dougherty, Under Secretary for Ireland, 17 December 1907, PRO, CO 904/221
125 Messrs Meredith to Malachy Kelly Esq, 24 March 1908, NAI, CSORP 1913/18119.

Office', and had nothing to do 'with friends such as some people seem to have counted among their collection' – a cloaked reference perhaps to Shackleton.[126]

After Blake's departure, Vicars had actually divided his work into two appointments. He brought in Sydney Horlock in January 1907 to carry out secretarial and clerical duties. Horlock appears to have required close supervision, working mostly in Sir Arthur's room, where Vicars could keep an eye on him.[127] The evidence from entries in the Registers of Grants and Confirmations between his appointment in January 1907 and premature departure the following November, reveals many errors. Frequently, Vicars appears to have checked over the blazons and other entries in the registers, to find errors and spelling mistakes, especially in mottoes, that were later amended by him in pencil. Whilst we cannot be certain all the errors were Horlock's, the frequency of the mistakes, in comparison with earlier and later work, suggests that whoever was making the entries was not familiar with heraldic jargon, and required scrutiny.[128]

A rather obscure figure was chosen to fill the vacancy of Athlone Pursuivant created by Blake's departure. This was Francis Bennett-Goldney, the Mayor of Canterbury between 1905 and 1910, who had no known connections with Ireland, bar his friendship with Vicars. The two probably became acquainted through membership of the Royal Society of Antiquaries, and as Goldney was used to civic processions and the rituals of ceremony, Vicars may have regarded him as a reliable person to meet the demands of this particular job. It would transpire that Goldney fulfilled just one public engagement in Ireland in his capacity as Athlone Pursuivant, when he appeared in the State procession through the streets of Dublin in May 1907 for the opening of the Irish International Exhibition by Lord Aberdeen. Vicars, as usual, was director of ceremonies for this event, publishing the arrangements in the press, and appearing prominently in the processional cavalcade to Ballsbridge where the exhibition was held. Supported by Goldney and Shacktleton, he appeared on the dais inside the exhibition pavilion alongside the Lord Lieutenant in the presence of hundreds of spectators for the opening formalities.[129] It was to be his last public appearance on a ceremonial occasion. Significantly, at the State closing of the exhibition, held on 9 November 1907, none of the staff of the Office of Arms was present. Goldney, Horlock and Shacklelton had resigned by the end of October, and while Vicars and his nephew Mahony, the Cork Herald, survived this purge, in the longer term his position appeared untenable.

---

126 Blake to Dougherty, 17 December 1907, PRO, CO 904/221.
127 Witness statement given by Mr Sydney Horlock, 11 July 1907, PRO, BS 22/4.
128 GO, MS 111J.
129 Dennehy, *Record: The Irish International Exhibition 1907*, pp. 62–7; 121.

Vicars's demands for an open inquiry were refused, but to satisfy public opinion, the Government conceded a viceregal commission. The 'Crown Jewels Commission' was held in the public office of the Office of Arms – scene of the crime – between 10 and 18 January 1908, and all employees and others associated with the Office were called to give evidence. The terms of reference of the Commission were narrow, making it clear that the underlying pretext was to ensure Vicars would be ousted. The brief was simply 'to investigate the circumstances of the loss of the regalia . . . and to inquire if Sir Arthur Vicars had exercised due vigilance and proper care as the custodian thereof'.[130] Rather than fully investigate how the theft had occurred, or explore the various other administrative shortcomings that may have provided the real context in which it occurred, the object of the Commission was to focus upon Vicars's culpability. There was little examination of the ongoing tensions between the Office administration and Board of Works, resulting in the failure of the latter to supply a safe for the strong room. More significantly, the absence of any detailed questioning or cross-examination of the several guards and sentries on duty at the Castle gate is striking.

Having been disrupted by the police investigation and media focus in July 1907, the Office of Arms was again under the spotlight in January 1908 for the duration of the Commission's sittings. Whilst the press was not admitted to the proceedings, journalists eagerly waited outside the Office. Within half an hour of the first session, Vicars's and his counsel – including Timothy Healy, K.C., M.P, barrister – caused a sensation by refusing to participate. Healy announced that his client could not take part because instead of investigating how the jewels had been stolen or subsequently disposed of, and furthermore ending scurrilous insinuations about his client's private life, the inquiry focused solely on his alleged responsibility for the crime. Refusing to have any further part in the proceedings, Vicars returned to his room on the first floor of the building, continuing to work as normal until the Commission's findings were published on 25 January. Miss Gibbon, loyal to the last, also refused to participate. Bennett-Goldney, Burtchaell, Horlock, Mahony and Shackleton were all called as witnesses and cross-examined. As suspected, the findings were damning, the commissioners concluding:

> We should have thought that in the case of Jewels like these . . . the
> responsible custodian would, instead of carrying about the key of the safe

---

130 *Crown Jewels Commission*, p. i.

'A story of bickerings, scandal and neglect'

Ceremonial opening of the Irish International Exhibition at Ballsbridge, Dublin, May 1907. This was Sir Arthur Vicars's last public appearance, and he can be seen to the right of the dais, on which the Chamberlain is probably reading the list of dignitaries. Directly behind Vicars is Shackleton, who appears to be bowing, perhaps as his name is called. Standing to attention on the left side of the dais is Bennett-Goldney. Picture from William F. Dennehy, *Record. The Irish International Exhibition 1907* (Dublin, 1907).

in his pocket, have deposited it with his banker or in some other place of security except on the rare occasions when it was necessarily in use.[131]

In contrast, Shackleton was specifically vindicated: 'He appeared to us to be a perfectly truthful and candid witness . . . there is no evidence whatever before us which would support the suggestion that he was the person who stole the Jewels', was the official conclusion in 1908.[132] It may have been a poor judgement. Four years later, Shackleton was imprisoned in England for fraud, and served 15 months' hard labour.[133] Five days after the publication of the inquiry, the life appointment of Sir Arthur Vicars was terminated.

An interesting, if anecdotal, oral history tradition that has been passed through generations of the Office staff is that the 'Crown Jewels' were not stolen at all. The tradition has it that the whole saga was a plot masterminded by the Establishment to get rid of Vicars, and that the precious jewels were safely concealed in a drawer in the table of the public room for the duration of the Commission's sessions.[134] Although unlikely, the story indicates the widely held perception that the whole episode was intended not only to teach Vicars a lesson, but ultimately also to banish him from office. After publication of the findings, public opinion was sympathetic to Sir Arthur, who, it was believed, had been made a scapegoat for administrative failings beyond his control.[135] An open judicial inquiry would at least have allowed the exploration of these other issues.

ABSENCE OF DOCUMENTARY EVIDENCE

Even today we can only glean hints of the true context in which the 'Crown Jewels' disappeared. It is impossible to reconstruct the actual course of events in the absence of vital documentary evidence, which is either missing or has been destroyed. Some eight Home Office files on the 'Larceny of the Crown Jewels' were systematically destroyed – indicated by annotations on the surviving files.[136] There are curious gaps in the documentation at the Office of

---

131 *ibid.*, p. ix.
132 *ibid.*, p. xi.
133 Cafferky, *Scandal and Betrayal*, pp. 206–7.
134 This story was transmitted to Alf MacLochlainn, former Director of NLI, by Sergeant O'Donohue, who became the Office's messenger-porter in 1937. I am grateful to him for recollecting it.
135 O'Malley, *Viceroys*, pp. 335–7.
136 PRO, HO 144/1648. An in-house annotation in red ink gives the numbers of files in this series that were destroyed.

Arms too. For example, the bound press book of Official Correspondence for the period, 1893 to 1909, stops suddenly in 1902, beginning again in February 1908 – a month after Sir Arthur's departure.[137]

More interesting still, the only volume preserved in its collections that is specifically devoted to the 'Crown Jewels' episode was actually compiled outside, and presented by a private donor as late as 1942. This is in fact the private scrapbook of correspondence and press cuttings compiled by Mr J.C. Hodgson, Librarian to the Duke of Northumberland. Hodgson was the last person to see the jewels, having been given a private tour of the Office by Sir Arthur on 11 June 1907, and Vicars contacted him to verify when 'he had seen them safe', and assist the police investigation. Intrigued by the story, Hodgson opened his scrapbook, which commences with his exchange of correspondence from Sir Arthur and concludes with press cuttings and commentaries that date as late as the mid-1920s.[138]

In the official file on the 'Larceny of the State Jewels', as held by the Chief Secretary's Office, and now in the NAI, there is only one document actually dealing with the theft itself. This is the initial police report compiled by Superintendent John Lowe, who was first on the scene. The remainder of the file, which includes a copy of the Commission's published report, is concerned with events several months and years after the event. There is much about Sir Arthur's petitioning to clear his name and reclaim his personal belongings (including a large collection of books and manuscripts) but little about any efforts to uncover the perpetrators.[139]

The events of 1907–8 cast a dark shadow over the remainder of Sir Arthur Vicars's life. After years trying to clear his name, or at least to secure a fair trial, Vicars lived out his days at Kilmorna, near Listowel, County Kerry. He married Gertrude Wright, sister-in-law of his nephew Pierce Mahony in 1917, but remained embittered to the grave. The manner of his death during the War of Independence in April 1921 later underlined the tragedy of his unhappy career. Dragged from his bed and shot in front of his wife as the house burnt behind them, Vicars's brutal murder by the IRA epitomised the injustice he had earlier suffered.[140] As with the theft of the Crown Jewels that ruined his reputation, the cowardly perpetrators of this crime were never identified, nor brought to justice.[141]

137 GO, Official Correspondence, uncat.
138 GO, MS 507.
139 NAI, CSORP 1913/18119.
140 Gaughan, *Listowel*, pp. 324–8.
141 Neligan, *Spy in the Castle*, p. 63.142 NLI, P.4944.

Many of Vicars's personal papers were destroyed in the fire. However, from the smatterings of his writings that do survive, including an exchange of correspondence with his fellow antiquary James Fuller, he was emphatic about Shackleton's involvement.[142] The contents of Vicars's last will and testament also reveal how his life was ruined by the 'cruel misfortune' of the theft, and his subsequent treatment by Government. He might have had more to bequeath, he stated, had it not been for 'the outrageous way in which I was treated by the Irish Government over the loss of the Crown Jewels . . . backed up by the late King Edward VII, whom I had always loyally and faithfully served'. To his death he believed that he had been made a scapegoat 'to save other departments' and shield 'the real culprit and thief Francis R. Shackleton (brother of the explorer who didn't reach the South Pole)!'[143]

The career of Sir Arthur Vicars, which had had started so promisingly, thus ended in disaster. There is ample evidence that it was sacrificed to save Government embarrassment, and avoid scandal. He was not the most popular member of the Castle staff, because of personal ambition, scholarly expertise and punctiliousness. Perhaps he should have been more careful about his chosen associates. However, it was wrong that he was held personally responsible for the theft of valuable jewels that had little to do with the heraldic business of his department, and most certainly unjust that he did not receive a public hearing. His real legacy for the Office of Arms was much more positive: contacts made with other scholars in the field; his endeavours to build up its collections; his conscientious care of the records; and, above all, his success in obtaining the prestigious Bedford Tower for its exclusive accommodation all combined to raise its profile.

The task of finding a successor proved difficult. In a private letter from Lord Aberdeen to the portrait, landscape and figure painter Dermod O'Brien, written on 18 December 1907, some three weeks before the Commission had even been convened, it was clear that Vicars's fate had already been sealed. Aberdeen offered the position of Ulster King of Arms to O'Brien, subject only 'to the approval of the King', and further stated that it would 'become vacant immediately'. The content of the letter reveals that the subsequent Commission was a complete sham. Aberdeen stated that the Office was to be 'reconstituted' and whilst not wanting to hurry O'Brien's response, to emphasise that 'this matter [wa]s really urgent', he required his acceptance by telegram within 24 hours – such was the official anxiety to fill Vicars's position immediately. To

---

142 NLI, P.4944.
143 NAI, Principal Registry will of Sir Arthur Vicars, probate granted 20 March 1922.

encourage O'Brien, he advised him that he would have 'full freedom for private practice in the matter of heraldry or any other pursuit', and for assistance with routine work, he could rely on 'an admirable deputy in the Chief Clerk and Assistant, Mr Burtchaell'. Finally, with specific reference 'as to the insignia', Aberdeen made the interesting comment that 'what remains, *or may be recovered* [my italics] can be deposited in a bank'. For as long as he remained Lord Lieutenant, Aberdeen assured him, he would 'certainly never wish to disturb the repository where they might be placed'.[144] O'Brien appears to have missed his acceptance deadline – perhaps he declined because of the controversy surrounding the Office – but it was known he did not care for a Government appointment.[145] Burtchaell was also considered, and given his knowledge of the Office and, experience as a genealogist might have been the obvious candidate for promotion. However, he suffered from epilepsy, and this condition rendered him 'unfit for taking part in court ceremonies'.[146]

The Office itself was never quite the same after the events of 1907–8. It took on an almost romantic aura – the scene of a major crime, and alleged scandalous behaviour. This legacy lasted for several generations. Indeed, even after Irish Independence, when Dublin Castle was handed over to the Free State Government, the Office of Arms remained the only building within the Castle precincts to be locked to the outside world, night and day.[147]

---

144 Lord Aberdeen, Vice Regal Lodge, Dublin, to Mr Dermod O'Brien, marked 'Private', 18 December 1907, NLI, O'Brien Papers. I am grateful to Fergus Gillespie for drawing this source to my attention.
145 Snoddy, *Dictionary of Irish Artists*, pp. 349–50.
146 Obituary for G.D. Burtchaell, *JSAI, 6th series, 12* (1922), p. 95.
147 Press cuttings, 1920s, SC.

THREE

'The future of heraldry depends on artistic excellence'

Sir Nevile Wilkinson and the art of heraldry, 1908–21

TRANSITION

Nevile Wilkinson had been painting the scenery for a pantomime at Wilton House in Wiltshire, the English seat of his father-in-law, the Earl of Pembroke, when the call came to present himself at the London office of Sir Anthony MacDonnell, Under Secretary for Ireland. Pembroke had earlier suggested him as a possible successor to Vicars at a Privy Council meeting, and the King, anxious for an immediate transition of authority, was in favour. It was rumoured that when one Privy Counsellor argued that Wilkinson had little knowledge of heraldry, the King responded it did not matter 'so long as he's honest'[1] Thus Nevile Wilkinson assumed the post of the King of Arms and Principal Herald for Ireland.

Wilkinson's prior collaboration with Sir John Ross of Bladensburg, Chief Commissioner of the Dublin Metropolitan Police 1901–14, on a published history of the Coldstream Guards, for which he provided illustrations, may also have been a factor in his appointment.[2] This link undoubtedly antagonised the aggrieved Vicars, who continued to protest that he had been made 'a scapegoat to save Ross of Bladensburg and the Board of Works',[3] and chose to be critical of the Wilkinson regime. His faithful typist, Miss Gibbon, who resigned in sympathy with him after the Commission continued to work with Vicars in pursuit of private genealogical research. He had hoped that other surviving staff members would also follow her example, regarding Burtchaell's decision

---

1   Bamford and Bankes, *Vicious Circle*, p. 146.
2   Ross and Wilkinson, *Coldstream Guards 1815–1895*.
3   Vicars, Grange Con, County Wicklow, to James Fuller, 6 July 1909, NLI, P. 4955.

Oak panelling from Old Bawn House, Tallaght, used by Wilkinson for painting the arms of successive kings-of-arms, which adorned his office in the Bedford Tower. *Courtesy, Klaus Unger, OPW.*

to stay as treachery. Vicars's tetchy comments about his former colleague reveal how badly the 1907 debacle had affected him:

> How Burtchaell could act in the mean and low way he has amazes me. I brought him into the Office and he was my assistant for 14 years, and I was awfully kind to him, notwithstanding his dreadful infirmity – but for me he would have succumbed in one of the several fits he had in the Office – his ingratitude when I think of it makes me shudder – however he can't and won't profit by it in the long run....[4]

In later correspondence Vicars revealed that he regarded Wilkinson as his usurper: 'nothing but a Guardsman', who in his opinion knew 'nothing of genealogy, English or Irish'. The indignant Vicars supposed that Wilkinson could not even 'properly blazon a coat of arms', and also observed that he lived 'chiefly away' from Dublin.[5] In 1911 he remarked that 'Wilkinson is never there, Burtchaell runs the whole show, and has no time for anything'[6] Wilkinson had travelled to Ceylon, to recover from an operation and build up his strength for a forthcoming royal visit to Dublin by King Edward VII.[7]

Vicars's begrudging remarks notwithstanding, Wilkinson would serve as Ulster King of Arms and Principal Herald of All Ireland for the next 32 years, with Burtchaell as his right-hand man for the next 13 years. Born in England in 1869, the son of a barrister, Wilkinson was a former captain in the Coldstream Guards whose services abroad had included a year in Ireland when he was stationed at the Castle Guard in 1891. His dashing good looks and impeccable manners made him popular at society events in Dublin, where he enjoyed the social round of dances, dinners, races and other sporting events.[8] On one occasion early in his career, he had been invited to dine at the top table with the Lord Lieutenant and his wife, Lord and Lady Zetland, at a Castle dinner – quite an honour for a young officer.[9] But Wilkinson was at home with the ceremonial niceties, and by 1903 his marriage to Lady Beatrix Herbert, eldest daughter of the Earl of Pembroke – one of the great urban landowners in Ireland at the time – had introduced him to the highest social

---

4   Vicars to James Fuller FSA, 26 June 1909, *op. cit.* In an uncanny twist of fate, Burtchaell died tragically in August 1921, just four months after Vicars's brutal murder in April of that year.
5   Various letters from Vicars to Fuller, 26 June 1909–10 December 1911, *op. cit.*
6   Vicars to Fuller, 12 September 1911, *op. cit.*
7   Wilkinson, *To All and Singular*, p. 191.
8   Wagner, *Herald's World*, p. 70.
9   Wilkinson, *To All and Singular*, pp. 36–40.

circles.[10] Since their marriage, the couple had spent each summer at the Earl of Pembroke's Irish county residence, Mount Merrion House at Stillorgan, County Dublin, and Wilkinson was 'known and greatly liked in Dublin in artistic and literary society'.[11]

Injured on active service during the Boer War, Wilkinson pursued his interest in art by studying etching and engraving at the South Kensington School of Art and Design. As a Conservative, he did not, by his own admission, share the same political outlook as the Government, and was thus not an obvious choice for the Aberdeen Administration.[12] However, both Lord and Lady Aberdeen approved of him, perhaps because he was available to take up the post immediately, saving the Castle any further embarrassment. They interviewed him on Thursday 30 January, recommending that he be appointed immediately. Anxious to accommodate the smooth transition of authority, Wilkinson crossed to Dublin the very next night 'in order to take over the vacant premises in the Upper Castle Yard', and make preparations for the start of the Castle Season.[13] This began less than a week later with a levée, when it was noted that Captain Wilkinson, 'the successor of Sir Arthur Vicars, had taken charge of the arrangements', that had been 'issued as usual from the Office of Arms'.[14]

So it transpired that on the same day that Vicars received his letter of dismissal, in which he was ordered to hand over the keys of the Office to his successor,[15] Captain Nevile Rodwell Wilkinson was officially appointed 'Ulster King of Arms and Principal Herald of Ireland'.[16] His patent of appointment, which empowered him to examine, view, correct and ratify the arms of eminent men, and carry out all other duties attached to his Office, concurrently revoked that of his predecessor.[17] In a separate arrangement with the Treasury, his appointment was made for life, and a salary of £750 per annum agreed.[18]

Following Vicars's dismissal on 30 January, the remaining Office staff – Burtchaell, Gibbon, and Mahony, along with the Office cleaner, Mrs Farrell –

10 French, *Nepotists*, p. 351; Galloway, *Most Illustrious Order*, p. 91.
11 *The Irish Times,* 1 February 1908.
12 Wilkinson, *To All and Singular.* p. 171.
13 *ibid.*, pp. 170–1.
14 *The Irish Times*, 5 February 1908.
15 J.B. Dougherty, Dublin Castle, to Vicars, 30 January 1908, NAI, CSORP 1913/18119.
16 *Dublin Gazette*, 30 January 1908.
17 GO, MS 154, pp. 151–3.
18 Treasury memorandum, NAI, CSORP 1913/18119.

were notified that the Office would be closed until after Wilkinson's arrival at noon on Saturday 1 February, and a notice to that effect was posted on the front door.[19] Wilkinson was struck by the public interest in his arrival at the Castle. He found himself surrounded by press reporters and photographers 'anxious for copy', and when he came to the glazed door of the Bedford Tower he was admitted, not by a member of staff, but a burly constable.

Gradually, the vacant appointments were filled up. A new messenger/porter, Sergeant Daniel Herlihy, was appointed in place of Stivey on 1 March 1908, and proved a loyal office keeper, his service continuing until 1936.[20] Sometime after this, Major Thomas Shepard, a retired major of the 4th Northamptonshire Regiment, was appointed. In the 1911 census he described himself as 'an assistant' at the Office of Arms, Dublin Castle.[21] As we shall see, he had technical expertise, and executed many of the early heraldic commissions issued by Wilkinson. Sergeant Bernard J. Tinckler, formerly of the Irish Guards, took the place of Miss Gibbon, although he had more responsibilities than she. He was appointed as Wilkinson's 'personal clerk' in 1908,[22] and later described himself as 'secretary to Ulster King of Arms, clerk and engraver'.[23] He was also artistically competent, and appears to have helped with the engrossing of patents, his technical expertise later commended by his colleagues.[24]

With so many new faces, it was Burtcheall who provided continuity between the old and new administrations, Wilkinson relying heavily on his advice, and often leaving him in charge. Indeed, in contrast to the constant scrupulous daily attendance of Vicars, Wilkinson soon established a pattern of absence. Between May and June 1908, he returned to London to recover from a bout of illness, when Burtchaell 'acted on his behalf' until he could make other 'necessary appointments' in relation to the Order of St Patrick.[25] He was absent again due to ill-health for six months between December 1910 and June

19 *The Irish Times*, 1 February 1908.

20 PRO, T 62/709.

21 NAI, 1911 Census Returns, County Dublin /85/6/5, Blackrock, Proby Square. Shepard was then aged 47, married with seven children between the ages of 10 and 20, all Roman Catholic.

22 NAI, CSORP, 1913 18119.

23 NAI, 1911 Census Returns, Dublin /41/24. Goldsmith Street. Tinckler was then aged 44, married with four children between the ages of six and 14, all Church of Ireland.

24 Burtchaell, Dublin, to Wilkinson, London, recounting Office administration during the War, 9 July 1920, GO, Accounts and Salaries File, uncat.

25 Wilkinson, Duchess Street, London, to Burtchaell, Office of Arms, 4 May 1908, GO, uncat. *op. cit.*

1911 (although he did make it to China during this period). His appearances in Dublin would become more erratic during the First World War, and its aftermath, when again bouts of illness and other activities distracted his attentions.

In June 1908, the Chief Secretary for Ireland, the Rt. Hon. Augustine Birrell, announced to the House of Commons that the Office of Arms must be reconstituted following the dismissal of the Ulster King of Arms in January 1908 and the resignations of the Athlone Pursuivant and Dublin Herald the previous November. The leader of the Irish Parliamentary Party, John Redmond MP, enquired if this meant that these offices had been abolished, but Birrell confirmed that they would be filled, with Crown approval. Mr William Bytes, the radical Liberal MP for Salford North suggested that the offices should simply be abolished, to save unnecessary expense. However, when it was pointed out that neither appointment entailed much expenditure (only £20 was paid to Athlone, whilst the Dublin Herald post remained an honorary position), parliamentary sanction for the new appointments was granted.[26]

The new officeholders were officially appointed on 18 June 1908.[27] Burtchaell was upgraded to the post of Athlone Pursuivant, in succession to Bennett-Goldney, and later, on 16 November 1909, he was given the additional position of 'Registrar of the Office of Arms'. The introduction of this new title (which related to the Office rather than the Order of St Patrick) was the first significant indication that the volume of genealogical and heraldic business undertaken by the Office was beginning to outweigh its ceremonial functions.[28] In the early years of his reign, Wilkinson chose to operate without an official deputy, although this was later to change during the First World War. However, Burtchaell, in effect, became the principal Office administrator.

Captain Guillimore O'Grady, another barrister-at-law, became the new Dublin Herald, in place of Shackleton. Formerly an officer in the South Irish Horse, O'Grady enjoyed his own private income derived from the family estate in County Clare. Considered to be a 'safe' appointment, he had some knowledge of genealogy and heraldry.[29] Vicars's nephew Peirce Gun Mahony had also stayed on as Cork Herald, although his was only an intermittent presence in the Office, and he later resigned, handing back his badge of office in October 1910.[30] He was then replaced by yet another appointee with a

---

26 *Hansard*, 1 June 1908, 189, 1720; 4 June 1908, 209, 208.
27 NAI, CSORP, 1908 Index.
28 GO, MS 154, p. 562.
29 *Who's Who,* 1929; Galloway, *Most Illustrious Order*, p. 92.
30 P.G. Mahony to Wilkinson, 7 October 1910, GO, Official Correspondence, uncat.

military background, Captain Richard Alexander ('Leo') Keith, an aide-de-camp to the Countess of Aberdeen, with a commission in the 3rd Battalion Seaforth Highlanders.

Like O'Grady, Keith was regarded as a safe replacement for this relatively nominal position, although he played little role in the daily routine of the Office, continuing to live in London, and fulfilling official ceremonial engagements in Dublin when required. There were just five investiture ceremonies for new knights of the Order between 1908 and the outbreak of the First World War. Indeed only a further six investitures were held in the years between 1915 and 1922. Keith was on active service during the War, and seriously wounded, so consequently he missed all of them.[31]

ADMINISTRATIVE PROBLEMS

Immediately on his arrival at the Castle on 1 February 1908, Wilkinson had to contend with an administrative problem that had followed on from Vicars's dismissal. Vicars did not comply with the rather stringent request of the Castle authorities to return to the Office to meet Wilkinson and hand over his keys. His personal attendance for this handing-over ceremony was rather a humiliating demand, and understandably he chose to avoid it. He did later return all keys for the building, including three strong room keys, but not in time for the opening of the Castle Season.[32] Wilkinson needed immediate access to the strong room to get the Sword of State and Maces for the official opening of the Season, and so he authorised another break-in to the strong room to recover them.

Continuing the rather bizarre saga of under-cover operations at the Castle, Wilkinson avoided the curiosity of the lingering press by waiting until the small hours of Sunday morning, when he rounded up a couple of labourers armed with crowbars. Accompanied by representatives of the Dublin Police and the Board of Works (presumably to act as witnesses), they forced their way into the strong room using crowbars, and successfully retrieved the symbols of State for use the next day in the Throne Room.[33]

A further administrative problem arose later, when Vicars demanded custody of all the papers that had accumulated in the Office during his

---

31 Galloway, *Most Illustrious Order*, p. 247.
32 Several keys were duly returned by Vicars on 5 February 1908, NAI, CSORP 1913/18119.
33 Wilkinson, *To All and Singular*, p. 174–5.

appointment. In addition to about 1,500 books, and some manuscripts that were his own private property and subsequently returned to him, Vicars also claimed a right to some 425 bundles of papers. He insisted these had been used for his own private genealogical practice, and argued that the papers related to the 'preliminary steps' of research which he had undertaken for clients, prior to the registration of entries. Wilkinson, however, resisted this, on the grounds that the material related to cases that had resulted in heraldic commissions being issued by the Office. He argued they were 'constantly referred to in questions which arise' during the course of business'.[34] The matter was not resolved without recourse to the legal process, in which Burtchaell gave evidence as an expert witness on behalf of the Office. He stated:

> Inquiries are constantly made as to the circumstances in which arms were granted or confirmed, and pedigrees registered, and the absence of such information would be an inconvenience to persons consulting the Office, and a loss of fees paid to the Treasury.[35]

The legal wrangle was finally resolved in March 1909, when Wilkinson, backed by the Crown Solicitor, informed Vicars that he could not remove 'official documents belonging to this Department, having been received by you in your official capacity as Ulster King of Arms, and during your tenure of the Office'. Only one letter and a rough pedigree together with its related documentation were officially returned to Vicars as private property after the inquiry.[36] The case set a precedent for the future, determining that what material created during the course of the Office's work was public property, rather than the private possession of the particular figurehead in charge of the Office, and protected against further loss.

However, it appears that Vicars may have removed other items prior to his departure. Many years later, a volume of pedigrees that belonged to the Office came up for sale through a London dealer. Known as the 'Barry' volume,[37] it had been missing since 1908. In 1930, it was finally returned to the shelf from which Wilkinson concluded it had been removed prior to Vicars's retirement. Being as fair to his predecessor's reputation as he could, Wilkinson speculated that it might 'inadvertently have been removed' by Vicars along with his own

34 Wilkinson to the Chief Secretary's Office, 12 February 1909, NAI, CSORP 1913/18119.
35 Report of G.D. Burtchaell, Registrar, 29 February 1909, GO, Official correspondence, uncat.
36 Wilkinson to Vicars, 9 March 1909, GO, Official correspondence, uncat.
37 Now catalogued as GO, MS 412.

private documents, owing to 'the confusion which then existed at the Office'. The dealer generously agreed to give it back. Perhaps he had little choice, for the leather label bearing the words 'Ulster's Office' on the cover clearly identified its provenance. Wilkinson assumed that the volume must have been sold at auction by Vicars 'shortly after his retirement', along with many of his other books and documents. Indeed, some 466 books and 63 lots of manuscripts – including the 'Autograph letters of Sir William Betham', comprising 3,000 letters on a range of heraldic, genealogical and antiquarian subjects (which were part of Vicars's private holdings), were sold in July 1908.[38] These particular valuable items were later re-acquired by the GO, and re-integrated into the collection. Vicars's remaining papers were later burnt in the fire that destroyed his home, following his murder in 1921.[39]

Having learnt from the misfortunes of the previous regime, Wilkinson made an early requisition for various items of security for the Bedford Tower. The Treasury approved of all of these demands without question, and they appear to have been fitted without delay by the Board of Works. They included a new burglar-proof safe 'of the strongest quality and sufficiently small to be placed inside the strong-room', and a small wall safe for the storage of all the Office keys. A new 'Bramah' lock was fitted to the strong room, for which six keys were made, replacing the existing 'very poor lock'. Three of the keys were kept for the Office staff, two went to the Board of Works and one to the Castle Detective Branch. New bolts were also affixed to various doors within the Office, including the basement and the door into Wilkinson's room from the balcony, while the window in the messenger's office was also secured, it being the last 'window low down at the back to remain unbarred'. The end of 1908 finally saw electricity installed to light the Bedford Tower, having been originally requisitioned by Vicars and refused in 1902. By 1908, it was deemed a necessity because 'since the robbery in the Office, one light had to be kept burning all night for security purposes'. Sanctioned as early as August 1908, the innovation of electric light not only reduced the risk of fire, but also improved atmospheric conditions in the building. In the confined and airless environment of the strong room, the dry gas fumes were actually injuring the bindings of manuscripts.[40] It can therefore be argued that the 'Crown Jewels' saga at least had longterm beneficial repercussions as far as the Office records were concerned.

---

38 Catalogue for sale of books and manuscripts from the private library of Sir Arthur Vicars, July 1908, GO, MS 507.
39 Wilkinson to Bernard Quaritch Ltd, Grafton Street, London, 11 February 1930, GO, Letters Relating to Sale of Book of Pedigrees, uncat.
40 Estimates approved 1908–09, GO, MS 328, pp. 30–3.

WILKINSON AND THE ART OF HERALDRY

Having seen first to his ceremonial duties connected with the first Castle Season, and also successfully superintended the investiture of Lord Castletown on 29 February 1908 (postponed and held over since July 1907 on account of the theft), Wilkinson then turned his attention to heraldic business. His first task was to clear outstanding commissions. Eight patents had been held over because of Vicars's dismissal, and these were signed by Wilkinson, and then despatched to clients. For example, a grant made to John Winthrop Hackett, Member of the Legislative Council of Western Australia, and formerly of Dublin, which had been authorised and designed by Vicars, was duly signed and registered by Wilkinson on 10 April 1908.[41]

Wilkinson made a valuable early contribution to the artistic and symbolic role of the Office of Arms. He had studied heraldry since his early retirement from the army in 1907. As a designer, etcher craftsman, Associate of the Royal Society of Painters Etchers, and later Vice-President of the Royal Society of Miniature Painters, he assumed office with a degree of flair and originality. This is demonstrated by the artistic quality evident in the Registers after his appointment. He also promoted the Office's artistic and cultural potential to learned bodies, and in 1910 advised the Royal Society of Antiquaries of Ireland that 'the future of heraldry depends on its artistic excellence'. In an illustrated paper, he emphasised the beauty that heraldry could bring to inanimate objects such as glass, stone, marble, china and wood.[42]

To demonstrate this potential, he undertook various projects to embellish the appearance of the Office itself, acquiring redundant oak panelling from the Old Bawn House at Tallaght, built in the 1630s for the Church of Ireland Archbishop of Dublin,[43] to fit out his room in the Bedford Tower. He then engaged various artists to paint the 'armorial bearings, names and dates of appointment' of each of his predecessors from Bartholomew Butler in 1552 to Vicars in 1893.[44] These beautiful heraldic paintings brought alive the wooden panelling, visually reinforcing the longevity and tradition of the Office of Arms. These continued to adorn the walls of this room until the Bedford Tower was renovated during the mid-1980s.

In spite of Vicars's initial external protestations, the Office of Arms gradually returned to a normal routine. The glare of the press died away, and the

---

41 Register of Grants, GO, MS 111J.
42 Nevile Rodwell Wilkinson, *Heraldry*, p. 53.
43 Arthur Vicars, *Old Bawn, county Dublin*, pp. 52–5. See also Leask, *House at Old Bawn County Dublin*, pp. 314–25.
44 Wilkinson, *To All and Singular*, pp. 178–9.

new staff settled down to their work. Its heraldic business recovered the hiatus created by the theft of the 'Crown Jewels' and subsequent distraction of the Commission. Compared with 18 commissions executed in 1908, some 28 patents were executed and registered by the Office of Arms the following year, and the work continued to be sustained until the First World War in 1914.[45] For example, in 1911 no less than 26 commissions were completed.

The increase may also have been a result of the publication of further legal opinion on the division of heraldic jurisdiction between the English, Scottish and Irish heraldic authorities. In November 1908, the Law Officers of the Crown declared that the authority to deal with new applications for arms would be determined in the first instance by the domicile of the applicant. Thus, all people resident in Ireland should apply to Ulster King of Arms. New grants of arms could also be made by Ulster to persons domiciled outside Ireland who could trace their descent from an Irish ancestor.[46]

Wilkinson brought in Major Shepard to execute the artwork on patents and registered copies. He continued to work for the Office of Arms until the First World War. Shepard had apparently applied in the past to Vicars 'for heraldic work', but the latter would not employ him because, in his view, 'he did not have a good style', and consequently had 'no work to give him'.[47] Contrary to this opinion, however, the registered arms as entered into the Registers of Grants and Confirmations following the 1908 transition show a very high standard of artistry, and have all the hallmarks of someone who was technically very gifted indeed. Shepard's first commission was a confirmation to the Revd Hugo Huband of Cambridge, formerly of Dublin, dated 15 July 1909, and is easily identified in the register because Shepard began the practice of annotating all his work. He added his initials, on either side of a shepherd's crook, below the symbols of the heraldic harp and crown, with the number of the commission. Whilst the first few registrations do show signs of someone undergoing tuition, being a little static, the quality soon improved. As one turns the pages of the Registers from 1908 onwards, the colour and embellishment are immediately striking.[48]

After Shepard had completed 27 commissions, a new register was opened, for which a new volume series was commenced, the reference '111A' assigned

45 GO, MS 111J.
46 C.E. Troup, Home Office, to the Secretary of the Treasury, communicating the opinion of the Law Officers on heraldic jurisdiction, 5 November 1908, GO, Material Relating to Heraldic Jurisdiction, uncat.
47 Vicars to James Fuller FSA, 6 July 1909, NLI, P. 4955.
48 GO, MS 111J.

to it.[49] Significantly the first entry in the new register was a certificate of arms that Wilkinson, who was already armigerous, issued to himself, so as to register his heraldic presence in Ireland, on 16 January 1909. This coat of arms is most artistic, featuring three whelk shells. The robustly drawn title page that proceeds it is an important artistic piece, marking the fact that it represents the first new volume of Wilkinson's reign. We know from the annotation that it was Shepard's work (see Colour Section).

The format of the entries also changed in the new register. The visual representation of each registered coat of arms was enlarged, filling an entire page, while on the facing page the text of the blazon was inscribed. This allowed each colour coat of arms to be executed in magnificent detail, and

gives a good indication of the quality of the patent issued to the client. Between 1909 and 20 October 1914 (when he completed his last commission in the Office registers) Shepard was responsible for making 151 registered entries.[50] Even when he returned to his regiment for active service during the Great War, Shepard's services were still required by the Office, initially at least. From Brighton, where he was stationed by January 1915, he completed several sketches of arms that were needed as a matter of urgency.[51]

In addition to Shepard, other artists involved in the commission to paint the armorial bearings of former Kings of Arms in Wilkinson's room may have included members of the McConnell family, of the famous heraldic studio on Lincoln Place. James McConnell (1842–1916) was an internationally recognised master of heraldic art and illumination, who, along with his three daughters, all of whom were trained heraldic artists, ran a successful independent heraldic studio near the back entrance to Trinity College, attracting students from all over Europe.[52] There was much demand for illuminated addresses and other presentation pieces in early twentieth-century Dublin, and the creative Wilkinson may have endeavoured to foster links between the studio and his Office.

47   Vicars to James Fuller FSA, 6 July 1909, NLI, P. 4955.
48   GO, MS 111J.
49   GO, 111A or Grants 'K' ('K' denotes the old series reference).
50   *ibid.*
51   Burtchaell to Major Thomas Shepard, 4th Northamptonshire Regiment, Brighton, 6 January, 1915, GO, Official Correspondence, uncat.
52   Swanton, *Emerging From the Shadow*, p. 32.

By early 1915, McConnell's eldest daughter, Mabel, was employed in the Office, in place of Shepard. McConnell's first artistic commission for the Office was to draw the arms for the Honan Hostel (a home for aged and destitute gentlemen, under the auspices of the Sisters of Charity) in Cork City, and granted on 9 January 1915 (see Colour Section).[53] This was a significant grant, demonstrating the changing times in which the Office was operating by 1915. It has a distinctive native style, featuring many Celtic ornamentations, and the motto is in Irish – another pre-Independence example of the use of the native language. The text of the motto was also significant – 'Do cum glóire Dé agus onóra na hÉireann' ('To the glory of God and honour of Ireland'). Significantly, the next time this form of words was used as a motto was for the intended arms for the President of Ireland, as prescribed by Dr Edward MacLysaght, first Chief Herald of Ireland, after the Office of Arms had been transferred from the authority of the British Crown to the Irish Government.[54]

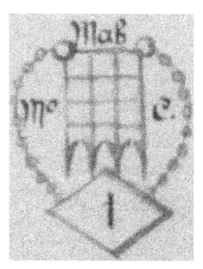

Like Shepard, McConnell followed the in-house style for registration, using separate pages for the visual representation of each coat of arms and for the text or blazon with which it was associated (in fact this style continued until 1933). She also applied her own annotation – the letters 'M' and 'Mc' appearing on either side of a portcullis (the heraldic devise representing a drawbridge).[55] After the death of her father in 1916, Mabel McConnell continued to run the family studio, in addition to fulfilling her role as herald painter in the Office of Arms, until her own death in June 1929.[56]

Autograph of Mabel McConnell, heraldic artist, 1915-29, detail from registration.

Other interesting heraldic commissions during Wilkinson's early days as Principal Herald of all Ireland, again reflecting the changing nature of social

---

53 GO 111B or Grants 'L', p. 7.

54 GO, MS 111G, p. 21.

55 Grant of arms to the Honan Hostel, Cork, 9 January 1915, GO, MS 111L, p. 7.

56 Wilkinson, Princess Street, London, to Mr Athawes, The Treasury, 3 London 1929, GO, Accounts and Salaries File, uncat.

and political life, included the grant of new arms to University College Dublin, founded under the Irish Universities Act 1908. This grant, featuring the harp of Ireland, was made in September 1911. It was followed soon afterwards by a grant to its parent institution, the new National University of Ireland, which replaced the Royal University, again founded under the terms of the Universities Act. This included the arms of Ireland as a charge, granted in May 1912 (see Colour Section).[57] In contrast, a grant to Queen's University Belfast, featuring the red hand of Ulster as one of its charges, was granted previously in March 1910.[58] Arms had been used by Trinity College Dublin since its foundation in 1592, and were certified by Sir Arthur Vicars in 1901,[59] while Sir Bernard Burke granted arms to Queen's College Cork (later University College Cork), in 1886.[60]

The introduction of the third Home Rule Bill in April 1912, heralding the success of constitutional nationalism and the potential for self-government, was a significant landmark in Irish political life. However, there was strenuous opposition to the proposed measure within the ranks of Unionism, especially in the north-east of Ulster. Determined resistance was shown on 'Ulster Day', 28 September 1912, when almost 472,000 people signed the Solemn League and Covenant – convinced 'that Home Rule would be disastrous to the material well-being of Ulster as well as the whole Ireland'. In addition to the Northern signatories, some 2,000 men of Ulster descent signed 'the Covenant' in Dublin. After the Ulster Unionist Council formed its volunteers into a united body known as the Ulster Volunteer Force in January 1913, various strategies of recruitment were devised to assist the 'Ulster cause'. This activity was supported by a small minority of Protestants in Dublin,[61] who participated in recruitment, distribution of literature, and other quasi-military activities connected with the anti-Home Rule movement.[62]

At this delicate stage in Irish politics, evidence from the surviving uncatalogued records in the Office indicates that it may have provided a distribution point for the circulation of literature opposing the anti-Home Rule movement. Hundreds of blank enrolment forms for membership of the 'British Volunteer

---

57 GO, MS 111J, pp. 62 and 87.

58 GO, MS 111K, p. 31.

59 Certificate of arms to the Provost, Fellows and Scholars of Trinity College Dublin, 10 January 1901, GO, MS 111J, p. 141.

60 Grant of arms to the President, Vice-President and Professors of Queen's College Cork, 27 March 1886, GO, MS 110, p. 110.

61 Stewart, *The Ulster Crisis, Resistance to Home Rule, 1912–14*, pp. 58–68.

62 *ibid.,* pp. 73, 109, 132–3.

'The future of heraldry depends on artistic excellence'

𝕭𝖗𝖎𝖙𝖎𝖘𝖍 𝕷𝖊𝖆𝖌𝖚𝖊 for the 𝕾𝖚𝖕𝖕𝖔𝖗𝖙 of 𝖀𝖑𝖘𝖙𝖊𝖗 and the 𝖀𝖓𝖎𝖔𝖓.

𝕭𝖗𝖎𝖙𝖎𝖘𝖍 𝖁𝖔𝖑𝖚𝖓𝖙𝖊𝖊𝖗 𝕱𝖔𝖗𝖈𝖊.

County or Town _____ Constituency _____

Occupation _____

Address _____

 THE UNDERSIGNED, hereby enrol myself as a Volunteer in the Force now being raised to assist Ulster in the struggle she is making to maintain the Union between Great Britain and Ireland. And in the event of the Government of Ireland Bill being passed into law without the sanction of the people of the United Kingdom being expressed at a General Election, I solemnly swear to hold myself in readiness to act anywhere and in any manner that may serve to this end. Further, I promise to stand by this agreement until such time as I notify my resignation in writing to my superior officer.

𝕲𝖔𝖉 𝕾𝖆𝖛𝖊 𝖙𝖍𝖊 𝕶𝖎𝖓𝖌.

Signed

Witness

Date

Printed recruitment form for the British Volunteer Force. Hundreds of these forms were found in the Office. *GO Collection.*

Force', distributed under the auspices of the British League for the Support of Ulster and the Union, in 1913, were discovered scattered throughout the building when the Office of Arms was transferred to the control of the Irish Government in 1943.[63]

Perhaps the territorial significance of the Office's other popular title of 'Ulster's Office' may have attracted such literature, but given the large quantities found, it seems more likely that a member of Wilkinson's staff was involved in the process of distributing it outside. There is no direct evidence of who may have been responsible, as none of the surviving forms contain signatures. Given

---

63 GO, Forms for the British Volunteer Force, uncat. Dr Edward MacLysaght discovered the material after April 1943. I am grateful to Alf MacLochlainn, former Director of NLI, for bringing this information to my attention.

that the Administration was firmly behind Home Rule, it is a little surprising that this activity was going on at all within the walls of the Castle. Wilkinson himself is unlikely to have been responsible. He was more interested in art than politics, an admirer of Lord Pirrie (the leader of the Home Rule movement in Ulster), and above all aware that his Office was 'in no sense a political one', but it is fair to speculate that he was not sympathetic to Home Rule.[64] Perhaps one of the several military personnel employed by him during this period may have been directly involved, and he turned a blind eye to it.

AN HERALDIC MUSEUM

Wilkinson's most important heraldic legacy to Ireland, derived from his interest in the artistic symbolism of heraldry, was the foundation of the Heraldic Museum. This was officially opened by Lord Aberdeen in the public office of the Office, on 20 April 1909, although Wilkinson had been working on its design from March 1908. The opening of the new museum did not generate much public comment at the time,[65] but it was of historic significance because it was the first of its kind in the world. To promote its uniqueness and prestige, Wilkinson insisted that items selected for display 'must have heraldic charges as the principal part of their decoration', and appealed for donations from members of antiquarian societies.[66]

His enthusiasm resulted in an impressive collection of drawings, bookplates, carvings, stained glass, china, embroideries, seals and engravings. Donors included Lord Iveagh, who funded the purchase of several rare artefacts, including an armorial champlevé enamel candlestick dating from the fourteenth century, a stained glass roundel featuring Swiss armorial bearings, and a Limoges enamel featuring the arms of a bishop. Wilkinson also secured institutional support from the National Museum of Science and Art, which provided the specifications for the custom-built display cases to exhibit the material, and from the British Museum, which presented wax impressions of medieval seals bearing heraldic devises.[67] In addition, the

---

64 Wilkinson, *To All and Singular*, pp. 203; 206.
65 The following week *The Irish Times* made no mention of it, whilst reporting other official engagements made by the Lord Lieutenant on that day, including the Anti-Tuberculosis Exhibition at the Rotunda, and the opening of the Dublin Spring Show.
66 Wilkinson, *Heraldry*, p. 54.
67 Wilkinson, Office of Arms, to Charles Read Esq, British Museum, 31 March 1908, GO, Official Correspondence, uncat.

HERALDIC MUSEUM,

OFFICE OF ARMS, DUBLIN.

Founded 1908.

THIS Museum was opened in the Public Library of the Office of Arms, Dublin Castle, by H. E. The Earl of Aberdeen, K.T., G.C.M.G., on the 20th April, 1909. It was founded with the object of bringing together a collection of specimens connected with Heraldry of artistic or historical interest, and is the first permanent institution of its kind.

The generosity of many interested in the project has enabled the Director during the past year to bring together a collection of much value both to the student and to the general public. Notable among the exhibits are a pair of embroidered Herald's Tabards of the time of George II. and George III. respectively; a XIVth century Pricket Candlestick in early Limoges Enamel; a rare Armorial Sévres Cup and Saucer, and several fine examples of Armorial Carving. A list of the more important gifts to the Museum is given overleaf.

The Director has presented to the Museum a collection of some 4,000 Irish Armorial Bookplates, which is now in course of arrangement.

There is no Grant of Public Moneys for the purposes of the Museum; the Trustees therefore hope that those who are interested in the study of Heraldry, and in the collection and preservation of Heraldic objects, will assist in the work so successfully begun, by becoming Annual Subscribers, or by Donations.

The Director will be glad to furnish any further information regarding the needs and work of the Museum.

Donations and Annual Subscriptions should be made payable to

THE HON. DIRECTOR,
Heraldic Museum,
Office of Arms,
Dublin Castle.

Subscription notice for the Heraldic Museum. *GO Collection.*

College of Arms donated a banner that had belonged to the King of Portugal, while the Office of the Lord Lyon assisted with the acquisition of a Georgian tabard.[68]

Funding for the new Heraldic Museum was entirely by private subscription, Wilkinson proudly declaring that 'no public money at all' had been used for its establishment, and as the word spread about its existence, the collections expanded. In 1912, the bust of Sir William Betham was bequeathed by the late Cecil William Betham of Stradbroke, County Dublin, and was initially displayed in the Heraldic Museum, although it later became a prominent feature of the entrance hallway, and is still on display in Kildare Street.[69] Additional

---

68 Subscription leaflet, including details of exhibits at the Heraldic Museum, 1910, GO, uncat.

69 GO, File Relating to the Heraldic Museum, uncat.

The Heraldic Museum, Dublin Castle, as designed by Nevile Wilkinson, which opened to the public in April 1909. *Courtesy, Bestick Williams.*

collections of bookplates, seals and manu-scripts followed from a variety of other sources. Wilkinson himself contributed generously, purchasing the illuminated vellum presenting the freedom of the city of Dublin to Dean Jonathan Swift, dated 1729, as well as hundreds of bookplates.[70]

At the official opening, Wilkinson delivered a long and reflective speech, in which he outlined the aims behind the Museum. Referring to the practice of his predecessors to consider as their private property 'all objects which have come into the Office except those which may be termed strictly official', the creation of a museum of artefacts was his attempt to rectify this practice. By appointing trustees to oversee its contents, his intention was to ensure they would be preserved for the people of Ireland 'in trust . . . so that when [his] time came to depart, should human nature prove too strong, the arm of the law would intervene and save the collection for posterity'. In the unlikely event of the 'abolition of the Office of Ulster', he also made provision that the trustees at the time should offer 'the whole collection to the National Museum of Science and Art', again to ensure that the contents would not be lost to Ireland.[71]

Advertising notice for the Heraldic Museum, posted on the door of the Office of Arms. *GO Collection.*

In addition to O'Grady and Burtchaell a third trustee of the new museum was Walter G. Strickland, Registrar of the National Gallery of Ireland and a leading art historian.[72] The fourth founding trustee was Sir William Thornley Stoker, Master of Surgery at the Royal University of Ireland – who had just been confirmed with arms himself, symbolically featuring the head of a druid (see Colour Section).[73] As Principal Herald of all Ireland, Wilkinson acted as Museum Director – a role continued by his successors.[74]

---

70   Wilkinson, *To All and Singular*, p. 179.
71   Speech delivered at the opening of the Heraldic Museum by its founder, Nevile Wilkinson, 20 April 1909, GO, File Relating to the Heraldic Museum, uncat.
72   Strickland, *Dictionary of Irish Artists* (Dublin, 1913).
73   Confirmation of arms to Sir W. Thornley Stoker, Dublin, 4 February 1909, GO, MS 111K, p. 83.
74   Subscription leaflet, including details of exhibits at the Heraldic Museum, 1910, GO, File Relating to the Heraldic Museum, uncat.

The Museum appears to have had the desired effect of introducing more people to the art of heraldry. Whilst not possible to establish the number of visitors to it at this time, Sergeant Herlihy's weekly salary was later increased from £1.1 shilling, to £1.4 shillings on account of his additional duties as attendant of the Museum, supervising the growing numbers of visitors.[75]

ULSTER'S CEREMONIAL ROLE

Proclamation notice of the death of King Edward VII, featuring the royal arms, and probably the work of Nevile Wilkinson, 6 May 1910. *GO, MS 154.*

Wilkinson found the routine of office work 'rather dull',[76] and was happy to entrust paperwork and general administration to the capable Burtchaell. He did, on the other hand, enjoy the ceremonial aspects of his position, and was never happier than when directing dignified and solemn processions. To add to the dignity of his position, he had secured a new tabard, bearing the arms of the royal standard, in February 1909. This was an altogether better fit than the one he had inherited from Vicars, who was of exceptionally small stature.[77] He also secured a new crown and badge of office at this time. Wilkinson's flair for ceremonial was demonstrated following the death of King Edward VII in May 1910, when he persuaded Lord Aberdeen to sanction 'Ulster's customary procession of proclamation through the streets of Dublin'.

Vicars had dispensed with this practice in 1901, following the death of Queen Victoria, for fear of public disturbance. However, by 1910, with Home Rule on the political agenda, it was in the Administration's interest to encourage opportunities for the populace to show their loyalty to the King. Lord Aberdeen consented to Wilkinson's suggestion. 'Gorgeously arrayed in the tabard', and attended by O'Grady, Wilkinson first proclaimed the King's death and accession of George V before a crowded balcony, where the Lord Lieutenant, and members of his household had gathered.

---

75   GO, Box Relating to Salaries, uncat.
76   Wilkinson, *To All and Singular*. p. 180.
77   Requisition, 15 February 1909, GO, MS 328, p. 36.

After this, he and O'Grady rode out on horseback to declare the solemn news again throughout the city. It was in fact the last occasion on which the Principal Herald of Ireland would perform such a function in the streets of the capital. Wilkinson and O'Grady also crossed to London for the funeral in St George's Chapel, and returned for King George V's Coronation in Westminster Abbey the following year.[78]

In July 1911, the new King's visit to Dublin again roused the Office of Arms and its staff to intense activity, much to Wilkinson's delight. While a stream of correspondence flowed between his staff and various departments of

Captain Nevile Wilkinson, Ulster King of Arms, proclaiming the accession of King George V, at the state entrance to Dublin Castle. Captain Guillimore O'Grady is behind him. Painting by H. Harris Brown, from plate in Nevile Wilkinson, *To All and Singular* (London, [1925]).

78 Wilkinson, *To All and Singular*, pp. 185–7.

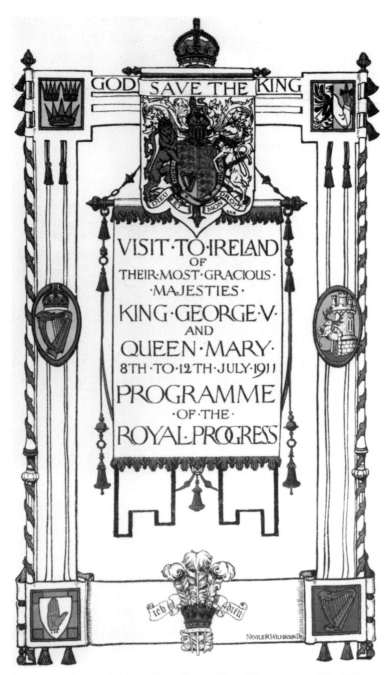

Programme for royal visit by King George V and Queen Mary, July 1911, as designed and executed by Nevile Wilkinson. *GO, Material Relating to Royal Visits.*

the King's household, Wilkinson devoted himself to designing the official programme handed to guests at various events. With beautiful heraldic emblems
on every page, the programme was a work of art, later complimented by the
Aberdeens.[79]

This visit was in fact the last royal visit to Southern Ireland by a reigning
British monarch. Reflecting the evolving radicalism of Irish politics, not everyone was happy to greet the King on this occasion The traditional State entry
to the city at Baggot Street Bridge, where the Lord Mayor delivered the keys
of Dublin to the King, had to be scrapped at the last moment because protest-
ing Republicans had daubed the seats for onlookers with fresh green paint.[80]
In other respects, Wilkinson regretted that the old order at the Castle was
changing for the worse. As he put it, very little effort was 'being made to
uphold the dignity of the ceremonial'. He disapproved of the Aberdeens' decision to relax the dress code for official functions, and lamented that they permitted 'the buzz of the camera' to record processionals and other events in the
Throne Room.[81]

BUSINESS DURING THE FIRST WORLD WAR

The usual festivities at Dublin Castle were suspended for the duration of the
War. Wilkinson returned to his old regiment for military duty as a Staff Captain at the Embarkation Department in Southampton in July 1914, eventually
serving at Gallipoli. For the duration of the War, he had little time to devote to
his Office in Dublin, especially as his military payment of £400 was initially
deducted from his civil income. He never had the same interest in the Office
after his return from the front, his private artistic interests taking first place.[82]

Under the misconception that his Office's duties had, in fact, completely
ceased, the Treasury refused to pay him his civil salary between October 1914
and February 1915. Officials believed there had been 'no ceremonies for many
months and were not likely to any in the near future'.[83] But this belied the
'very considerable flow of work in correspondence, with proving descents,
supplying arms, arranging changes of names'. Wilkinson was at pains to point
out that his local staff – Burtchaell, together with his assistant, Sadleir were

---

79 Official programme for the royal visit to Dublin, July 1911, GO, uncat; Aberdeen
    and Temair, *More Cracks With We Twa'*, p. 143.
80 Wilkinson, *To All and Singular*, p. 200.
81 *ibid.*, pp. 195–6.
82 *ibid.*, pp. 206–7; 222.
83 Treasury memorandum, PRO, T 11744.

doing their best to execute this work in Dublin – and he was paying them from his own salary.[84]

Encouraged initially by Sir Arthur Vicars to develop his interest in heraldry and genealogy, Thomas Sadleir had maintained his contacts with the Office, particularly through 'Mr Burtchaell' as he referred to him in early correspondence and for whom he conducted some genealogical research on the Pink family as early as 1902. He even advised Sir Arthur about aspects of the Vicars genealogy, and was responsible for compiling other family pedigrees that were entered into the Office registers between July and November 1904.[85] Perhaps as a result of this collaboration, he had been invited to the investiture of the Earl of Meath on 13 April 1905. His links with the Office continued after Vicars's dismissal, when he was invited to the investiture of Baron Castletown, just after Wilkinson's arrival, on 29 February 1908.[86]

By 1913, Sadleir was working in the Office on a daily basis, and on first-name terms with his colleague George Burtchaell. It is difficult to establish exactly when this happened because he was not paid an official salary.[87] Later correspondence confirms that Burtchaell 'brought him in during 1913 as [his] understudy', paying him £100 per annum. This represented a considerable proportion of Burtchaell's own income of £166 per annum. However, he was 'quite content' about this, because it relieved him from 'constant daily attendance in the Office', freeing his time to pursue his legal career (culminating in his appointment as King's Council in 1918), as well as considerable scholarly publications, principally in the *Journal of the RSAI*.[88] Burtchaell did, however, continue as the Office Registrar, quietly and diligently attending to Office business when required.[89]

With an Office income of just £100, Sadleir was also permitted to pursue his own private research interests, which were considerable, although probably not very lucrative. As well as publishing countless research papers on a range of historical, genealogical and architectural subjects, Sadleir was also touring the country to inspect and research Ireland's finest Georgian mansions,

---

84 Memorandum on herald's work, [February] 1915, *op. cit.*

85 W.D. Pink to Sadleir, 15 December 1902; Vicars to Sadleir, 9 Gardiner's Place, 2 July 1904, SC. Two volumes belonging to Vicars, containing will abstracts and 'Irish genealogical notes' and dated 27 February 1903, and 17 March 1903 respectively, seem to verify the commencement of his associations at this time, GO, MSS 424; 527.

86 Invitations to investitures, SC.

87 Information from Randal Sadleir, his son.

88 *Who Was Who, 1916–28.*

89 Slevin, *George Dames Burtchaell*, pp. 19–22.

'The future of heraldry depends on artistic excellence'

A youthful Thomas Ulick Sadleir worked in an unpaid capacity for the Office whilst an under-graduate at Trinity College Dublin. Here he is seen in 1906, when he was called to the Irish Bar. *Courtesy, Randal Sadleir.*

and the genealogies of the families who lived in them. The information he collected was published (with Page Dickinson) as *Georgian Mansions* in 1915.[90] By 1920, he had published an edition of Lord Mount Cashell's tour in Europe 1801–03,[91] and was working on several other collaborative projects, including, with Burtchaell, *Alumni Dublinenses* – the register of students, graduates, professors and provosts at Trinity College Dublin, which was eventually published in 1924.[92]

The War 'upset everything' about the quiet Office routine, because not only was Wilkinson absent, but 'the skilled assistance of Shepard and Tinckler' was also lost, and 'so far from having any relief, the whole of the work devolved upon the deprived', as Burtchaell referred to himself and Sadleir.[93] Pressure of work for the staff combined with Wilkinson's absence was blamed in official circles for the 'terrible lache' that occurred when the outgoing Lord Lieutenant Lord Aberdeen was promoted to the title of Marquis of Temair. 'Temair' translates to in Irish as 'Tara', and 'all classes of Irishmen' considered it 'an insult' that such a title could be borne by a Scotsman – an error for which Wilkinson was heavily criticised.[94]

These events forced him to make more formal arrangements for the administration of the Office. When he returned briefly to Dublin to take part in the ceremonial departure of the new Marquess of Aberdeen and Temair, and having secured his civil salary of £540 plus military pay of £400 from the Treasury, Wilkinson officially appointed Burtchaell as the Deputy Ulster King of Arms and Principal Herald of all Ireland, to carry on the business of the Office in his place, on 19 February 1915.[95] Burtchaell thus effectively became a figurehead – empowered to sign patents of grants and confirmations, authorise changes of name and other legal business. He even lodged the fees of the Office to his personal bank account, for convenience – a practice frowned upon by Treasury accountants when they discovered it.[96] In a separate warrant,

90 Sadleir and Dickson, *Georgian Mansions in Ireland*. Although the text of this book is confined to the finest country houses, Sadleir includes a subtle line drawing of his place of work, the Bedford Tower, on the title page.
91 Sadleir (ed.), *An Irish Peer on the Continent*.
92 Burtchaell and Sadleir (eds.), *Alumni Dublinenses*.
93 Burtchaell to Wilkinson, recounting Office administration during the War, 9 July 1920, GO, Accounts and Salaries File, uncat.
94 Treasury memorandum, PRO, T 62/709; Wilkinson, *To All and Singular*, pp. 267–8.
95 Appointment of Burtchaell as Deputy Ulster, 19 February 1915, PRO, T 160/192.
96 GO, Material Relating to Financial Arrangements For Mr Burtchaell, uncat.

Burtchaell appointed Sadleir 'to be Registrar of the Office in Ireland during the time that he [Burtchaell] should hold the position as Deputy Ulster'.[97]

In his capacity as Deputy Ulster, it was Burtchaell who signed and issued a certificate of arms to Sadleir, on 6 July 1915.[98] But while Burtchaell filled Wilkinson's place as figurehead and signatory, Sadleir was responsible for much of the day-today work – supervising staff, conducting research, and replying to correspondence. Indeed, one correspondent referred to him as 'top dog at Ulster Office' by January 1916.[99]

Whilst these men assumed these additional administrative responsibilities in Dublin, initially they appear to have performed them without

George Dames Burtchaell, Athlone Pursuivant 1908-21, and Deputy Ulster King of Arms 1910–11, 1915–21, was Sadleir's mentor, and also responsible for Office administration during Wilkinson's early absences. *JSAI, 6th series, 12* (1922).

additional pay. Indeed, it transpired 'during the whole period from October 1914 till October 1916', when Burtchaell was effectively responsible for the Office, that he received no extra salary for his additional responsibilities, paying Sadleir himself to act as Registrar, while he acted as Deputy Ulster. This situation was rectified to some extent in October 1916, when Burtchaell received

---

97 Appointment of Sadleir as Registrar, 24 April 1915, GO, MS 154, p. 97
98 GO, MS 111K, p. 13.
99 Arthur R. Moore, 'on active service' to Sadleir, 51 Lansdowne Road, 15 January 1916, SC.

an additional £60 for clerical assistance, and Sadleir's income was boosted to £150. Later, Burtchaell confided in Treasury officials that he felt let down that Wilkinson would not agree to fix all the salaries of the Office staff.[100] Wilkinson's military duties seemed to place a distance between him and the local staff in Dublin that was never fully rectified afterwards.

He returned to Dublin only once more before the end of the War, to make an appearance for the ceremonial display at the public entry to Dublin of Lord Wimborne, who succeeded as Lord Lieutenant, in April 1915. He almost missed this event, however, for the car in which he was travelling to Kingstown to meet the incoming viceroy broke down at the Merrion Gates, forcing him to hail a passing motorist. As a result, Ulster King of Arms arrived on the pier in full regalia in the back of a two-seater.[101] It was, in fact, Wilkinson's last public appearance until 1921. Under Lord Wimborne, arrangements were made for the fitting out of the State Apartments as a military hospital, run by the Red Cross.

Whilst the ceremonial aspects of the Office of Arms receded, the genealogical and heraldic demands on Burtchaell and Sadleir appear to have continued during the War years. After an initial dip in the number of heraldic commissions during the first year of the War to just 14, they picked up again, averaging 19 until 1919. Recorded income receipts reveal a fairly constant rate of genealogical work throughout the War.[102] To cope with the increased interest in genealogical enquiries, Burtchaell initiated new typewritten *pro-forma* application forms on which those wishing to register their pedigrees or determine other genealogical information, as well as applicants for arms, were required to fill out their particulars.[103]

POLITICAL DISRUPTIONS

The relative peace of the Castle routine was disturbed by the events of the Easter Rising in 1916, when a handful of revolutionaries changed the course of Irish history by storming the General Post Office in Sackville Mall and proclaiming the birth of the Irish Republic on 24 April 1916. Attempts had been made to storm the Castle too, when a policeman on duty at the entrance from Cork Hill was shot through the heart, but the gates were shut before the rebels got inside. Instead they occupied the City Hall, commanding the entrance into the Castle

---

100 Treasury minute, PRO, T 160/192.
101 Wilkinson, *To All and Singular*, p. 220.
102 Treasury receipts, Ulster King of Arms, PRO, T 60/192/7335.
103 Typewritten forms and orders, GO, MS 319.

Pro-forma application form for arms, as devised by
George Dames Burtchaell, *c.* 1919. *GO, MS 319.*

and neigbouring houses in Castle Street. This occupation effectively imprisoned the Castle staff and troops inside at the time for the best part of a week.[104]

As it was Easter Monday, none of the Office staff was in the Castle at the time and they remained on enforced leave until 20 May as a result of the Rising. However, the Bedford Tower provided a defensive vantage point where the Castle Guard patrolled to fend off attacks from snipers in Castle Street during the siege. Soldiers occupied several offices in the building when not on duty on the roof. When Burtchaell was eventually allowed back in early May he reported to Wilkinson that 'cooking operations' in his room had 'not improved the carpet', and that a 'certain amount of notepaper' had disappeared.[105]

---

104 O'Brion, *Dublin Castle and the 1916 Rising*, pp. 92–121.
105 Burtchaell to Wilkinson, 8 May 1916, quoted in Wilkinson, *To All and Singular*, p. 220.

The disturbances of 1916 were the prelude to the Troubles in Ireland that culminated, after the end of the European War, in the War of Independence of 1919–21. The execution of the leaders of the Rising in 1916 turned public opinion towards revolutionary nationalism, and Sinn Féin stormed to victory in the general election of December 1918. The Republicans refused to take their Westminster seats, meeting at the Mansion House in Dublin for the first public session of Dail Éireann, the parliament of the Irish Republic, on 21 January 1919. On the same day, the first shots were fired in Tipperary, heralding the start of the Irish War of Independence.[106]

The hostile political climate had a negative effect on Office administration. The services of staff at all levels were lost. Both Captain Tinckler and Major Shepard resigned permanently in January 1919. Mr Farrell the coal carrier, announced his resignation the following September.[107] Burtchaell's resolution for the first day of January 1920 was to hope there 'would never be a worse year for the country' than had been experienced in 1919.[108]

CHANGING TIMES

Against the deteriorating background of Anglo-Irish relations, the British Government enacted the Government of Ireland Act, in May 1920. This made provision for two Home Rule Parliaments, one for the six counties of the north-east, which became Northern Ireland, and the other for the remaining 26 counties. In anticipation of the intended Home Rule Parliament for Dublin, a new administrative infrastructure was introduced to Dublin Castle.[109] In June 1920, Sadleir observed: 'the first step towards Home Rule has been the setting up of an Irish Treasury in the Castle'. Internally, there were high hopes that this local Treasury presence would result in an increase of salaries all round, as post-War inflation was making it difficult to make ends meet. Sadleir himself was on just £150 per annum, although he did at least have his private research interests upon which to fall back on. Nevertheless, he had a constantly overdrawn bank account.[110]

---

106 Ward, *Irish Constitution*, pp. 104–5.
107 Wilkinson to Captain Tinckler and Major Shepard, 2 June 1919, accepting their resignations, and the resignation of Richard Farrell, 1 September 1920, GO, Personnel File, uncat.
108 Burtchaell to Wilkinson, 1 January 1920, GO, Salaries and Wages File, uncat.
109 McColgan, *British Policy*, pp. 1–4.
110 Sadleir, Office of Arms, to Wilkinson, London, 11 June 1920, GO, File Relating to Accounts and Salaries, uncat.

In July 1920, it was reported that the new Assistant Under-Secretary, A. W. Cope, had visited the Office, on which occasion he had 'seemed interested in the Museum'.[111] Significantly, whilst Wilkinson remained in London during this period, it was Burtchaell who endeavoured to impress upon the new Castle administrators the importance of paying reasonable salaries to the staff, especially the painter and the clerk. His efforts paid off, as the allowance for clerical assistance was increased following Cope's visit, from £450 to £620 per annum on 25 July 1920. This allowed Sadleir to be paid £200 as Registrar, and Burtchaell £130 as Deputy Ulster and Athlone Pursuivant. In addition, the clerk typist was to receive £120 rather than £80 and the herald painter £170 rather than £100.[112]

Wilkinson resented the interference of the new Castle administration in the affairs of his Office, which he insisted should be accountable only to the Crown and not subject to any audit. He 'had a lot to say about the effect of placing the Crown under the Executive', threatening to 'bring the matter before the King', which did not endear him to the Treasury.[113] Instead of appointing a full-time member of staff, he brought in an unqualified ex-major, Gerald Burgoyne, late of the 3rd Dragoon Guards, to fill the vacancy created by Shepard's departure.

This gentleman was described in Treasury files as 'middle-aged' and 'of independent means, living on his own yacht in Kingstown Harbour!' Recommended to Wilkinson by the Church of Ireland Dean of Dromore, Dean Henry Biddall Swanzy (a respected antiquary and amateur genealogist) Burgoyne came with the commendation that he was prepared to work in an unpaid capacity.[114] The curious title of Deputy Cork Herald was resurrected for him, and he was given a room in the Office in May 1921.[115] This honour may have justified Burgoyne's presence in the royal cavalcade when King George V visited Belfast a month later. On this occasion he appeared on horseback, in full regalia, virtually at the top of the procession.[116] A Miss McCormack had replaced Tinckler as the clerk/typist early in 1920, but she was soon enticed away by higher salaries on offer at the Chief Secretary's Office. As Wilkinson

111 Burtchaell, Dublin Castle to Wilkinson, London, 9 and 20 July 1920, *op. cit.*
112 Burtchaell to Wilkinson, 25 July 1920, *op. cit.*
113 Treasury memorandum, 1921, PRO, T 5880.
114 Wilkinson recounting terms of Burgoyne's employment to the Under Secretary's Office, 26 February 1921, GO, Personnel File, uncat.
115 GO, MS 154A, p. 127.
116 *Belfast Newsletter*, 23 June 1921.

was reluctant 'to make any permanent appointment for this post, until times [became] more normal', Burgoyne stepped in to assist with the routine office work at this juncture.[117]

Whilst 'a charming man socially',[118] Burgoyne had no administrative skills, admitting his typing was very slow.[119] His unofficial status meant that he kept rather irregular hours, and he even arranged for others to substitute for him. For example, when he disappeared to go sailing during May 1921, he paid an ex-nurse to fill in for him. This was not too popular with Sadleir, as she could 'not be relied upon to do any work properly'. By 13 August 1921, when Burgoyne was cruising off the Isle of Man, Sadleir was forced to complain that most of the work fell on his shoulders.[120]

The Troubles had impinged directly on the Office of Arms during one particular attack. In February 1920, three officers patrolling outside the Guard House were shot dead 'not 150 yards' from the window of the public office' where Major Burgoyne was reading a manuscript.[121] Sergeant Herlihy was later commended for the role he played in recovering the bodies whilst allegedly 'under fire in the Office of Arms', and he laid them out 'in the hall where his duties were carried on'.[122] There was further cause for gloom when Sir Arthur Vicars, who had lived quietly at Kilmorna House, near Listowel, County Kerry, following his dismissal in 1908, was brutally murdered by a local band of the IRA outside his home on 14 April 1921.[123]

A Parliament in Dublin had been envisaged for the 26 counties, under the Government of Ireland Act 1920, and, in addition, a 'Council of Ireland' to represent matters of common interest between North and South was to have been created; but these institutions did not materialise. The Dublin Parliament met only once, being boycotted by the vast majority of MPs, and was abandoned on 13 July 1920. Significantly, the Office of Arms was specifically dealt with in the plans for the Council of Ireland. Alongside such institutions as the PRO and NLI (which held documentary evidence relating to people throughout the island), it was regarded as politically neutral and suitable for

---

117 Wilkinson, London, to the Under Secretary's Office, Dublin Castle, 26 February 1921, GO, Personnel File, uncat.
118 Treasury memorandum on Office staff, PRO, T 160/192.
119 Major General Gerald Burgoyne to Wilkinson, London, 24 February 1921, GO, Personnel File, uncat.
120 Sadleir to The Treasury, 13 August 1921, PRO, T 160/192.
121 Burgoyne to Wilkinson, 24 February 1921, GO, Personnel File, uncat.
122 Wilkinson to Mr James Rae, Treasury, recounting Herlihy's service, 16 December 1928, PRO, T 62/709.
123 *The Times*, 15 April 1921.

administration by the all-island Council.[124] However, as the Council never met, this particular administrative plan for its future came to nothing.

In spite of the administrative difficulties that his Office was encountering by this time, Wilkinson only appeared in Dublin for the last of the ceremonial events associated with the Lord Lieutenant's household. On 2 May 1921, he was back in Dublin to receive and swear in the new Lord Lieutenant, Viscount FitzAlan of Derwent, who, under the terms of the Government of Ireland Act, was to relate to both the Dublin and Belfast Parliaments. Although Burtchaell, as Athlone Pursuivant, attended Wilkinson, the ceremony was low-key and devoid of any splendour, reflecting the fact that the office of the Lord Lieutenant was about to end.

Whilst the proposed Dublin Parliament was boycotted, Wilkinson did get the opportunity for final shows of splendour in Belfast. He was present in Belfast City Hall for the formal swearing-in of the newly elected MPs of the Belfast Parliament, on 7 June 1921. During King George V's historic visit to Belfast later in the month, Wilkinson was among the notables who met the royal party at Belfast Lough – one reporter commented that his dress was 'quaint but gorgeous'. It was Wilkinson who planned and directed the 'imposing ceremonial' for the official opening of the Northern Ireland Parliament by the King on 20 June, on which occasion there were notable levels of security. Wilkinson was also reported to have kept 'close touch with their majesties throughout the royal visit', responsible for directing the protocol at a number of other events, including an investiture ceremony at the Ulster Hall when he was promoted to Commandership of the Royal Victorian Order, having been made a Companion the previous year.[125]

Wilkinson alleged that the political difficulties in Dublin made it necessary for him to retreat to London to plan these events, as he was not prepared to trust officials in Dublin 'to preserve the secrecy of official documents'.[126] Whilst this may have been true, another reason for his absence was his preference for living in London by this time. The continuing disturbances in

---

124 Rt. Hon. Sir Henry Robinson, 'Powers of the Council of Ireland' memorandum, 17 January 1920, PRO, CAB 27/68. The other institutions intended for similar administration were: the Office of the Registrar General, the National Gallery, Labour Exchanges, the Geological Survey, the National Museum, the School of Art, the Congested Districts Board, the Land Commission, Registry of Deeds, the Ministry of Transport, the Dublin Metropolitan Police, the Botanic Gardens, College of Science, fisheries, prisons, lunatic asylums, and the Board of Charitable Donations and Bequests.
125 *Belfast Newsletter*, 23 June 1921.
126 Wilkinson, *To All and Singular,* p. 265.

Dublin resulted in nightly curfews. Social events were curtailed, whilst the atmosphere in the environs of the Castle with defensive sandbags and scaffolding everywhere was depressing.[127] It was hardly surprising that the sociable Wilkinson declared London as his preferred place of residence. Treasury officials queried his behaviour, however, when he claimed travelling expenses from London to Belfast to attend to the King's visit, noting that London was 'not his official headquarters'. But no action was taken, and the expenses appear to have been paid.[128]

Meanwhile, Wilkinson's staff in Dublin was becoming increasingly disgruntled by his absence. By July 1921, one Castle official commented 'Ulster's Office [was] in a rotten condition', but that the present moment was not the time to try to clear it up.[129] The following month, officials complained that he 'was an unworthy recipient of His Majesty's pay', spending all his time in London and seldom attending the Office. He drew £600, plus a war bonus, for doing ' practically nothing', while his low-paid officials had to do all the work.[130]

The tragic death of George Dames Burtchaell as a result of a tram accident near his home in Donnybrook village on 18 August 1921 exacerbated the administrative difficulties of the Office at this time, and put a lot of pressure on Sadleir. Although not in attendance on a daily basis, Burtchaell had an unrivalled genealogical knowledge, acquired during his long service at the Office since 1893, and he had schooled Sadleir to follow him. Sadleir later used the preface of the *Alumni Dublinenses* to pay tribute to his mentor, declaring him to have been 'probably the most accomplished genealogist Ireland has known'.[131]

As it had been Burtchaell's rather unorthodox practice to lodge the fees of the Office to his own account, Sadleir was unable to access any funds until after probate was proved, causing further administrative difficulties. Thereafter he reverted to lodging the fees in the Bank of Ireland, 'to the credit of Ulster King of Arms', as had been the practice during 'the reign of Vicars, Ulster'.[132]

Burtchaell's death marked a clear division between the ceremonial and heraldic remit of the Office of Arms, as Sadleir was reluctant to take on any court duties. When Wilkinson asked him to take over the duties of Athlone,

127 Anon, 'Last days of Dublin Castle', p. 183.
128 Report of Treasury audit, 12 October 1921, PRO, T 160/190.
129 James MacMahon, Under-Secretary to Cope, 6 July 1921, GO, File Relating to Accounts and Salaries, uncat.
130 Treasury memorandum, 13 August 1921, PRO, T 160/192.
131 Burtchaell and Sadleir, *Alumni*, p. vii.
132 Sadleir, to 'My dear Waterfield', Treasury, Dublin Castle, 19 August 1921, GO, Accounts and Salaries File, uncat.

'until such time as I am able to appoint a successor',[133] Sadleir hoped he 'should not be asked to take part in public processions and state ceremonies', as he had more than enough on his plate. This included 'the work of supervising, in Ulster's absence, especially of the work of the artist, such as illuminating and engrossing', in the absence of the elusive Captain Burgoyne.[134] Sadleir may also have been reluctant to pay for a ceremonial uniform, which would have cost about £150 and was a prerequisite for taking up the position.[135]

It transpired that the post of Athlone Pursuivant, in existence since 1552, would never again be filled. Instead, the two offices of Registrar and Deputy Ulster were merged into one appointment, at the fixed salary of £300, and filled by the humble Sadleir from 21 September 1921. In contrast to the splendour of the tabard, Sadleir was content to wear his barrister's gown when conducting the business of the Office of Arms.[136]

Burtchaell's death forced Wilkinson to co-operate with the Treasury to ensure that satisfactory financial arrangements were made for Sadleir, and to bring in additional clerical support. Sadleir insisted that the post of clerk-typist be filled immediately, and William Moore, formerly assistant at Marsh's Library, was appointed to this post.[137] Although only a clerical appointment, the clerk/typist was crucial to the efficient running of the Office, and unfortunately Moore was unsatisfactory – Sadleir later reporting him indolent, and of 'no assistance whatever'. But, at least the position had been filled, setting a precedent for the future. In the ensuing political transformation of Ireland, which resulted in an increased demand for the Office's genealogical and heraldic services, Sadleir would need all the help he could get.

---

133 Wilkinson to Sadleir, 23 August 1921, SC.
134 Sadleir to Wilkinson, 29 August 1921, GO, Personnel File, uncat.
135 Opinion of P. Waterfield, The Treasury, to Cope, 13 September 1921, PRO, T 160/192.
136 Recollection of Randal Sadleir.
137 Letter of appointment from Sir Neville Wilkinson to William Moore, 40 Fitzwilliam Square, 23 September 1921, GO, Personnel File, uncat.

FOUR

'The Office of Arms, its treasures, documents and records has not yet been taken over. . .'

After 1922

INDEPENDENCE?

In the aftermath of the Anglo-Irish War, 1919–21, and the intensive negotiation that followed it, agreement was finally reached between the Irish and British Governments in the form of the Treaty signed on 6 December 1921.[1] The Treaty gave dominion status to the 26 counties, styled the Irish Free State. Unlike the Northern Ireland Parliament, whose legislature was still subject to ratification at Westminster, the Free State gained independent sovereignty rights, subject to inclusion within the British Commonwealth of Nations, and similar to those of Canada.

The Irish Free State (Agreement) Act of 31 March 1922, which gave the Treaty the force of law, stretched the framework of dominion status, allowing for state-derived Government, which went much further than in other dominions. Power was transferred to the Provisional Government, which became the Free State Government in December 1922.[2] The new Government was empowered to run its own parliament, Dáil Éireann; to nominate its own Governor-General, in place of the Lord Lieutenant; and to establish a new office of the President.[3] Many Government Departments and other services hitherto administered by the British were simply transferred to the Provisional Government, the Transfer of Functions Order of 1 April 1922 enabling the process of transfer to commence.[4]

The King, however, remained the head of the Irish Executive, whose

---

1 McColgan, *British Policy*, pp. 1, 90–1.
2 Harkness, *Restless Dominion*, p. 24.
3 Lee, *Ireland 1912–1985*, p. 50; Sexton, *Ireland and the Crown*, p. 173.
4 'Transfer of services hitherto administered by the British government in Ireland', proclaimed by Provisional Government, 16 January 1922, NAI, CSORP 1921/3864/2, quoted in McColgan, *British Policy,* pp. 96–7.

The Office of Arms continued to occupy the Bedford Tower, in Upper Castle Yard, which along with other Castle buildings was handed over to Michael Collins in 1922. However, its authority continued to be derived from the Crown, and its expenses and staff salaries were paid by the British Treasury until 31 March 1943. *NLI, Lawrence Collection, IMP 10.*

formal powers continued to be derived from English Common Law.[5] It was within this political context that the Office of Arms continued to operate, as it had done in the past, as an imperial service deriving its authority from the Crown. In spite of the dramatic political changes that had occurred around it, this situation was set to last until 1 April 1943, when it was the last Office of State to be transferred from British to Irish control. In the intervening period, the Office continued to occupy one of the most prominent buildings in the Upper Castle Yard – which became the seat of many Free State Government Departments. Its salaries and expenses continued to be remitted by His Majesty's Treasury. Yet the Office provided heraldic and genealogical services for individuals and institutions in both Northern Ireland, the Free State, and indeed for people of Irish descent living abroad. The political circumstances that led to this position were complex, and the purpose of this chapter is to explore them in some detail.

AN END TO CEREMONY

The new Free State Constitution impinged directly on the Office of Arms because it abolished the office of the Lord Lieutenant from December 1922. The ceremonies, processions, and spectacles so carefully superintended by Ulster King of Arms in the past became 'distant memories', as one contemporary lamented, after 1922.[6] As we have seen, they were declining anyway in advance of Independence. The new constitutional position ended them for good. In dramatic contrast to the splendour of several ceremonies before the War years, simplicity was the order of the day when Viscount FitzAlan of Derwent, the last Lord Lieutenant, formally handed over Dublin Castle to Michael Collins and the other representatives of the Provisional Government on 16 January 1922.[7] In his capacity as Ulster King of Arms, Sir Nevile Wilkinson was present for the passing of the old political order. FitzAlan symbolically gave Collins the keys of the Castle in the seclusion of the Privy-Council chamber, located above the archway between the Upper and Lower Yards; but there were no duties for Wilkinson to perform.[8]

The event was also striking for the absence of any trappings of tradition or ceremonial grandeur. *The Irish Times* remarked: 'no one seemed to know what

---

5   Ward, *Constitutional Tradition*, p. 169.
6   Countess of Fingall, *Seventy Years Young*, p. 334.
7   *The Irish Times*, 17 January 1922; Anon., 'Last days at Dublin Castle', pp. 187–90.
8   Wilkinson, *To All and Singular*, pp. 264–5.

arrangements had been made for the historic ceremony of the passing of British authority to Irish control'. A red carpet had been laid out, but there was no pre-scribed court dress, no rituals, no trumpets or courtiers when the Castle was 'quietly handed to eight gentlemen [who had] arrived in three taxicabs'.[9] After the event, FitzAlan was driven out through the Castle gates for the last time, in a cavalcade of vehicles.[10] Wilkinson returned to London a few weeks later, and thereafter his appearances in Dublin would be few and far between.

The Office of Arms did not play any role in the ceremonial arrangements connected with the new political regime in the South. The arrival of the first Governor-General of the Free State, Timothy Healy, for example, was a low-key affair, devoid of any ceremony as had been indicated on the occasion of the arrival of the last Lord Lieutenant the previous year. The King had pre-sented Healy with his Seal of Office in London, but no ceremony followed his arrival in Ireland. Unlike the practice in other dominion states, no formal open-ing of Parliament occurred in the Free State. Whilst Healy did address the joint houses of the Oireachtas when it opened on 12 December 1922, and again in October 1923, these were token gestures, and the practice was discontinued thereafter.[11]

The Governor-General had no association with the Order of St Patrick, unlike the new Governor of Northern Ireland, the Duke of Abercorn, who was sworn in and invested as a knight at his audience with the King in London on 21 December 1922.[12] Healy probably had no regrets about this – his last encounter with the affairs of the Order had been back in 1908, during the Crown Jewels Commission, when, as Sir Arthur Vicars's barrister, he had unsuccessfully defended his client. The Order's future was weakened by the new Free State Constitution, and this had repercussions for the Office's cere-monial significance. Article Five stipulated that 'no title of honour may be con-ferred on any citizen of the Irish Free State', except with the approval of the Government.[13]

At the conferences held in June 1922 to iron out outstanding issues arising from the Transfer of Government Order – prior to the Free State coming into being – the issues of honours, titles, grants of arms and the future of the Order of St Patrick were discussed at length by British and Provisional Government

---

9   *The Irish Times,* 17 January 1922; see also Robins, *Champagne and Silver Buck-les,* pp. 164–5.

10   *ibid.*

11   Sexton, *Ireland and the Crown,* pp. 90–1.

12   *The Times,* 6 December 1922.

13   *Free State Constitution, Irish Free State (Saorstát Éireann) Act,* 1922.

delegates.[14] The Irish delegates were firmly of the view that dignities and titles of honour were outside the scope of the new Constitution. Making specific reference to the future of the Order of St Patrick, their policy was to allow it to lapse completely.[15] In contrast, the British delegation argued that the Crown might continue to grant honours to Irish citizens 'in respect of services rendered to Great Britain'.[16] The issue would be a thorny one. Whilst the Order did not cease immediately, only three new knights were invested after 1922. Significantly, each of them was a royal prince: the Prince of Wales in 1927, Prince Henry, Duke of Gloucester in 1934 and Prince George, the Duke of York, in 1936 – the last knight. The investiture ceremonies also took place in London, without any recourse to the Free State Government.[17]

IMPACT OF POLITICAL CHANGE ON THE OFFICE OF ARMS

Given that its ceremonial work had come to an end as a result of Independence, it was widely expected that the Office of Arms would simply close or, like the Order of St Patrick, be allowed to lapse after 1922. In February 1922, Lord Walter Fitzgerald commiserated with Sadleir that he was 'sorry to hear of the likely abolition of Ulster's Office', which he felt would be a 'great loss to pedigree compilers'. He hoped, however, that its Funeral Entries and other sources would 'continue to be available to searchers in the Royal Irish Academy or the Record Office'.[18]

Other correspondents were concerned about the contents of the Heraldic Museum in the light of the political changes at the Castle in January 1922. One donor enquired if his collection of Irish coins 'is at all likely to become confiscated under the new Constitution authorities', as he would not like to lose them.[19] Reflecting concerns for the safety of the Museum and its contents, Sir Nevile Wilkinson deposited a number of items in the Records Office in November 1921. These included an illuminated address presented to Lord Aberdeen,

---

14 Memorandum entitled 'Extract from secretary's note taken at meeting of conference on Ireland with Irish ministers held on Saturday, 10 June 1922 at 3pm', PRO, PREM/2/75.
15 Opinion of the Attorney General on the Order of St Patrick, 21 May 1928, NAI, DT S578A. For general background see Galloway, *Most Illustrious Order*, pp. 106–7.
16 PRO, PREM 2/75.
17 Galloway, *Most Illustrious Order*, p. 246.
18 Lord Walter Fitzgerald, Kilkea Castle, to Sadleir, 4 February 1922, SC.
19 R.W. Jackson, 'Morfa Nevin', North Wales, 15 January 1922, to Wilkinson, GO, Material Relating to the Heraldic Museum, uncat.

the Lord Lieutenant 1905–15, by the Lord Mayor and Burgesses of Cork.[20] The current provenance of Dean Swift's Freedom of the City in St Patrick's Cathedral, Dublin, rather than the Museum (where it had been Wilkinson's most prized exhibit) may also result from this period of flux.[21]

Whilst concerned for the safety of pieces on display in the Museum, and aware of the general pessimism about the Office's future, Wilkinson was determined that it would not close, and made clear the symbolic role that he envisaged for it in the new political climate. Lest its 'proper status and functions' might 'not be fully understood by those of His Majesty's ministers . . . at present engaged [to] transfer authority to the Southern Parliament of the Irish Free State', he prepared a detailed memorandum, sent to the Home Office in January 1922, on the eve of the transfer of political power being formally arranged. Whilst Wilkinson may well have been driven by self-interest to protect his lifetime appointment, his constitutional arguments helped to defend the status of the Office of Arms, in spite of the changed political context.

Wilkinson's memorandum emphasised the long history of the Office of the Ulster King of Arms, which had evolved since 1552. He emphasised that his appointment, like those of his predecessors, had been made for life by royal prerogative, according to letters patent under the Great Seal that could not be revoked. Furthermore, and of greater political significance for the changing nature of Irish politics, North and South, he stressed that as the King's heraldic representative, he functioned for 'the whole of Ireland', and as such 'formed a valuable connecting link' between 'the Governments of Southern and Northern Ireland'. To emphasise this significance, Wilkinson even suggested that the style and title of his appointment might be altered to reflect the new constitutional position, so that he would be re-named the 'Ireland King of Arms and Ulster Principal Herald', thus encompassing his 'All Ireland status within the Empire'. He stressed that the Office could simply not be abolished, insisting that it must be allowed continue 'as present constituted', with its records remaining *in situ*, operating as an imperial service for the whole island.[22]

Although the 'style and title' was not changed at this time, Wilkinson's defence of his rights as a royal appointee within an all Ireland context had far-reaching effects, influencing British Government policy on the matter and helping to ensure the *status quo*. Memorandums were circulated to the Home

---

20 NAI, 999/664. This item survived as it was probably in the PRO Registry, awaiting cataloguing, at the time of the bomb that destroyed the other contents.
21 The item now forms part of the Living Stones exhibition in St Patrick's Cathedral, Dublin.
22 Wilkinson, Office of Arms, Dublin Castle, to His Excellency, Viscount FitzAlan of Derwent, Vice-Regal Lodge, Dublin, 19 January 1922, PRO, HO 267/46.

Office, Colonial Office, Treasury, and Dominions Office, advising that 'Ulster will not be transferred' as he 'will remain an imperial officer', in May 1922.[23] Another memorandum stated categorically that 'Ulster King is reserved', and that whilst 'a dominion [might] say he is not wanted . . . [it] can't say he must go over'. Ulster was not, as far as the British Government was concerned, to be 'transferred and [by] O[rders] in C[ouncil] never will be'.[24]

DUBLIN'S BID FOR TRANSFER

Whilst there was clarity in London that the Office of Arms had been retained as a Crown service, by contrast there was initial confusion about its status in Dublin. For some civil servants, it seemed that the Transfer of Functions Order of 1 April 1922, catering for the practical transfer of the Courts and many other departments and services, would simply apply to the Office of Arms too. For others, this tiny department, with its small staff, low budget and rather esoteric functions, was not high on the list of priorities. As Harkness has commented, there was less concern with the 'trappings and details' at this point. The Free State had been created, and the fine-tuning would follow later.[25]

Indeed, some institutions, including the Land Commission, the Mercantile Marine Branch of the Board of Trade, and the Registry of Deeds, were initially specifically reserved by the British Government to safeguard the interests of Northern Ireland, while the functions of the Clerk of the Crown and Hanaper (responsible for issuing writs, and housing the Great Seal of the Imperial Government), and the Quit Rent Office (responsible for Crown revenue), were reserved in the interests of the Crown. The Post Office Savings Bank and Trustee Savings Bank remained reserved until 31 March 1923, the final date on which 'transferable services' could be transferred to the Provisional Government, under the terms of the Treaty.[26] These departments were catered for by specific legislation or were subsequently transferred to Irish control or, as was the case of the Office of the Clerk of the Crown and Hanaper, simply abolished the Office of Arms, by contrast, was not the subject of any legal instrument.

Understandably, some officials in Dublin assumed that the Office of Arms had been transferred in accordance with the Transfer of Functions Order of

---

23 Treasury minute, 2 May 1922, PRO, T 164/24/1.
24 Home Office memorandum concerning Orders in Council for Ulster King [of Arms], undated, [1922], PRO, HO 267/46.
25 Harkness, *Restless Dominion*, p. 26.
26 McColgan, *British Policy*, pp. 99–104.

Office stamps for incoming and outgoing post emphasised its imperial links until 31 March 1943.

1 April 1922, especially given its location at Dublin Castle, and they began to treat it as if it was theirs. The Ministry of Home Affairs of the new Provisional Government issued two transfer orders to the Office concerning aspects of its administration, indicating their thinking. The orders were received by Thomas Sadleir, the Registrar, whose reluctance to comply with them soon indicated the obscure position that the Office of Arms would present in the fledgling State.

The first order, dated 21 March 1922, concerned Office stationery, instructing that the use of envelopes headed 'On His Majesty's Service' should be discontinued immediately. Instead a rubber stamp was to be obtained from the Stationery Office in Dublin Castle, which would 'delete this heading and inscribe Rialtas Sealadach na hÉireann [Provisional Government of Ireland]'.[27] A similar circular was sent to all Government Departments and the Courts at this time, and in due course they obtained printed envelopes bearing the Irish harp and 'Éire' to replace the stationery of the old political regime. The Office of Arms, however, successfully avoided this particular transition until 1943.

Adhering to its position as an imperial service, Sadleir was determined that all its outgoing letters (received by Government officials both in Dublin and London) continued to bear the Crown, with the words 'Ulster's Office', or sometimes 'Office of Arms'. 'In addition, items of incoming post were also stamped with the traditional in-house stamp, bearing the royal symbol after 1922. On several occasions when supplies of official stationery were low, Sadleir even resorted to using redundant headed paper from the Chamberlain's Office, abolished in 1922, until fresh supplies for the Office of Arms became available.[28]

It later became cheaper for the Office to requisition all of its stationery from England. Reflecting a general tightening on its expenditure in 1924, for example, the Treasury ordered that 'its printing and stationery supplies' must be requisitioned from the Stationery Office in Manchester, rather than the

---

27   Ministry of Home Affairs, Irish Provisional Government, to Ulster King of Arms, 21 March 1922, SC.
28   Various letters from Thomas Sadleir, to Treasury officials, 1923, PRO T 160/190.

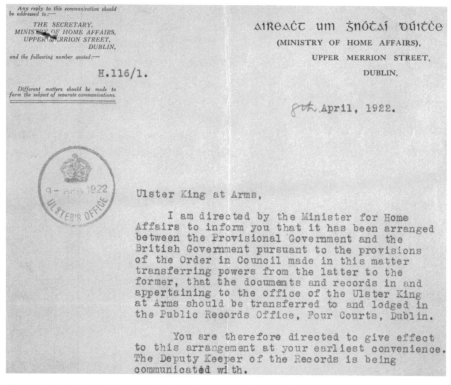

The order that directed the transfer the documents and records to the PRO, might have changed all for the Office of Arms had it been complied with, but it was not. Ministry of Home Affairs to Ulster King of Arms, 8 April 1922. *Sadleir Correspondence.*

Stationery Office in Dublin, because the Free State prices had become too high.[29] The Office did lose the privilege of sending its post free of charge, enjoyed by all vice-regal household departments until December 1922. With this exception, however, Sadleir determined that no other administrative alterations would affect the Office in the light of political change. Indeed, he later informed one correspondent that 'the only change made in 1922 was that we lost the right to send letters free (i.e. on H.M.S.)'.[30]

---

29 N.G. Scorgie, Deputy Controller, H.M. Stationery Office, Westminster to the Registrar, Office of Arms, 13 March 1924, including detailed comparative costs of stationery between H.M. Stationery Office, Manchester, and the Stationery Office, Dublin, and ordering that future orders be made at Hollinwood only, GO, Personnel File, uncat.

30 Sadleir, Office of Arms, The Castle, Dublin, to Major Hackett, Cabinet Secretariat, Government House, Hillsborough, 10 Aug, 1938, PRONI, CAB 9R/52/1.

The second order that the Office received from the new Ministry of Home Affairs indicating its intention of a takeover concerned the transfer of the records and manuscripts. Issued on 8 April 1922, in accordance with 'arrangements' agreed with the British Government, this order instructed that 'the documents and records in and appertaining to the Office of Arms . . . should be transferred to, and lodged in, the Public Records Office, Four Courts, Dublin'.[31] The order was swiftly followed two days later by the visit of a PRO official who took 'stock of [the] documents'.[32] When informed by Sadleir of this particular development, Wilkinson protested vehemently, believing that it fulfilled his worst fears for the integrity of his Office. In a strongly worded letter to the outgoing Lord Lieutenant he argued:

> It is clearly impossible for the work of my Office to be carried on without such records and documents. . . . Grants of arms and such like, cannot be issued without the consent and approval of His Majesty. I presume therefore that it is the intention of the Provisional Government to abolish my Office. If this is the case . . . I should be deprived of a life appointment.[33]

When the Home Office investigated this matter, British officials also came to the conclusion that no such arrangements about the Office or its contents had actually been agreed. Although the Irish Law Officer, Hugh Kennedy, had 'pressed for the transfer . . . of papers, which he stated were of general historical interest', it was clear that no 'agreement [had] been reached with Provisional Government'. In these circumstances, the Home Office requested that any question of a transfer must be deferred until Wilkinson (who by late April was recovering from major surgery) was well enough to return to Dublin to discuss the issue.[34] A Cabinet directive, issued on 1 June 1922, stated categorically that this Office had:

> not been transferred to the Provisional Government under the Orders in Council of 1 April, and the records and other documents in his [Ulster's] possession, so far as they appertain to his heraldic functions will remain in his custody.[35]

---

31 Sadleir, Dublin Castle, to Wilkinson, London, 10 April 1922, enclosing ministerial order dated 8 April 1922 concerning transfer of records to the Public Records Office, SC.

32 Sadleir to Wilkinson. 10 April 1922, SC.

33 Wilkinson to Viscount FitzAlan, 11 April 1922, PRO, HO 26746.

34 Viscount FitzAlan, Vice Regal Lodge, Dublin, to Tallents, Home Office, 13 April 1922, *op. cit.*

35 Direction of Mr Churchill, Secretary, Dominions Office, as conveyed by Mr L. M.

The Colonial Office advised other British Government Departments that:

> The functions of this officer who is not engaged in the administration of any public office, and is properly to be considered rather in the light of an appendage to the Court, have not been transferred to the Provisional Government, under Orders in Council of April 1922.[36]

It was of high importance to the British Government that Northern Ireland's ceremonial and heraldic needs be provided for: 'so far as the North is concerned, Ulster apparently remains a necessity', stated one Treasury memorandum. Wilkinson's participation in the opening of the Belfast Parliament and the visit of King George V in June 1921 had emphasised this in a ceremonial context. As we shall see below, he would also provide expert advice about aspects of protocol and precedence, and design a heraldic identity for the new Northern Ireland State, and some of its institutions.

Whilst clear about the necessity for continuing his appointment in relation to Northern Ireland, the British Government was less certain about the attitude of the Southern Government. The Treasury further speculated that:

> it is quite possible they [the Free State] will have no use for him at state and public functions, and it is also possible that interest in Southern Ireland in family trees may flag . . . if this is so, the necessity for continuing his Office disappears.[37]

But the Free State most certainly would have a role for the Office, especially in the light of events of that followed the outbreak of the Civil War between pro-and anti-Treaty forces on 14 April 1922. This resulted in the catastrophic destruction of the Public Records Office of Ireland, which was reduced to ashes on 30 June 1922.

CIVIL WAR

The Civil War deferred any political decision being made about the future of the Office and its records indefinitely. The correspondence of Thomas Sadleir at this time provides graphic detail about political events as they unfolded in Dublin. To reassure Wilkinson about the records, Sadleir informed him a few

---

Freer, Secretary Cabinet Committee for the Provisional Government of Ireland, to Secretary Ministry of Home Affairs, Dublin, 1 June 1922, PRO, T 164/24/1.

36 Treasury minute concerning Colonial Office circular about the transfer of the Office of Arms, dated 1 June 1922, PRO, T 162/316.

37 Treasury minute, 8 May 1922, PRO, T 14/24/1.

Mantelpiece recovered from the rubble of the Four Courts in 1922, transferred to the Heraldic Museum at the Office of Arms. *Courtesy, Irish Architectural Archive.*

days after receipt of the order to transfer them to the PRO, that he did not believe it would happen. Given the disturbed state of Dublin, and especially as the Four Courts complex, including the PRO, had forcibly been seized by anti-Treaty forces, he concluded:

> I do not think anything will be done for some time with regard to our records being transferred, the Record Office being in the hands of "irregulars". For several nights past there have been frequent and prolonged bursts of firing, which is most alarming.[38]

38 Sadleir to Wilkinson, 20 April 1922, SC.

By early May, the city was 'on the verge of a crisis', and access to the Castle restricted by barricaded entrances, all employees being searched on entering and leaving, although Sadleir did manage to keep the Office open on a daily basis.[39] Operations became more difficult by mid-June. A battle was raging, and 'the din too awful' to concentrate on any work, whilst several patents for grants of arms had to be postponed because Sadleir could get no 'stamping' – the impress for stamp duty done. For a short time, arrangements were made for some patents to be stamped in England, although this procedure was later stopped and stamping resumed in Dublin in 1923.[40]

On 30 June 1922, the Four Courts, including the PRO, which had been used for storing ammunition by the anti-Treaty forces, was bombarded and burnt to the ground. This event and other disturbances throughout the city forced Sadleir to close the Office of Arms early:

> I carried on at the Office until 1.30pm . . . when fighting spread all up Dame Street and we were warned by the Provisional Government that we might have to leave at any moment. I therefore closed the Office and at some risk made my way via Dame Lane and Nassau Street to Westland Row, where I was able to get a train . . . as no trams were running.[41]

The noise of firing continued for several days, and the Office did not re-open until 6 July.[42] The Bedford Tower may in fact have been occupied during the intervening period, because later Éamon de Valera recollected 'the bleak grey days' in 1922, when he 'stood in the Bedford Tower in Dublin Castle and gazed on the burning ruins of the Four Courts'.[43]

The destruction of the PRO made it all the more fortunate that the transfer order relating to the Office of Arms records had not been complied with in April 1922. Indeed, the events of 1922 elevated the archival impotance of its holdings significantly. The pedigrees based on abstracts from the prerogative wills, marriage licences and grants of administration so carefully compiled from the originals by William Betham during his tenure of office, became in effect primary sources for future generations of researchers, replacing the material lost in the

---

39   Sadleir to Wilkinson, 1 May 1922, SC.
40   Sadleir, Lansdowne Road, Dublin, to Lady Beatrix Wilkinson, London, 25 June 1922; Sadleir to Wilkinson, 24 July 1922, SC.
41   Sadleir, Lansdowne Road, Dublin, to Lady Beatrix Wilkinson, London, 30 June 1922, SC.
42   Sadleir to Wilkinson, 24 July 1922, SC.
43   *Dáil Debates*, 8 May 1929, 29, 1587.

PRO. Within weeks of the disaster, Sadleir was advertising in the press that 'as well as supplying heraldic services', the Office of Arms was in many cases able to furnish copies of, or extracts from, wills and manuscripts – the originals of which were lost of destroyed in the Four Courts fire.[44] In particular, the chart pedigrees compiled by Betham from the Irish Prerogative Court wills – invaluable sources in their own right – had 'increased in value since the destruction of the original wills'.[45]

Immediately after the events of 30 June, he was able to respond positively to a British Treasury circular enquiring whether any of the Office's records had been destroyed during the bombardments, and whether the Office had been able to carry out any work since then. In early July, Sadleir reported:

> None of our records have been destroyed, as they are all in the fire-proof strong room. . . . The volume of work here seems unlikely to diminish, in fact owing to our having copies of many of the records destroyed at the Four Courts, I think that our clients will probably increase in number.[46]

Sadleir later sent a circular to Irish peers informing them that their pedigrees and other registered papers had not, unlike the patent rolls in the PRO, been disturbed or destroyed during the recent troubles in Ireland. They remained available for research at the Office of Arms, which would also continue to compile Ulster's Roll – the official list of Irish peers. This task proved increasingly difficult, however, in the light of political events. Sadleir frequently complained to the House of Lords that he no longer knew to whom he should apply regarding 'official knowledge' about the claims of representative peers to vote at the election of representative peers. The Office of the Clerk of the Crown and Hanaper, based at the Four Courts, had been allowed to lapse after the bombing in 1922. He thus found it impossible to obtain the necessary information to maintain Ulster's Roll accurately. [47]

In an ironic twist of fate, an eighteenth-century mantelpiece that had been salvaged from the rubble at the Four Courts was later transferred to the Office of Arms to decorate the Heraldic Museum in the Bedford Tower. The Museum

---

44   Various press cuttings, SC.
45   Sadleir, 'Ulster's Office records', p. 435.
46   Sadleir, Office of Arms, to A.P. Waterfield, Treasury, Dublin, July 1922, PRO, T 164/24/1.
47   Sadleir, Office of Arms, to Lord Lisborne, London, August 1922; Sadleir to the Lord Great Chamberlain, House of Lords, 7 November 1924, GO, File Relating to the Irish Peerage and Claims to Vote, 1924–39, uncat.

seemed the appropriate resting-place for the beautiful black and white marble columned piece with representations of the Knights Templars.[48] It remained there until the Office was re-located to Kildare Street in 1981.

GENEALOGICAL RESEARCH AND PROPOSED 'FUSION' WITH THE PRO

There is some evidence that the number of enquiries received by the Office increased in conjunction with the political uncertainty of the time. Even before the destruction of the PRO, members of the Irish gentry who chose to leave Ireland as a result of the political trouble (some of whom may have known Sadleir personally as a result of his earlier research on the Georgian houses of Ireland, and his ongoing research for the *Alumni Dublinenses*) contacted him with queries before their departure. He observed that 'a rash of work' often followed an outbreak of violence. For example, seizure of the Masonic Hall in April 1922 resulted in the Office being 'unusually busy' in the weeks thereafter. In May 1922, there were 68 pieces of work outstanding, and with Dublin hotels 'full of Irish gentry refugees en route to England', arrears of work mounted.[49]

With the destruction of the PRO, the Office's work increased again, as Sadleir had anticipated. By August 1922 the Office's annual month-long summer holiday had to be postponed, partly because the heraldic painter had so many patents to finish, and partly because Sadleir had so many queries to answer.[50] At this time he was forced to work until 12.30 every night to keep up with increasing volumes of work.[51]

In spite of the British policy to retain the records at the Office and Wilkinson's insistence that this be adhered to, the increasing genealogical research demands on Sadleir's time – and perhaps his growing frustration with Wilkinson's absence and unwillingness to organise additional support for him – gave rise to a radical proposal to fuse the Office of Arms with the PRO. By November 1922, the latter institution was attempting to rebuild itself – a project in which Hugh Kennedy, the first Law Officer of the new Free State, was personally interested. He and Sadleir appear to have had earlier discussions about the future status of the Office of Arms, perhaps in the context of the early

---

48 Drawing of cornices, architraves and other details of the mantelpiece in the Heraldic Museum, Dublin Castle, by C.F. Quinlan, 1938, NLI, Maps and Drawings, 1208.

49 Sadleir to Wilkinson, 16 May 1922; copy of letter from Major A. Burgoyne to Wilkinson, 21 May 1922, SC.

50 Sadleir to Wilkinson, 27 July 1922, SC.

51 Sadleir to Wilkinson, 1 August 1922, SC.

anticipation that the Office would simply close and its records be transferred to the PRO. He reminded Sadleir of earlier plans:

> I have often been anxious to have a chat with you on the subject of your Office. I had practically arranged to give effect to your suggestion about the Record Office and setting up a genealogical department there when the War began and the Record Office went up in smoke.[52]

In response to this, Sadleir consulted Herbert Wood, the Deputy Keeper of Records at the PRO, and then submitted a hand-written report to Kennedy entitled 'Scheme For Making the Office of Arms a Branch of the PRO'. This proposed 'a fusion' of the Office of Arms, with the Records Office, because so many of its documents replaced those lost in the PRO.[53]

It is unlikely that Wilkinson, recovering from his operation in London, was ever consulted about this. Indeed, reflecting the ongoing tensions that existed between him and Sadleir about workloads and salaries, it is hardly surprising that the scheme also proposed abolition of Ulster's appointment, with its high income 'at present enjoyed'. Instead a 'Genealogical Superintendent', who would be paid an annual salary of £500, was envisaged to replace both Wilkinson's post and that of the Registrar. Presumably Sadleir envisaged that he might fill the new post of superintendent, the cost of which (in contrast to Ulster's salary of £750) would, he advised, lead to an immediate saving of over £500 for the Free State Government.

He further proposed that a clerk typist and herald painter would assist the Superintendent as before. In addition, a new post of assistant clerk would be introduced to help process the increasing numbers of genealogical enquiries. Again reflecting his frustration with the existing regime, Sadleir proposed higher fees for the new service. He regarded the current scale of fees in the Office of Arms (including ten shillings per search for arms and pedigrees, and five shillings per general search) as 'ridiculously small', and suggested it 'might be vastly increased'.[54]

---

52 Hugh Kennedy, Law Officer's Department, Upper Merrion Square, to Thos. U. Sadleir Esq., Office of the King of Arms, Dublin Castle, 20 November 1922, UCD, P4/810 (1).

53 Sadleir, Office of Arms, to 'My dear Kennedy', 27 November 1922, enclosing memorandum, UCD, P4/811 (1).

54 Memorandum entitled 'Scheme for making the Office of Arms a branch of the Public Record Office', drawn up by Thos. U. Sadleir, in consultation with Mr Wood, Deputy Keeper of the Records, and submitted to the Law Office, 27 November 1922, UCD, P4/811(4).

Although these proposals came to nothing, the concept of developing the Office of Arms as a genealogical service within a larger record repository was thus established as early as 1922. This would later become a reality when the Office was finally transferred to the Irish Government in 1943 and began its association with the National Library of Ireland. That these plans were even mooted at this earlier period emphasises that by the early 1920s the volume of the Office's business was principally genealogical, rather than its more traditional heraldic and ceremonial work. For the moment, British Government policy, influenced by the sentiments of Wilkinson, was to maintain the *status quo*.

SERVICES FOR ALL IRELAND?

As Ulster King of Arms and Principal Herald for All-Ireland, Wilkinson's continued absence from Dublin seemed a contradiction in terms. However, his London base did allow him to maintain contacts more easily with representatives of the new Government of Northern Ireland, enabling him to oversee the ceremonial opening of Parliament and the historic visit of King George V to Belfast in 1921. He later drew up a new scale of precedence for the Northern State, to be observed at official functions in Belfast City Hall in January 1923, and provided advice on precedence issues for the Governor-General's Office, including the correct manner in which to address the daughter of a duke, marquess or earl.[55] Although this advice was transmitted to Belfast from London, official registration was made in the Register of Warrants in the Office of Arms in Dublin.[56]

It was from London too that Wilkinson initiated several aspects of Northern Ireland's new heraldic identity, although his staff in Dublin was responsible for executing the work. These commissions paved the way for the subsequent cross-Border significance of the Office of Arms, which, by virtue of the Free State's dominion status, continued to operate for All-Ireland, irrespective of Partition. Wilkinson designed the cap badge for the newly constituted police service for Northern Ireland, the Royal Ulster Constabulary, in November 1922.[57] He also

---

55 Commander Oscar Henderson, Governor General's Office, Belfast, to Wilkinson, Duchess Street, London, 24 October 1924 and copy of Wilkinson's reply, November 1924, PRONI, CAB/9R/12/2A.

56 Royal warrants determining a scale of social precedence and local precedence for Northern Ireland, 30 January 1930, GO, MS 154A, pp. 128–33.

57 Ministry of Home Affairs, Belfast, to Major Sir Nevile Wilkinson KCVO, 6 Duchess Street, Portland Place, London, acknowledging designs for the RUC, 9 November 1922, SC.

drafted designs for the Northern Ireland flag in February 1923,[58] and its Great Seal in April 1923.[59]

Wilkinson held initial discussions about the designs for a new coat of arms for Northern Ireland with the Duke of Abercorn and other Northern Ireland officials at the Home Office in London from January 1924. However, much of the work on this particular commission was executed in Dublin.[60] For example, Sadleir wired detailed descriptions of the provincial arms of Ulster, including the red hand of Ulster, to Wilkinson prior to his meetings with officials in the Home Office, for which Wilkinson was much indebted.[61] It was also Sadleir who submitted the final designs for the arms of Northern Ireland from Dublin Castle to the Cabinet Secretary in Belfast, for the Northern Government's approval in April 1924, after Wilkinson had gone abroad.[62]

After the artwork had been approved, the royal warrant for the arms of Northern Ireland was signed by King George V, and issued through the Home Office in London on 2 August 1924. Concurrently, a copy was registered in the Register of Arms at the Office of Arms in Dublin.[63] In the same way, supporters for the arms, featuring an Irish elk and lion, were also granted by the Crown, issued by Wilkinson through the Home Office, and concurrently registered in Dublin in 1925.[64]

In contrast to this work for Northern Ireland, the Free State Government commissioned little heraldic work. Later, when discussing the designs for the arms of Northern Ireland, Sadleir commented that 'there are no arms on record for the Irish Free State'.[65] In November 1922, in conjunction with his ambitious genealogical proposals for the Records Office, Sadleir had been asked by the first Law Officer, Hugh Kennedy, to advise him about the arms of Ireland, for possible use on a new Free State flag. Sadleir responded to this with a

---

58 Sadleir to Wilkinson, 23 February 1923, conveying the thanks of Duke of Abercorn's private secretary, for all the trouble he had taken with the flag, SC.

59 Sadleir to Wilkinson, 19 April 1923, confirming that designs submitted for the great seal for Northern Ireland are to be settled shortly, SC.

60 Wilkinson, London, to Sadleir, 14 January 1924, SC.

61 Wilkinson to Sadleir, Office of Arms, 24 January 1924, SC.

62 Sadleir to Cabinet Secretariat, Government House, 19 April 1924, PRONI, CAB 9R/12/2A.

63 Royal grant of arms to Northern Ireland, 2 August 1924, 'registered and recorded by Sir Nevile Wilkinson, who has cognisance of matters of this nature', GO, MS 111C, p. 49.

64 Royal grant of supporters to Northern Ireland, August, 1925, GO, MS 111C, p. 66.

65 Sadleir, Office of Arms, Dublin Castle, to A.T. Butler, Windsor Herald, College of Arms, 12 July 1932, SC.

detailed report about the history of the arms of Ireland, accompanied with sketches of the earliest drawings of them from the Office's registers.[66] His report urged retention of the arms of Ireland that had been in use from medieval times – a gold harp with silver strings, on an azure blue background, rather than the favoured green flag associated with the 1916 Rising.[67]

However, the tricolour of green, white and orange, being representative of popular revolution, was chosen by the Dáil, and adopted by usage rather than by statute in May 1923.[68] It is interesting to learn, however, that whilst Sadleir's sketches were not used for the flag, the Free State Government did use them for the design of its new Seal, although this was acknowledged, nor did any registration of the Seal follow at the Office of Arms. Apparently, Miss McConnell was approached in a private capacity to execute these designs for the Free State Great Seal by Free State officials. Several others artists were also approached and the Gaelic scholar, Professor Eoin McNeill was asked for his opinion.[69] The drawings were then sent to the Royal Mint for processing, which caused consternation in the Colonial Office, because no prior permission had been sought from the British Government. In turn, Wilkinson remonstrated with Sadleir for not keeping tighter control on the actions of his staff, to which Sadleir protested he could do nothing, given that Miss McConnell had been commissioned independently of the Office. In May 1923, he informed Wilkinson:

> It now transpires that certain small sketches of the earliest examples here of the arms of Ireland ordered some months ago by the Free State Ministry, to be used in making a proposed Irish flag, have been utilised in designing the Great Seal of the Free State.

But he added that he knew nothing about this until the last moment.[70] So the Free State chose not to engage with the Office of Arms directly in securing designs for its early symbols of State. The McConnell Studio in Lincoln Place was contracted, amongst others, for the work instead, and the design for the Postmaster's General 'as prepared by Miss McConnell, Ulster King of Arms Office' remains on the Government file concerning State Seal designs.[71]

---

66 Sadleir, Office of Arms, Dublin Castle, to Hugh Kennedy, Law Department, Merrion Street, 25 November 1922, UCD, P4/810 (2).
67 Draft of document about the harp as the national emblem, and possible use on a flag, undated, in the hand of Thomas Sadleir, GO, Box Relating to Flags, uncat.
68 *Dáil Éireann Debates,* 21 May 1923, 15, 739.
69 NAI, S1587A.
70 Sadleir to Wilkinson, 15 May 1923, SC.
71 NAI, S1587A.

Incidentally, the same studio also supplied Celtic designs for the first Free State postage and fiscal stamps.[72]

The Free State Government did, however, have to co-operate with the Office of Arms in relation to the procedures for allowing citizens to change their surnames and arms – a process requiring the royal warrant. Applications for warrants for this purpose were relatively rare, usually to fulfill the terms of a will, and claim inheritance to an estate, but they had to be registered in the Office and in the Register of Royal Warrants, and usually involved a concurrent new grant of arms. In accordance with the changed constitutional position after 1922, the Governor-General, rather than the Lord Lieutenant, transmitted applications to the Office for processing and registration. Thus, we find the first such warrant issued by the Office of Arms after Independence, in August 1923, authorising Godfrey Robert Wills-Sandford of Ballinlough, County Roscommon, to change his surname to Sandford-Wills and bear the arms of Wills. This was signed by the King, sealed with the Great Seal, but also counter signed by His Excellency Timothy Healy, Governor-General of Ireland, and registered in the Office register.[73] A similar warrant was registered for Hubert Edward Madden Bourke, to take the name and arms of Burrowes, in March 1925.[74]

These documents emphasised the Office's status within the Free State – its authority remained derived from the Crown. Later, in an effort to downplay the Office of the Governor-General, the Free State Government replaced the Governor-General's signature on such documents with the signature for the Minister for Justice, and ordered that in addition to the Great Seal they should also be affixed with the Seal of the Free State. Thus, when Edith Julia Dobbin, of Ballygarth Castle, Julianstown, County Meath, applied to the Governor-General to assume the surname Dobbin-Pepper and to bear the arms of Pepper in October 1926, her warrant, as issued by the Office of Arms, was duly signed by the King and sealed with the Great Seal. In addition, it was counter-signed by the Free State Minister for Justice, Kevin O'Higgins, and sealed with the Free State Seal.[75]

Whilst the local signatory had changed, and a second Seal was affixed to symbolize the input of the Free State, the authority under which it was issued continued to be Crown – for the time being at least. Even the British Treasury, which demonstrated an increasing reluctance to invest in this obscure little Office in Dublin, given the post-War economic depression affecting the United

---

72 Lawrenson Swanton, *Emerging From the Shadow*, p. 32.
73 GO, MS 154A, pp. 143–5.
74 *op. cit.*, pp. 146–7.
75 *op. cit.*, p. 149.

Kingdom, was forced to accept in 1924 that 'for political reasons, the abolition of any personal links between the sovereign and the I.F.S. would be undesirable at this juncture'.[76]

RELOCATION TO NORTHERN IRELAND CONSIDERED

It was to keep alive this imperial link between Free State dominion and Crown that 'the question of an establishment of an Office of Arms in Northern Ireland' was not pursued either.[77] The possibility of transferring the Office to Belfast was discussed at a senior level, between the Belfast Government and Home Office officials, in 1923. One advocate of a relocation to the North was the Church of Ireland Primate of all Ireland, the Most Revd Charles D'Arcy, who resided in Armagh – ecclesiastical capital of Ireland. In March 1923, he proposed that St Patrick's Cathedral, Armagh, might provide a suitable religious centre for the threatened Order of St Patrick, to which its regalia, records and officers (including Ulster King of Arms) could be transferred for their safety, 'owing to the changes in the South of Ireland'.[78]

No further action was taken in this regard, however. The Prime Minister of Northern Ireland, Sir James Craig to whom supporters were later granted, designed and registered at the Office of Arms, Dublin Castle in 1927 following his elevation to the peerage as Lord Craigavon[79] was not in favour of initiating any appointment that 'would carry a new salary against Northern Ireland funds'.[80] British Government policy was firmly against any move that would weaken the dominion links that it provided in Dublin. Indeed, the Home Office urged the North to maintain the *status quo*, hoping that it would not 'stir up this question' which was a 'difficult one requiring a wary step and great time'. The Northern Ireland Government was informed that the 'Ulster King held his appointment direct from the Crown, normally speaking for life' and that his position was 'quite different from that of the ordinary public servant'.[81] Whilst in the past Wilkinson's preference for living in London had been the source of contention with British Government officials, especially in the Treasury, by the

---

76 Treasury minute, 14 March 1924, PRO, T 162/709.
77 Oscar Henderson, Government House, Hillsborough, to W. B. Spender, 6 March 1923, PRONI, CAB 9R/12/2A.
78 Charles F. Armagh, Archbishop of Armagh, on board the 'Larne Steamer', to Mr Tallents, Governor General's Office, Belfast, 28 March 1923, PRO, HO 267/46.
79 Grant of supporters to Lord Craigavon, 5 April 1927, GO, MS 111C, pp. 90–2.
80 Spender to Henderson, 8 March 1923, PRONI, CAB 9R/12/2A.
81 Buckland, Home Office to Tallents, 10 March 1923, PRO, HO 267/46.

Grant of Supporters.   Craigavon.

Grant of supporters to Lord Craigavon, as designed for and registered in the Office of Arms, Dublin, 5 April 1927. It features 'dexter a constable of the Ulster Special Constabulary, with his hand resting on a rifle, sinister, a private of the Royal Ulster Rifles, armed and accoutred both proper'. *GO, MS 111C.*

1920s it actually became a means of reassuring Belfast. Thus, the Home Office admitted that whilst it was true that the Office was located in Dublin, 'the present holder of the office has . . . done most of his work in London.'[82]

Some Northern Ireland clients would later prefer that there had been a relocation, on account of the obligatory payment of stamp duty – an issue that became quite contentious for some. Stamp duty had been included in the fees of the Office of Arms since the eighteenth century. Following Independence, a new Free State stamp impress was introduced in Dublin, it being the right of a dominion to control its own stamping. After some initial difficulties during the Civil War, this was affixed to all legal instruments and other documents, including patents of arms issued by the Office of Arms, for which £10 stamp duty was charged per patent.

The Free State stamp was a distinctive symbol, featuring a green harp, surrounded by green shamrocks. When the proprietor of the *Belfast Telegraph*, Sir Robert Baird, received his grant of arms in 1925, he was delighted with the 'elaborate document' but less than gratified with the 'large £10 Free State stamp containing a green harp etc' affixed to it, and he complained to the Government of his own State.[83] The matter was referred to the Home Office in London, but after investigation officials there were 'unable to discover any legal basis for stamping elsewhere than in the Free State' because it remained a dominion. Whilst the new choice of green shamrocks might not be to everyone's taste, it remained legally acceptable for the Free State, which claimed the stamp duty, to decide what kind of stamp should be used. The official policy remained that it should be the objective 'to maintain as far as possible the traditional position and functions of Ulster', including local payment of stamp duty.[84]

The Northern Ireland grant of arms and subsequent grant of supporters did not, it has to be said, end up with green shamrocks on them. Although registered at the Office of Arms in Dublin, the transmission of the original patents through the Home Office in London avoided the embarrassment of any Free State identity being affixed to them. Instead, it was found 'necessary that [each] should be impressed with a £10 stamp by the Inland Revenue Department'.[85] Significantly, the Office's prescribed fee of £44 for each grant was also waived,

---

82 *op. cit.*

83 C.G. Duggan, Ministry of Finance of Northern Ireland, Belfast to Mr S. G. Tallents, Imperial Secretary, Belfast, 10 July 1925, PRO, HO 267/46.

84 C.M. Martin-Rae, Home Office, London, S.G. Tallents, Belfast, 15 September 1925, *op. cit.*

85 H. Maxwell, Home Office, London, to S. G. Tallents, Imperial Secretary, Belfast, 7 August 1924, PRO, HO 267/46.

Grant of supporters to the Government of Northern Ireland. Registered by the Office of Arms, Dublin, August 1925. *GO, MS 111C.*

on the grounds that the Northern Government was already contributing to imperial expenditure under the terms of the Government of Ireland Act 1920, and should not be liable to further charges.[86] Such were the diplomatic niceties that the Office of Arms was forced to observe in the new political climate.

HIS MAJESTY'S TREASURY AND ATTEMPTS TO CURTAIL EXPENDITURE

By his own admission, political events in Ireland had affected the health of Sir Nevile Wilkinson, and he was largely absent from Dublin in the years and months that followed Independence. He had been living at his London residence in Duchess Street after the First World War, making periodic visits to Dublin until the early months of 1922, after which he was increasingly reluctant to go. One of his complaints was that 'irregulars' had occupied the Kildare Street Club, where he sometimes stayed, and had stolen his clothes.[87] Wilkinson was a sensitive soul, easily affected by the radical changes going

---

86 G.C. Duggan, Stormont Castle, Belfast, to The Secretary, Treasury, Whitehall, 20 March 1924, *op. cit.*
87 Wilkinson to S. G. Tallents, 11 September 1922, *op. cit.*

on in the world around him, and this in turn was detrimental to his health. The serious illness that had necessitated an operation in April 1922, was, he informed the paymasters at the Treasury, 'in the opinion of the doctors due to the great nervous strain caused by the Rebellion'.[88] This prevented him even answering correspondence until June, or undertaking any work in relation to the Office of Arms until September of that year.[89]

Whilst fond of Ireland, Wilkinson found it difficult to come to terms with the new political regime that had replaced the world of levées, drawing rooms, balls and dinner parties that he was used to. His prolonged absence from Dublin after Independence indicates a reluctance to engage with the new political situation. When asked to defend his position, Wilkinson described himself as 'the link between the Court and Ireland', and anticipated a revival of ceremonial duties. His anticipation of a fairytale court did not convince Treasury officials, who concluded that 'his anticipations appear to be based on nothing stronger than a belief on his part that there is to hand a revival of the Irish aristocracy'.[90]

As had been the case during the First World War, Wilkinson's absences put extra pressure on his staff, especially Sadleir, who informed one confidant in November 1922: 'Ulster has not been over since 11 March [1922] so I presume he will not return'.[91] In fact Wilkinson returned to Dublin only twice between March 1922 and April 1925. He was back for a week in July 1923, when Sadleir was gratified that he had 'thought the Office well run during [his] absence', and for a month in November 1923, prior to a Treasury audit.[92] He returned 'to pick up the threads', as he put it, between 15 April and early June 1925,[93] following a three-month trip to the United States – the first of a series of international escapades with Titania's Palace, the work for which he is best remembered.

Wilkinson had been painstakingly constructing the 'Palace' – a magnificent 16-room doll's house in miniature – since 1907. Various parts of this had been exhibited over the years,[94] and when Wilkinson was supposedly recovering from

---

88 Wilkinson, London, to Mr Fass, Treasury, 14 December 1923, PRO, T 160/192.
89 Copy of letter from Lord FitzAlan, 1 Buckingham Palace Gardens, London, to 'Wilkinson', 16 September 1922, in which he states he is glad to hear Wilkinson is better, PRO, HO 267/46.
90 Treasury minute, 26 February 1924, PRO, T 62/709.
91 Thos. U. Sadleir, Office of Arms, Dublin Castle, to Mr Hugh Kennedy, Law Officer, 27 November 1922, UCD, P4/811(3).
92 Sadleir, Dublin Castle, to Wilkinson, London, 9 July 1923, SC; Sadleir to Mr Athawes, Treasury, 23 November 1923, PRO, T 160/190.
93 Wilkinson to W.B. Spender, Stormont, 8 April 1925, PRONI, CAB 9R/12/2A.
94 Gordon Bowe and Cumming, *Arts and Crafts*, pp. 203–4, Galloway, *Most Illustrious Order*, pp. 134–5.

illness, Queen Mary opened the complete work at a special event in London on 6 July 1922.[95] Following the London showing, Wilkinson then embarked on taking the 'Palace' around the world. After his first American trip in 1925, he returned for an extended 16-month tour between February 1928 and May 1929, followed by South America during the spring and summer of 1931, and Australia and New Zealand in the winter of 1934.

Whilst these foreign visits raised thousands of pounds for handicapped, neglected or unhappy children,[96] they had nothing to do with his responsibilities for the Office of Arms, and once again his absences hindered its administration. In a telling memo to the Treasury that reflected ongoing difficulties, Sadleir vented his frustrations, in May 1923:

> I venture to bring to your notice the heavy arrears in this Office. One grant of arms, three confirmations, and 28 searches for arms or pedigrees, for all of which fees have been paid, remain uncompleted.

Drawing attention to Wilkinson's continued absence, he urged that his own salary might be increased – given he was doing the work of three men 'his own, Ulster's and Athlone's' – and that the arrears might be addressed. Lest there be any misconception about Wilkinson's perceived ceremonial role, Sadleir had this to say:

> I have no information, whatever, that he has attended any court for a considerable time, though I know he spent a great part of last year in Bath, and is at present in the south of France![97]

Subsequent enquiries at Buckingham Palace revealed that Wilkinson's claims that he had to attend on His Majesty were misleading: 'there are no Court duties here which can be held to be responsible in the slightest degree' for his absence from his office in Dublin.[98]

The same month, the Exchequer and Audit Department conducted an external audit. This identified a 'general laxity in the administration of the

---

95 Snoddy, *Dictionary of Irish Artists*, p. 540.
96 Nevile Rodwell Wilkinson, *Titania's Palace. Illustrated Guide* (21st ed., London, 1926), p. 4. Aside from his travels, Wilkinson was also busy publishing during the 1920s a series of fairy stories based on the imaginary adventures of Yvette: *Yvette in Italy and Titania's Palace* (London, 1922); *Yvette in Switzerland and Titania's Palace* (Oxford, 1926); *Yvette in Venice and Titania's Palace* (Oxford, 1927), as well as his memoirs in 1925. He published again in the 1930s: *Yvette in the USA* (London, 1930), and *A History of the Guards' Chapel, 1838–1938* (London, 1938).
97 Memo to the Treasury in the hand of T.U. Sadleir, PRO, T 160/192.
98 Treasury memo, *op. cit.*

Office of Arms', which it reported it had long been suspected. Sadleir was asked to explain these errors, and pointed out how difficult it was to keep the accounts in order 'on account of Ulster keeping the cheque-book in England', which made it impossible to know what cheques had been drawn.[99] Whilst the auditors were satisfied that there was no question of dishonesty and that the errors were 'solely due to mismanagement', Wilkinson's absence was called into question: 'Ulster's exercise of his control from London and elsewhere does not make for efficiency'.[100] Comparison of the Office's receipts and expenditure revealed that its income had fallen, although this undoubtedly was also linked to the uncertain political climate. Compared with receipts of £565 for the year 1921–2, its income dropped to £370 for the year 1922–3, and just £250 for the year 1923–4, its lowest recorded income since formal records were returned to the Treasury by Burke in 1872.[101]

In spite of his failings, Wilkinson held onto his life appointment. Commenting on his conduct as 'an international showman' on world tour, whilst receiving 'full pay and travelling expenses' from the British Government, some officials were scathing, and bemoaned the fact that he they could not touch him. But in 1926, having been warned of his official position as a Crown appointee by letters patent under the Great Seal, and of his friends in high places,[102] the Treasury concluded that it was 'extremely doubtful . . . we could encompass the revocation of his letters patent in view of his influence in important quarters'.[103]

Whilst resigned to the fact that Wilkinson's position was 'to all intents and purposes a sinecure', the Treasury was determined to curtail the general expenditure of the Office. Thus, after the audit in 1923, Wilkinson was ordered to ensure that the closing balance each month 'matched the Office's bank balance'.[104] Printing and stationery supplies were to be purchased from Manchester rather than Dublin from 1924. In 1925, attempts were also made to disconnect the Office telephone (installed since 1903), because the fees charged by the 'Free State people' for use of the internal exchange in Dublin Castle were 'becoming absurdly high' by 1925. Treasury officials pushed to discontinue the

---

99 Sadleir to Mr Athawes, Treasury, 23 November 1923, PRO, T 160/190.
100 Treasury minutes on audit at the Office of Arms, December 1923, PRO, T 160/192.
101 Receipts and expenditure of Ulster King of Arms, *op. cit.*
102 C.M. Martin Jones, Dominions Office, to James Rae, Treasury Chambers, Whitehall, 12 February 1926, PRO, DO 35/14.
103 Treasury memorandum, June 1926, PRO, T 160/192.
104 Treasury minute, Mr Athawes to Mr Fass and Mr Hieneyet, 19 February 1923, *op. cit.*

telephone altogether, informing Wilkinson there was no necessity for him 'to be constantly in touch with all the departments in Dublin Castle'.[105]

Wilkinson successfully defended the Office's need for a telephone. He happened to be in Dublin at the time, en route to America, and argued that the telephone was indeed a necessity:

> We receive a good many calls each day from solicitors and others making inquiries on behalf of clients, which result in fees. These come as far away as Cork and Limerick. Another and perhaps more important reason for the retention of the telephone is that it is frequently used by Belfast to make inquiries about questions of ceremonial and precedence in the six counties, queries which need immediate answers. The use of a long telegram in such cases would cost more to the public.[106]

He was also anxious that the Office should not lose business to the English heralds operating at the College of Arms, who, unlike their Irish counterparts, had remained financially independent and had to generate their own fees. They were only too glad to supplement their private incomes when Irish business came their way, and were allegedly spreading stories that the Office of Arms in Dublin had closed in the aftermath of Independence. Wilkinson warned that this would cost the Treasury by reducing public fees, and that if his number and address were removed from the telephone directory, this might lend 'colour to the [English heralds'] story'.[107] A compromise was eventually reached, and instead calls were to be put directly through the central telephone exchange in Dublin from 1925. The Office was also obliged to keep a detailed record of incoming and outgoing calls, underlining its precarious financial situation and adding to Sadleir's workload.[108]

THE DIASPORA AND LINKS ABROAD

In spite of the difficulties that Wilkinson's absences caused to daily administration, his international travels, particularly those to America, did have far-reaching consequences for promoting Irish heraldic and genealogical services throughout the world. His travels do indeed appear to have generated more business at home.

---

105 E.V. Athawes, Treasury Chambers, London, to Wilkinson KCVO, Office of Arms, Dublin Castle 7 May 1925, GO Personnel File, uncat.
106 Wilkinson to Athawes, 8 May 1925, *op. cit.*
107 *op. cit.*
108 Athawes to Wilkinson, 12 May 1925, *op. cit.*

Work for the diaspora included this confirmation of arms to Thomas Hughes Kelly Esquire, of New York City, whose ancestors came from Trillick and Fintona, County Tyrone, and descended from the ancient family of Kelly of Mullaghmore, County Galway. Registration of this patent confirmed information that had not 'been heretofore recorded in the Office of Arms, 8 October 1925. *GO, MS 111C.*

Whilst regretting that the Office of Arms had lost its ceremonial prestige as a result of the new Free State constitutional position, Wilkinson was confident that it could continue to 'occupy its accustomed place, and carry on the tradition of 400 years undisturbed by the social upheaval of the past ten years'. This was possible, he believed, by virtue of the genuine desire of Irish people to preserve the tradition of their ancestors, a particular characteristic of the Irish living outside of Ireland.[109] He had encountered this first hand on his travels, especially in the United States, where many people detained him to ask questions about their ancestral links with Ireland. From Colorado in February 1925, for example, he reported: 'I venture I could start a most lucrative heraldic office out here', given the great interest there is in pedigrees and arms'.[110] On return from 'his wonderful tour of America', he informed the Treasury that he had been 'able to give lecture on heraldry as far as San Francisco, which should bring in new clients'.[111] Indeed, the American clients began to roll in, a flurry of business following from the States of California, Illinois and New York, and the city of Philadelphia between 1925 and 1931.[112]

As well as processing heraldic work and related genealogical research for aristocratic Americans trying to establish claims to inherit the estates in Ireland that had belonged to their ancestors,[113] an increasing number of requests of a more general nature were also received. These came from people of humbler stock who were attempting to make first contact in Ireland in a bid to trace their Irish ancestors. Their voluminous and varied requests necessitated the Office printing up thousands of the forms that had first been drawn up by Burtchaell c. 1919. On these 'Form Cs', as they were called, enquirers filled in basic information, to allow staff to assess whether or not it would be possible to carry out further research for them in repositories such as the PRO and Registry of Deeds as well as the Office of Arms itself. The demand for this initial assessment increased and by the 1930s one newspaper article commented that the Office was dealing with an average of 100 enquiries per week from genealogically-minded Irish people all over the world.[114]

Contrary to the perception that ancestral research for the diaspora is a recent phenomenon linked to the development of mass communication from the 1950s,

109 Wilkinson, *To All and Singular*, pp. 182–3.
110 Wilkinson, Colorado, to Sadleir, Dublin, 25 February 1925, SC.
111 Wilkinson, Office of Arms, Dublin Castle to E. Athawes Esq., Treasury Chambers, Whitehall, 15 April 1925, GO, Personnel File 1, uncat.
112 GO, MS 111C.
113 Various press cuttings, SC.
114 *The Irish Times*, 30 October 1938.

evidence from the Office of Arms suggests that the trend was well in train from the 1920s. In 1928, for example, the Heraldic Museum was included by local tourist agencies in Dublin on their tour itineraries of the city for the first time, which Wilkinson predicted would 'mean a large increase of clients next season'. He reminded the Treasury of the importance of these connections:

> The work of the Office has recently been augmented by American clients, who have been attracted to the Office partly by lectures on heraldry I have given in America, and partly by visits to the Heraldic Museum, which . . . I founded in Dublin Castle.[115]

OFFICIAL SALARIES AND OTHER ARRANGEMENTS

In spite of these developments, staff salaries were not increased. A salary table for the period 1919–39 shows no change, apart from an increase in Wilkinson's salary from £600 to £739 in 1937, as a reward for loyal service following the coronation. Sadleir received a constant £300 as Registrar, and the heraldic painter £170 throughout the period. The typist's salary ranged between £96 and £126, depending on qualifications.[116]

Static and unpensionable posts did not attract good employees. Whilst Major Burgoyne was happy to assist with general administration and the technical execution of patents without remuneration, he grew discontented with the political uncertainties, and had 'gone to England' by July 1922 Sadleir bemoaned the fact that 'he would be much better employed here'. In consequence of the poor-quality work of Moore, the clerk-typist, Sadleir ended up doing most of it.[117] When Moore took extended sick leave from January 1923, Sadleir discovered that many documents for which he was responsible had been misfiled, and wasted time searching for them. He reported: 'the accumulation of work in the Office quite depresses me. It is far more than I can cope with'.[118]

It was at this point that he resorted to paying two workers from his own pocket to assist with the accounts and in-house researching, a new precedent that, as we shall see, would be continued by his successors once the Office was taken over by the Irish Government in 1943. The cost of this was a burden on his already meagre personal salary. In July 1923 he warned Wilkinson that 'as

---

115 Wilkinson to Mr James Rae, Treasury, 16 December 1928, PRO, T 62/709.
116 Civil estimates for the upkeep of the Office of Arms, 1919–39, GO, Box Relating to Expenses and Salaries, uncat.
117 Sadleir to Wilkinson, 27 July 1922, SC.
118 Sadleir to Wilkinson, 22 January 1923, SC.

the expense of paying Miss Elliott and Miss O'Rourke, really leaves so little out of my £300 p.a. . . . unless you can induce the Treasury to raise my salary, I really cannot go on'.[119]

The arrival of John McNeill as grade-one clerk-typist in July 1923 was a boost to Sadleir, as he proved quick and intelligent, his 'clear hand' allowing him to assist with engrossing documents. But his appointment would be a brief respite, as he was lured to the Player's Factory, where a higher salary and pension prospects were on offer, in May 1924. A succession of clerk-typists then followed, but there was little continuity as most stayed for no more than a year. Miss Johnson, who replaced McNeill, was an 'excellent employee', according to Sadleir, because she could assist with searches as well as type; but she was forced to resign on her engagement, in January 1927. Her replacement, Miss Kinnear, who had a degree, stayed only for a year because of the low salary and was gone by August 1928.

The next clerk, Miss Marsh, who had actually been working privately for Sadleir on the accounts since April 1928, was formally appointed in September 1928. She proved versatile, her duties including typing, filing, interviewing clients in the absence of the Registrar, and even specialist heraldic and genealogical work, as well as keeping the books in order. However, she only lasted until April 1929, when the Treasury terminated her contract to curtail personnel expenditure. Her departure caused real dismay, forcing a lot of work to be suspended. By January 1931 a Mr Lobo was in employment, but he resigned when the Treasury proposed cutting his salary in January 1932.[120]

A POLITICAL ANOMALY

Whilst these in-house trials and tribulations continued for Sadleir, the Free State Government was beginning to examine the anomalous position that the Office of Arms presented, and to consider how it might effectively bring it under its own control.[121] Technically, the Bedford Tower building had, along with the other Castle buildings, been transferred for the use of the Provisional Government in January 1922. At one point, a Home Office memo indicated that the British Government was prepared to pay the rent for it, informing the Treasury that 'we will pay rent of his Office if necessary'.[122] However, reflecting the

---

119 Sadleir to Wilkinson, 23 June 1923, SC.
120 GO, Personnel File 1, uncat.
121 File of papers relating to the transfer of the Office of Arms, 1922–43, NAI, DT S3926A.
122 Home Office memorandum, PRO, HO 267/46.

The opening page of this Register of Arms includes, in the centre of the smaller box, the arms of Ulster King of Arms, used inter-changeably by the Office of Arms until 1943. The Office arms featured: or a cross gules on a chief of the last a lion passant guardant between, on the dexter a harp, and on the sinister a portcullis, all of the first. When used by the Office, the motto 'Miserere Mei Deus' (Have Mercy on Us) was also included. In the larger box above the royal arms are reproduced in splendid colour. The Office of Arms derived its authority from the Crown until 1943. *GO MS 111K.*

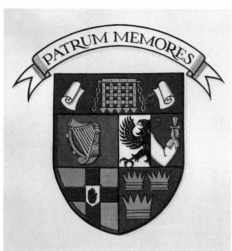

The arms of the GO, as registered in February 1945 featured quarterly, the four provinces of Ireland, *viz.* 1) Leinster; 2) Connaught; 3) Ulster; 4) Munster; and on a chief gules a portcullis or between two scrolls proper, that on the dexter bend sinisterwise and that on the dexter bendwise, with the motto above the shield 'Patrum Memores' (Mindful of the Fathers). *GO, MS 111Q.*

STATE RECEPTION OF THE REMAINS OF
H.E. RICHARD SOUTHWELL EARL OF MAYO.
K.P. VICEROY OF INDIA. 25ᵀᴴ APRIL.1872.

Colour detail from the funeral entry for the Honourable Richard Southwell sixth Earl of Mayo, who was born in 1822, and became Viceroy and Governor General of India in 1868. He was assassinated in the Andaman Islands, while on a tour of inspection, on 8 February 1872. Following a period of lying in State, he was buried at Johnstown Church, near Naas, County Kildare, on 26 April 1872. The entry was executed during Sir Bernard Burke's tenure of office. *GO, MS 77.*

The tabard of royal arms was worn by the King of Arms for all ceremonial occasions. This one belonged to Sir Arthur Vicars, Ulster King of Arms 1893–1908, who was of exceptionally small stature. *Heraldic Museum.*

Detail from registration of the grant of arms issued by Sir Arthur Vicars to Sir J. T. Bankes, of Dublin, showing the coat of arms designed for him, and opening words of the grant. *GO, MS 110.*

This Dresden china figure was one of a series of figures of royal courtiers, produced as an upmarket souvenir, following the coronation of George VI in 1937. It features Sir Nevile Wilkinson, Ulster King of Arms 1908–40, in coronation dress, with white knee-breeches, tabard, his crown of office, collar of 'S's', and bearing his baton. *College of Arms.*

Robustly-drawn title page of the first full register compiled during the tenure of Sir Nevile Wilkinson, Ulster King of Arms 1908–40. This artistic piece, which includes the royal arms, the arms of the Office, and several of its personnel, was executed by Major Thomas Shepard, heraldic artist between 1909 and 1915. *GO, MS 111J.*

The arms of Sir William Thornley Stoker, Master of Surgery at the Royal University of Ireland, of Dublin, and a founding trustee of the Heraldic Museum, included a striking druid's head on the shield. They were confirmed by the Office on 4 February 1909, two months before the Heraldic Museum opened. *GO, MS 111A.*

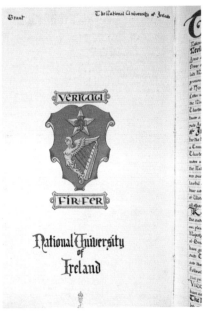

The arms of the National University of Ireland, as registered in the Office of Arms in May 1912, included the heraldic harp as its principal charge. *GO, MS 111J.*

The first example of the artwork of Mabel McConnell, heraldic artist at the Office 1915–29, includes several Celtic features, and her distinctive autograph – the letters 'M' and 'Mc' on either side of a portcullis (drawbridge). Granted to the Honan Hostel, Cork, 9 January 1915. *GO, MS 111B.*

The arms of Éamon de Valera. His personal interest whilst Taoiseach in the future of the Office of Arms under Irish control, was an important factor in its survival after 1943. *GO, Register of the Arms of the Presidents of Ireland*.

The heraldic emblem of 12 stars on a blue background is the symbol of Europe *par excellance*. It was designed by Ireland's Chief Herald, Gerard Slevin, for the Council of Europe in 1954. *Courtesy, Photo European Parliament*.

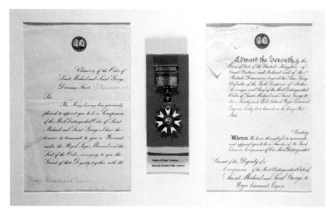

Badge of Knight Commander of the Order of St Michael and St George, issued in 1911, and earlier warrant of Knight Companion, issued in 1905, to Roger Casement, 1864–1916, for diplomatic and humanitarian services. Casement did not accept them personally, and formally renounced them in 1915. Following his trial and execution for treason in 1916, he was officially stripped of these honours, and his family handed them back to the British Government. Thereafter, the Office of Arms was considered the best place for their safekeeping, but given the political sensitivities, they were not displayed. Instead, they were carefully concealed behind a panel in one of the display cases in the Heraldic Museum, and only recovered when the Office moved out of the Castle in 1981. *Heraldic Museum*.

The arms of Northern Ireland, as they appear in the Register of Arms, granted on 2 August 1924. The Office's work in designing an heraldic identity for the new Northern Ireland State is symbolic of its anomalous position in the Irish Free State, but also demonstrates how it transcended politics. *GO, MS 111C.*

Q 20
The arms
of Ireland
n. b.
The number
of strings should
be fifteen

Prud
9 Nov. 1945

Draft sketch of the arms of Ireland, prior to registration in the Office under the authority of the Irish Government, in 1945. The annotation by Dr Edward MacLysaght, Chief Herald of Ireland 1943–54, recommends that no more than 15 strings should be shown for heraldic purposes. *GO, File Relating to the Arms of Ireland.*

Symbolic of its cross–Border identity, the Ulster Transport Authority chose to re-register its arms in the GO, as granted and first registered by the College of Arms in London, in June 1960. The GO issued a most ornate certificate to record this. *GO Collection.*

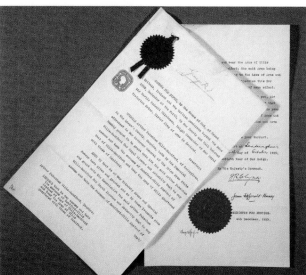

Royal warrant authorising a change of surname and arms, as issued through the Office after Independence. This document is symbolic of the Office's constitutional position after 1922. For legal authenticity, although it bears the signature of the King, and is affixed with the Great Seal, it is counter-signed by the Free State Minister for Justice, and also bears the Seal of the Free State. *GO, MS 154A.*

Recent grant to the College of Anaesthetists, issued by the GO in 1999. The principal heraldic charge is the poppy head – symbolic of sleep, while the healing hand of medicine, and cloud of anaesthesia are also in evidence. The supporters are dolphins, taken from the arms of the MacDonnells of the Glens. Dr John MacDonnell, an ancestor of the present MacDonnells, was the first man to administer an anaesthetic in Ireland, on 1 January 1847. The patent is signed by Fergus Gillespie, Deputy Chief Herald. *GO, MS 111Y.*

The colour and contrast of the Heraldic Museum, Kildare Street, Dublin.

uncertainty about its future, the Free State Department of Finance, in whom the building had become vested in 1922, decided not to ask for any. Instead, an informal arrangement was made whereby the Minister of Finance simply loaned the premises occupied by the Office of Arms to the British Treasury.[123]

As a result of this development, various departments did try to claim accommodation within the building. This annoyed Wilkinson, who complained, in December 1923, that his 'Office accommodation had been encroached upon', the Land Registry Office occupying a room in the basement, and the Dáil Courts Commission taking over two of rooms on the attic floor, in spite of his 'strong protest'.[124] To facilitate the latter development, partition walls were taken down in the attic between the Office and the former Chamberlain's House, which became the Gas, Weights and Measures Commission after 1922. The former Guard House was allocated to the Department of Finance in 1922, and became the Special Commission of Income Tax. In spite of these developments, however, the bulk of the Bedford Tower building, including its offices on the first floor and three remaining ones in the attic, in addition to the Museum, strong room and messenger's room on the ground floor, were all retained, remaining isolated from other parts of the building.

This seemingly anomalous situation was too much for some, and helped to fuel anti-Treaty political agendas.[125] By June 1924, for example, one suspicious civil servant, Séamus Hughes, informed Eoin McNeill, the Minister for Education:

> The Office of Arms . . . with its treasures, documents and records has not yet been taken over by our Government, or, if it has, is now not under our control. I understand the staff is still being paid by the British, which is wholly inappropriate.[126]

Other negative rummors circulated. It was claimed that public access to the Office was not permitted, and even speculated that it represented the last bastion of Unionism at the Castle – perhaps a throw-back reference to the Home Rule campaign during 1912–3, when the Office had apparently been a focal point for circulating anti-Home Rule literature. It was further alleged that when President W.T. Cosgrave and officials had paid a courtesy visit to inspect it during the summer of 1924, they had not been permitted to view the strong room.

---

123 Opinion of Attorney General, 23 January 1928, NAI, DT S3926A.
124 Nevile Wilkinson, Ulster, 6 Duchess Street, London, to H. E. Fass Esq, The Treasury, 14 December 1923, PRO, T 160/192.
125 Opinion of E.J. Kelly, 29 May 1928, NAI, DT S3926A.
126 Séamus Hughes to Dr. Eoin McNeill, Minister for Education, 27 June 1924, *op. cit.*

In a letter to the President's Department, Thomas Markham, an intelligence officer who was later discredited by the Free State Government, made sensational claims about how the Office of Arms 'had reverted to British control', in spite of the fact that Michael Collins had instructed him personally to keep a vigilant eye on it.[127]

But these conspiracy theories were the work of anti-Treaty civil servants, and found to be unreliable.[128] The public had not been able to make personal searches in the past, and this position did not change after 1922. However, for a moderate fee, the staff undertook searches on behalf of enquirers.[129] Visitors were still permitted to visit the Heraldic Museum, the opening hours for which were extended by the mid-1920s – from 10am to 5pm Monday to Friday (less an hour for lunch), and from 10am to 1pm on Saturdays.[130] Access to the strong room would not have been in order for anyone, President or otherwise, simply because it was bad archival practice and probably regarded as such by the conscientious Sadleir. Nevertheless, the fact that such stories circulated at all reflected the political anomaly that the Office began to present in the public mind.

---

127 Thomas Markham to Secretary, President's Department, 2 July 1924, *op. cit.*
128 It transpired that both Markham and Hughes were friends, and unable to substantiate their outlandish stories. For general background, see Regan, *Irish Counter-Revolution*, pp. 98–100.
129 See Clare, 'Irish genealogy', p. 45.
130 GO, Personnel File 2, uncat.

FIVE

'Threatened with extinction'?

Constitutional logistics, 1928–43

THE ANOMALY CONTINUES

In 1930, *The Star* (a weekly journal devoted to current political, economic and social affairs in the Free State) articulated general political feeling about the status of the Office of Arms when it remarked:

> Surely it is high time that the office of Ulster King-at-Arms was trans-
> ferred to the Irish Government. We do not know what has led to the sur-
> vival for almost eight years of a little institution like the Arms Office
> under British control at Dublin Castle. The principle seems to be the
> provision of coats of arms for wealthy Americans of Irish origin, but
> there seems to be no good reason why that particular work could not go
> on under Irish control and why any fees obtained for it should not go
> into the national exchequer.[1]

The reason for the continued anomalous position of the Office was, as we have seen, related to the Free State's dominion status and the fact that Ulster King of Arms was a royal appointment that could only be terminated by the death or retirement of Sir Nevile Wilkinson. Whilst Irish officials became increas-ingly aware of this situation, and endeavoured to change it, constitutional restraints resulted in a protracted process of negotiation between 1928 and 1 April 1943, when the Office of Arms was finally transferred.

The peculiar status of Wilkinson was the source of passing comment within Irish Government circles by the late 1920s. In November 1927, Hugh Kennedy, then Chief Justice and formerly first Law Officer of the Free State, was asked by Ernest Blythe, the Minister for Finance, about 'what arrange-ments' had been 'made with Sir Nevile Wilkinson'. Kennedy replied that there

---

1 *The Star Weekly*, 31 January 1930; similar views were expressed in *The Irish Times*, 5 February 1930.

had been none, but in a bid to clarify the complexity of the situation, explained what had happened at the 1922 conferences held in the Colonial Office.

At these conferences, Kennedy alongside Kevin O'Higgins, then Minister of Economic Affairs, and E.J. Duggan, then Minister of Home Affairs, discussed matters arising out of the working arrangements for the transfer of officials with British delegates, the latter including Prime Minister David Lloyd George and Winston Churchill, then secretary of the Colonial Office. When the discussions eventually came around to the question of Ulster King of Arms, the delegates agreed verbally that he would remain 'an officer of the Crown, with whom [the Free State] would have no concern', because the British 'intended to control the granting of titles of honour and the granting of arms, which in their constitutional theory flow[ed] solely . . . from the Crown'.

Kennedy had also been led to believe that Wilkinson would function from London, 'his only real remaining interest being in Northern Ireland', whilst the building that housed his Office 'was understood clearly by everybody' to be passing to the Free State Government, along with 'the whole of the Castle buildings'. Kennedy was deeply concerned about safeguarding the Office's records and other historical objects such as book-plates, embroidered tabards and other items (demonstrated by his abortive plans with Sadleir to transfer the material to the PRO in 1922). As far as Kennedy was concerned, the records were the priority:

> After some discussion, it was expressly and definitely agreed that there would be no attempt on the part of the British to claim the contents of this office; that they were an Irish historical collection, which we should take over.[2]

Following the destruction of the Four Courts, and also the protestations of Sir Nevile Wilkinson to preserve the integrity of his Office, for which, he argued, its records were essential, nothing further had happened. After 1922, Kennedy confessed that the 'matter dropped', other more pressing issues taking precedence in the immediate aftermath of independence. Five years later, it appeared to Kennedy that the most advantageous course of action was

---

2   Hugh Kennedy, Courts of Justice, The Castle, Dublin, to Ernest Blythe, Minister for Finance, Government Buildings, Merrion Street, 29 November 1927, NAI, DT S3926A. An earlier document in the Kennedy papers reiterates this account of the conferences held in June 1922, Hugh Kennedy, Law Officer's Department, Upper Merrion Street, to 'Mr O'Sullivan', Ministry of Home Affairs, Dublin Castle, 23 August 1922 UCD, P4/175(3).

to postpone the matter until some future date, when the entire transfer of the Office, including its functions, records and contents, might be secured.[3]

Given its imperial status and close links with the Crown, it is hardly surprising that the Office of Arms played virtually no official role in providing services for the Free State Government. As we have seen, the Government had no contact with the Office at all, apart from the aborted plan to transfer its records, friendly co-operation between Kennedy and Sadleir about designs for a possible Free State flag, and very occasional formalities (involving the Minister for Justice to authenticate royal warrants) for changes of name and arms. Indeed, when Government departments in Dublin received genealogical and heraldic enquiries, they were 'embarrassed' about referring correspondents on to 'a British service', preferring instead to advise correspondents to contact solicitors or record agents.[4]

MOVES TOWARDS TRANSFER

Successive Free State governments tried and failed to secure the transfer of the Office during the late 1920s and throughout the 1930s. This was in spite of a changing political climate in Ireland, which was becoming more Republican. By the late 1920s, the Government of W.T. Cosgrave was battling to stay in power against the rising tide of the new Fianna Fáil party, founded by Éamon de Valera in 1926. Fianna Fáil did well at the two general elections held in 1927, posing a serious challenge to Cosgrave's Cumman na nGaedhael party, which had survived in government only because of support from the Labour Party. Labour had little regard for the monarchy, demonstrated by the refusal of its parliamentary representatives to take the oath of allegiance to the King. Cosgrave was thus under considerable pressure to take a firmer stand on Irish sovereignty and do away with outstanding imperial links in Ireland, such as the Office of Arms.

In 1928, attempts to reconstitute the Order of St Patrick were firmly resisted by Cosgrave's Cabinet, which backed its Attorney General's opinion that the 'moribund' Order had no future in the Free State and should disappear.[5] Indeed, when Cosgrave received information that the infamous 'Crown

---

3   Hugh Kennedy, Courts of Justice, The Castle, Dublin, to Ernest Blythe, Minister for Finance, Government Buildings, Merrion Street, 29 November 1927, NAI, DT S3926A.

4   Minute relating to communications received by the Irish Government, intended for the Office of Arms, February 1937, NAI, 54618A.

5   Cabinet minute, 21 May 1928, NAI, DT S5708. See also, Galloway, *Most Illustrious Order*, pp. 123–4.

Jewels' had been found (information that later turned out to be untrue), he instructed that they should be purchased by the Government, if only to ensure that any attempt to use them to revive the Order might be quashed.[6]

Wilkinson's punctilious requests for permission from the Governor-General to accompany Titania's Palace abroad, submitted prior to his many trips away, increasingly ruffled the constitutional feathers in Dublin.[7] Adhering to the imperial status of his Office, and respecting the Free State's dominion status, Wilkinson was merely paying a courteous formality, having already secured sanction from the Dominions Office, the Governor of Northern Ireland, and the King. But by addressing these requests to the Governor-General, he was in effect bypassing the Free State Government. In 1928, when he approached 'His Excellency' in this way before his extended trip to America, the Free State Government had had enough. It was striving to diminish the position of the Governor-General, and Wilkinson's direct requests to him – to which it had no option but to accede – were embarrassing. Indeed, they raised:

> in an acute manner the ambiguous position of the Office of Arms and of Sir Nevile Wilkinson, who is apparently paid by the British Treasury, and subject to its control, yet occupies quarters in Dublin Castle.[8]

Reflecting a hardening of attitude on the whole question of the anachronistic Wilkinson and his anomalous office, a series of memorandums, official opinions and related correspondence followed, as the Free State endeavoured to secure the transfer of the Office to its control. When the matter came before the Cabinet on 1 September 1928, it announced simply that it had 'decided to take over the service of the Office of Arms from the British Government, as from 1 October 1928', and sent a despatch to the Dominions Office to that effect.[9]

The matter of a transfer would not be as simple as the Free State Government had hoped, however. The British Government delayed responding to Dublin's despatch until August 1929, the sudden request having necessitated that it conduct 'some research into the constitutional status of the Office in question'.[10] In fact the representatives of several British Government Depart-

---

6   *ibid.,* p. 90.
7   For example, Sir Nevile Wilkinson, Duchess Street, London to 'His Excellency', Mr Tim Healy, Governor General, Vice-Regal Lodge, Dublin, 13 January 1928, NAI, DT S3926A.
8   Opinion of Attorney General, 23 January 1928, *op. cit.*
9   Report of Cabinet meeting, 1 September 1928, *op. cit.*
10   Lord Passfield, Secretary of State for Dominion Affairs, Downing Street, London, to the Minister for External Affairs, Dublin, 19 August 1929, *op. cit.*

ments (including the Treasury, the Colonial Office, the Home Office and Number 10 Downing Street) were called together to discuss the issue in April 1929. The meeting came to the conclusion that 'on political grounds' – the weakening of imperial links with other dominion states – it would be inadvisable to transfer the Office at this point. Whilst citizens in dominions such as Canada and Australia were able to use the College of Arms for their heraldic needs, the tradition in Ireland since 1552 had been that it had its own King of Arms, appointed under royal patent. History could not suddenly be rewritten, leaving this dominion without a King of Arms, which it was feared might result in 'very awkward repercussions in other matters and with other dominions'.[11] Significantly, Canada became the first country in the Commonwealth to be granted a new heraldic authority of its own, but this did not happen until 1988, when by royal letters patent, Queen Elizabeth II transferred the exercise of her heraldic prerogative to the Governor-General of Canada.[12] Back in the 1920s, it was not desirable for the British Government to create such a precedent.

Replying on behalf of the British Government in 1929, Lord Passfield, Secretary-of-State for the Dominions, rather 'bamboozled' the Free State Government with political arguments, stating that the transfer request was based on a 'misapprehension as to the relation between Ulster and the Crown'. Ulster King of Arms was a servant of the King, who functioned as part of royal prerogative and was not subject to ministerial control. Thus, his appointment could not be transferred. Even if Ulster and his staff were to receive their salaries from the Irish Government rather than the British Exchequer, Passfield concluded that this would not alter that fact that the appointment was made by royal patent, which could not be revoked.[13]

The opinion of John A. Costello, who had succeeded Hugh Kennedy as Attorney General in 1926, defined Irish counter-argument by this time:

> It is highly anomalous that an Office performing purely Irish functions should be paid for, and the fees gained by such Office received, by the British Treasury. I am clearly of opinion that the Office ought to be taken over by the Irish Government. I do not think that the North have much interest in the matter. If they have any objection to being under the jurisdiction of the Ulster King of Arms functioning for Dublin, it could

11 Treasury minute, 19 April 1929, PRO, T 162/709.
12 *Canadian Heraldic Authority*, p. 3.
13 Lord Passfield, Secretary of State for Dominion Affairs, Downing Street, London, to the Minister for External Affairs, Dublin, 19 August 1929, NAI, DT S3926A.

easily be arranged that armorial matters in connection with the North might be dealt with by the British College of Arms.[14]

Not deterred by Lord Passfield's response, the Irish Government tried again, sending a further despatch to the Dominions Office in January 1930. This reiterated the Irish difficulty with the fact that the expenses of the Office appeared in the annual estimates of the United Kingdom Parliament, while its employees were accommodated in premises belonging to the Free State Government. Again, it proposed to take over the Office of Arms:

> as soon as conveniently may be and make provision for the expenses of the office in the estimates to be presented to Dáil Éireann in respect of the forthcoming financial year.[15]

Another conference of British Government Departments met in March 1930, and was actually forced to concede that the Office was not entirely independent of ministerial control, because warrants to authorise changes of surname and arms had, since 1925, been counter-signed and sealed by the Free State Minister for Justice.[16] Although the occasions on which these were issued were relatively rare – only four changes occurred between 1922 and 1929 – because of the procedure the British were inclined to urge a more cautious approach. As a compromise, the conference proposed that, on the occasion of a vacancy, the position of Ulster King of Arms, 'in so far as he acted under the instructions of . . . the Free State', might be re-examined. Dublin was asked at this point either to consider a conference with the British Government to discuss the issue further, or to simply agree that the existing position would remain unchanged during Wilkinson's tenure 'on the understanding that the whole question should be reconsidered on the occurrence of a vacancy'. Furthermore, this last despatch reminded Dublin that the interests of people domiciled in Northern Ireland had to be safeguarded. The Office of Arms, it concluded, provided heraldic services for the entire island of Ireland: 'the functions of Ulster extend to the whole of Ireland and are not limited to the area of the Irish Free State'.[17]

---

14 Opinion of John Costello, Attorney General, 1 February 1929, *op. cit.*
15 Despatch of the Department of External Affairs, to the Dominions Office, 29 January 1930, *op. cit.*
16 Note of meeting held in the Home Office, and attended by representatives of the Home Office, Dominions Office, the Treasury, the Prime Minister, and the Central Chancery of the Orders of Knighthood, 26 March 1930, PRO, DO 35/359/6.
17 Despatch of the Dominions Office, Downing Street, to the Minister for External Affairs, 4 July 1930, NAI, DT S3926A.

The Irish file on the Office of Arms question reveals that no conference took place, and there was agreement that until Wilkinson either died or retired, the transfer would not be considered. The all Ireland status of the Office made it an attractive symbol of unity in Dublin. Whilst important to clear up outstanding matters, the question of the Office of Arms was not high enough on the political agenda to warrant either Cosgrave's Coalition Government or de Valera's Fianna Fáil Government, which succeeded it in 1932, pursuing it in depth after Wilkinson's departure. Thus, following the exchange of inter-Governmental despatches in 1930, there was no further Anglo-Irish communication on the matter until 1938.[18] Indeed, in spite of its continued anomalous position, the Office of Arms was discussed only once again at Cabinet level in 1931,[19] and mentioned only twice in Irish parliamentary debates before 1943. These latter were merely passing references: once in the Dáil, during question time in 1938, and once in the Seanad, in relation to securing its records; in 1939.[20]

Clearly anticipating that a takeover would eventually transpire, but also indicating that the process would not be immediate, the Secretary of the President's Department in the Free State, Michael McDunphy, had corresponded with Sadleir about the arms of Ireland, in June 1931, thus:

> The question will, no doubt, arise for decision some time, and for this purpose it would be desirable to have before us a memorandum regarding heraldic and other implications of a State coat of arms, especially how they have come to be established in Great Britain, and other countries, and by what authority.

McDunphy also requested details about the shape, colour, and any other heraldic details that, in Sadleir's opinion, would be useful for his Government to know.[21] As he had done in the 1920s, Sadleir again supplied the relevant heraldic information. He advised 'the harp has been from very early times the national emblem ... symbolical of the spirit of the song'. Regarding the colour, he continued: 'the Irish flag has always been blue, that is ultramarine'.[22] This exchange of correspondence was on file when the Irish Government eventually registered the arms of Ireland under its own authority

---

18 M. Moynihan, Secretary, Department of the Taoiseach, to J. P. Walshe, Secretary, Department of External Affairs, 5 February 1942, *op. cit.*
19 Report of Cabinet meeting, 24 April 1931, *op. cit.*
20 *Dáil Debates,* 24 May 1938, *71,* 1535; *Seanad Debates,* 11 July 1939, 23, 808.
21 McDunphy to Sadleir, 13 June 1931, GO, Box Relating to Flags, uncat.
22 Sadleir's reply, undated, *op. cit.*

From medieval times, the harp has been regarded as the heraldic symbol of Ireland. It is the only national emblem in the world to consist of a musical instrument. This heraldic shield, incorporating the arms of Ireland, formerly hung over the Speaker's chair, in the Irish House of Commons during the period of Grattan's Parliament, 1782-1800. After it was sold at auction in 1916, Nevile Wilkinson made several unsuccessful attempts to purchase it for the Heraldic Museum from its new owner, A.W. Turner, a collector in Brighton, England. A note on the back of the shield records: 'The Ulster King of Arms wanted to purchase after I bought at sale and made me promise to give him first refusal before selling to any rebel Irishman. A.W.T.'. When Turner died in 1948, his family offered it to the Taoiseach, Éamon de Valera, who accepted it on behalf of the nation and it is now on display in the Heraldic Museum.

144

in 1945. By then, Sadleir's heraldic advice may have influenced the design of the flag introduced for the Irish President, who had become Head of State in the context of constitutional changes after 1937. The Presidential flag featured the heraldic and considerably older symbol of the harp on a blue background.[23]

FINANCIAL SQUEEZE

Back in 1928, accountants in His Majesty's Treasury were disappointed that the Free State had not secured the transfer. The tone of their minutes and correspondence by the late 1920s and into the 1930s reveals that they wanted rid of Wilkinson by this time, regarding him as 'an absentee par excellence', whose influence in high places frustrated their attempts to have him dismissed. His employment record on file at the Treasury spoke for itself. There had been a succession of repeated absences, on army service during the Great War, on sick leave during the early 1920s, and then latterly on his 'world tours', for which he had 'armed himself . . . with the King's permission to go'. But it was impossible for officials to take any action.[24] In this context, it is not surprising that in 1928 they proposed 'reducing the staff' of the Office, and 'sending its illumination and engrossing work to artists in England', presumably the College of Arms, to cut expenditure.

To his credit, Wilkinson successfully defended his staff members and paid tribute to their work, although he was unable to secure any increase in their salaries. Of Miss McConnell, the herald painter, he commented: 'the Office is very fortunate in securing so clever a painter . . . at her present meagre salary'. In spite of eye trouble, she worked in defiance of doctor's orders to 'keep pace with the very large amount of illuminating work' that was coming in by the later 1920s. The Office's 'high artistic reputation' was, he assured the Treasury, 'mainly due to her exceptional skill', and he warned that to send Irish work for execution in England would 'raise a hornet's nest politically' in Ireland. He referred to ongoing 'encroachments by the Heralds' College' – the College of Arms in London – onto Irish heraldic jurisdiction, which, he claimed, reduced Irish receipts. One flagrant example of this was the College of Arms grant of arms to the Irish tenor John McCormack.

Although an American citizen since 1917, McCormack was born in Athlone, began his career in Ireland, and was, as far as Wilkinson was

---

23 See Hayes-McCoy, *Irish Flags*, p. 227; Ó Brógáin, *Irish Harp Emblem*, pp. 47–61.
24 Treasury minutes on the conduct of Sir Nevile Wilkinson, PRO, T 62/709.

concerned, 'Irish of the Irish'. Such an encroachment rather than his absence, he suggested, might account for reduced income in Dublin. McCormack had in fact received an honorary grant from the College, for which he would not have paid, so Wilkinson's example was not a good one.[25] However, he was adamant that his Office's chief importance should be seen not from 'the fees it collected' but rather by the 'imperial service' it provided for people throughout Ireland, and indeed for people of Irish descent throughout the world.[26] Given that receipts of income had actually increased to £347 for the year 1926–7, on account of growing American business, the Treasury backed down and concluded that its proposed reductions were 'not practical' at this juncture.[27]

To compound its frustrations, the Treasury was asked awkward questions about the anomalous position of the Office of Arms by informed British taxpayers. In June 1929, a letter addressed to the Chancellor of the Exchequer made some pertinent enquiries, such as 'how £1000 a year spent by the British Treasury in Ireland for Ulster King of Arms' could be justified, given that he was 'always travelling abroad or away from the Office?' It demanded that the 'Irish Government should pay [for] it now'.[28] When asked to comment about these allegations, Wilkinson pointed out that they came from an 'infected source' – a cousin of the late Sir Arthur Vicars – and that Vicars, as his 'disgraced predecessor', had 'spent many years trying to oust [him] from office'.[29] It was an interesting connection with the Office's more sensational past, and added fuel to the fire of the Treasury officials, who were glad of any justification for either getting rid of it or at least making it more financially viable.[30]

The prevailing economic climate in the aftermath of the Wall Street Crash and subsequent depression in the United States had reduced the Office's heraldic clientele at this time. To avoid the risk of 'scaring away possible clients', Treasury accountants were dissuaded from increasing fees. Disappointed, they resigned themselves to putting up with Wilkinson's unorthodox methods of managing an Office that was recouping little income, until such time as it was transferred to the Free State.[31]

---

25 Honorary grant of arms, crest and badge, to John McCormack, New York, 28 July 1927, CA, Grants, 94, p. 297.
26 Wilkinson to Mr James Rae, Treasury, 16 December 1928, PRO, T 62/709.
27 Treasury minute, 10 January 1929, *op. cit.*
28 W.H. Vicars, Bath to the Rt. Hon. P. Snowden, Chancellor of the Exchequer, 24 June 1929, *op. cit.*
29 Sir Nevile Wilkinson, Office of Arms [c/o London], to Sir James Rae, Treasury, 19 July 1929 *op. cit.*
30 Treasury minute, 4 August, *op. cit.*
31 Rae to G.C. Whishardt, Downing Street, 20 July 1929, *op. cit.*

Although reference to the King was removed from the Irish Constitution in 1936, this did not affect the operation of the Office of Arms, which continued to issue patents of arms in the name of the King until 1943. This wooden piece, depicting the royal arms, remained on display in the Heraldic Museum until 1981 – symbolic of the Office's royal roots. *Courtesy, Irish Architectural Archive.*

Sadleir remained responsible for the day-to-day administration of the Office in Dublin. Correspondence between him and Wilkinson indicates that they entered into a private 'gentlemen's agreement' during periods when Wilkinson was abroad or on sick leave. When exactly this commenced is difficult to ascertain, but it may explain why Sadleir opened a bank account in London in 1928 to facilitate his own payments.[32] We know from later

32 E.V. Athawes, Treasury Chambers, Whitehall to Thos. Sadleir, confirming that

correspondence that the payments amounted to about half Wilkinson's salary, less income tax, so at least Sadleir was receiving fair remuneration for his additional responsibilities by this stage.[33] He was also actively pursuing his private research interests, including all the 'Irish researches' for Philip Guedalla's biography of the Duke of Wellington, *The Duke*, first published in 1931, which may have supplemented his income.[34]

Once the post-depression lull had passed, Sadleir was able to employ his own assistant to cope with increasing Office workloads. A 'very large accumulation of work' induced him in 1930 to take on a young history graduate from Trinity College, Miss Beryl Eustace (later Phair after her marriage in 1958), whom he paid from his own pocket to assist with searches and incoming enquiries.[35] This would be a propitious appointment, as Miss Eustace became an expert genealogical researcher. Under Sadleir's guidance, she compiled several in-house indexes, including the index to all of the will abstracts in the Office.[36] Her association with the Office continued after its transfer to the Irish Government. Indeed, her professional contact and friendship with Edward MacLysaght, first Chief Herald of Ireland, and his successors continued until her death in May 1990, and provided continuity between the old and new regimes.[37]

Wilkinson's absences from the Office continued in the 1930s. When he applied for leave to visit Australia in 1932, the Treasury reluctantly allowed

---

his monthly salary will in future by paid to Messrs Coutts and Company, London, 9 June 1928, SC.

33 Treasury minute, 30 March 1940, PRO, T 162/709.

34 Guedalla, *The Duke*, p. ix.

35 Wilkinson confirmed that he was glad that increased work justified the employment of Miss Eustace, Sir N. Wilkinson, London, to T.U. Sadleir, Office of Arms, Dublin, 22 September, 1930, SC.

36 GO, MS 429.

37 With guidance from Sadleir and later Edward McLysaght, Miss Eustace compiled several valuable in-house indexes, including the index to all the will abstracts in the Office, which remains an invaluable finding aid, because it is organised by surname. A condensed version of this was later published, bringing the holdings of the Office to a wider audience. Eustace also edited and published several other sources for the IMC that remain invaluable for genealogical research. For background, see McLysaght, *Changing Times,* p. 183. P. Beryl Eustace, 'Index of will abstracts in the Genealogical Office, Dublin', *Analecta Hibernica, xvii,* (1978); other published works as follows: Edward Keane, P. Beryl Phair and Thomas U. Sadleir (eds.), *King's Inns Admission Papers 1607–1867* (Dublin, 1982); Eilish Ellis and P. Beryl Eustace (eds.), *Registry of Deeds Dublin, Abstracts of Wills, iii, 1785–1832* (Dublin, 1984).

him full salary 'on the understanding that [it] would be the last occasion'.[38] It was in fact his last foreign tour, but his influence in high places later prevailed when he was awarded a pay rise of £139 following the coronation of King George VI in 1937, bringing his annual salary to £739.[39] In recognition of his prominent participation at the coronation, which was the last royal event ever attended by an Ulster King of Arms with jurisdiction for all Ireland, a Dresden china figure was produced as an upmarket souvenir. Part of a series of figures of royal courtiers, and unmistakably Wilkinson, it shows him in coronation dress.[40] It has now become a collector's item.[41] Wilkinson was actually accompanied to the coronation by Major Guillimore O'Grady, his Dublin Herald. Significantly, Sadleir wrote on their behalf using the virtually redundant headed paper of the Order of St Patrick to petition places for them in the coronation procession at Westminster Abbey.[42] It would be the last such ceremonial event attended by any representative of the Irish heraldic authority.

REPUBLICAN POLITICS

During the time of Wilkinson's grand participation in world tours and appearances at coronations, political life in the Free State was undergoing dramatic change. The rising tide of Republicanism had resulted in the anti-Treaty Fianna Fáil Party winning the general election of 1932. Once in power, the new Government took radical steps to remove the Free State from the Empire, abolishing the oath of allegiance, and terminating payment of the controversial land annuities, paid by Irish tenant farmers to buy out their holdings.[43] Anglo-Irish relations reached a low ebb when Britain and Ireland became locked in a punishing economic war lasting until April 1938. Whilst relatively unimportant in the context of these political events, outstanding anomalies such as the Office of Arms might have been expected to be resolved by the new Government.

---

38 A.F. James, H.M. Treasury, reporting on the conduct of Sir Nevile Wilkinson, 26 September 1940, PRO, T 62/709.
39 Civil estimates for the upkeep of the Office of Arms, 1937, GO, Box of uncatalogued material relating to expenses and salaries.
40 For a description of Wilkinson's impressive appearance at the coronation, see Countess of Fingall, *Seventy Years Young*, p. 334.
41 One such figure is now in the collection at the College of Arms, London. I am grateful to Mr Thomas Woodcock, Norroy and Ulster King of Arms, and Mr Robert Yorke, Archivist, for drawing it to my attention (see Colour Section).
42 Petition for places to be assigned to Wilkinson and O'Grady, at the coronation, written on their behalf by T. U. Sadleir, 27 October 1936, PRO, C 195/5/11.
43 Ward, *Constitutional Tradition*, p. 225.

However, change did not occur quickly. In December 1935, the question of the Office's status was examined following receipt of an application for a royal warrant to process a change of surname and assumption of arms. This was from Richard Mervyn Hardress Waller, who wished to adopt the surname and arms of the Tynte family in order to inherit the estate of the Tyntes of County Kildare.[44] Waller was not prevented from receiving the royal warrant on this occasion – the Government recognised that to block it would have caused 'serious hardship', preventing him from securing his inheritance. However, the Secretary of the President of the Executive Council's Department, Michael McDunphy, questioned the fact that 'two Departments of State' – the Department of External Affairs (which transmitted the warrant to London for royal assent), and the Department of Justice (which processed it for legal purposes within the Free State) – appeared to be 'actively collaborating with the Office of Arms for the purpose of invoking the King's warrant in matters affecting the private interests of Saorstat citizens'. Exploring the matter further, McDunphy concluded the Fianna Fáil Government had inherited the policy of its predecessor:

> that the anomalous position of the Office of Arms, which is a British service, housed in, and operating from, a Government office in Dublin Castle, should be definitely terminated . . . [and that] steps be taken to bring a definite conclusion to the negotiations with the British Government for the transfer of that Office, to the control of this Government which commenced as far back as November 1928.[45]

Again, however, no immediate action was taken. The issue slipped from political consciousness, public demand for changes of name and arms being relatively rare. Indeed, between 1925 and 1935 only five warrants, including Waller Tynte's, signed by the King and counter-signed by the Minister for Justice as the Free State signatory, were registered at the Office of Arms.[46] Following Waller's warrant, another application was not received until February 1938. This, as we shall see, resulted in a new instrument being drawn up, in the light of constitutional developments.

---

44 Copy of the royal warrant to licence Richard Mervyn Hardress Tynte (formerly Waller) to bear the arms of Tynte, 4 December 1935, submitted to the Department of the President, NAI, DT S3926A.

45 Michael McDunphy, Department of the President, to the Secretary, Department of External Affairs, 14 December 1935, *op. cit.*

46 All were registered in the volume entitled 'Royal Proclamations'; covering the period 1910–46, GO, MS 154A.

REMOVAL OF THE KING FROM INTERNAL POLITICS

The abdication of King Edward VIII in December 1936, prior to his coronation, was used by the Irish Government as the means of eliminating all references to the Crown from its internal affairs. The Constitution (Amendment No. 27) Act 1936 deleted all references to the King and Governor-General in the Constitution of 1922. To maintain some link with Britain and the Commonwealth, a concurrent piece of legislation, the Executive Authority (External Relations) Act 1936, retained the King 'as a symbol of the co-operation' between Éire and other Commonwealth States'. King Edward's successor, George VI, thus continued to act for the Irish Free State in relation to its external or foreign affairs.[47]

With specific reference to the Office of Arms in the context of these changes, de Valera's advisers noted that its functions were 'not confined to the Irish Free State', but extended 'to the whole of Ireland'.[48] Rather downplaying its role, and clearly unaware that its heraldic practices had continued to flourish since 1922, one memorandum stated that no grants of arms had been issued since the foundation of the State. Furthermore, it continued, only occasional confirmations of arms, and warrants for changing surnames and arms, were issued in addition to genealogical research. A few weeks after introduction of the new constitutional amendments, in January 1937, de Valera personally directed that 'the Office of Arms be excluded from the general legislation dealing with the King's former powers'.[49] The Department of External Affairs later confirmed that no further development had taken place 'in the matter of taking over the service'.[50]

Enactment of the 1937 Constitution, introduced in the Dáil in May 1937, and which came into force following referendum, on 29 December 1937, did however, result in a major change in the format for the registration of a change of name and arms. The new Constitution repealed the Free State Constitution of 1922, and declared Ireland or Éire (its designation in Irish) to be 'a sovereign, independent, democratic state'.[51] In future 'all powers, functions rights and prerogatives' formerly exercised by the Free State, as a dominion, were

---

47 Ward, *Constitutional Tradition*, p. 229.
48 Memorandum by Michael McDunphy, Department of the President, 31 December 1936, NAI, DT S3926A.
49 Memorandum on 'Royal grant of permission to bear arms' by Michael McDunphy, Department of the President, to the Secretary, Department of External Affairs, 4 January 1937, *op. cit.*
50 Memorandum of the Department of External Affairs, 19 January 1938, *op. cit.*
51 Article 5, *Bunreacht na hÉireann*.

vested in the people of Ireland.[52] For the purposes of executing legal instruments, the people, represented by the Government, replaced the King. A new instrument replaced the royal warrant formerly used.

Thus, when Geoffrey Henry Julian Skeffington Smyth applied to take the surname and arms of Fitzpatrick to fulfill the terms of the will of his grandfather, Lord Castletown, and so to inherit his estate, a new style of licence was designed, issued in the Irish language – the first official national language under the new Constitution – and registered in the Office register for the purpose. Instead of the King, the Taoiseach (Prime Minister), Éamon de Valera, signed the licence, and it was sealed with the Government Seal.[53] It was then directed to the Office of Arms for registration, 'in the same manner as royal licences had formerly been', and duly entered in the volume formerly used for royal warrants.[54] Thus, continuity of registration was maintained although the authority under which it was issued had changed. Irish Government officials specifically paid tribute to Sadleir for his assistance in facilitating the changes to in-house documentation.[55]

It is worth noting, however, that no engrossed entry of the licence was entered into the Register. Instead, the typewritten licence, bearing de Valera's signature and the Presidential Seal, was simply stapled into the volume formerly used for royal warrants and proclamations. Sadleir's disapproval of the new political regime in the Office of Arms, may perhaps explain the unimpressive method of recording the first instrument made solely under Irish Government authority.

The new Constitution had created the President as the Head of State to take precedence over other persons in the State, and the Presidential Seal Act 1937 made provision for a Presidential Seal to authenticate official and judicial documents, such as orders, commissions, warrants and other instruments.[56] The Seal, as demonstrated by the example on Skeffington Smyth's licence, was in the form of a circle, embodying the national emblem, the harp, with the name of the State underneath, and surmounted by a ring of Celtic ornamentation. The image of the harp was based on the instrument known as the Brian Ború harp, housed in Trinity College, while the surrounding ornamentation had been

---

52 Article 49, *op. cit.*
53 Memorandum relating to procedure regarding grant of licences authorising change of name and assumption of arms, 5 April 1938, NAI, DT S3926A.
54 GO, MS 154A.
55 The Secretary, Department of External Affairs, to the Secretary, Department of the Taoiseach, 5 May 1938, NAI, DT S3926A.
56 McDunphy, *The President of Ireland*, p. 87.

adapted from details on the Ardagh Chalice.[57] Unlike the Great Seal designed and registered for Northern Ireland in 1924, the new Seal of Éire was made under the auspices of the Government, without any consultation or subsequent registration in the Office.

The Office had no contact with presidential matters until after it was transferred to the Irish Government, when the arms of President Séan T. Kelly, the second President of Ireland, were registered in 1945. The first President, Douglas Hyde, a personal friend of Sadleir's, already had personal arms.[58] There was no new registration of his arms to mark his elevation to the highest Office in the State. Although his inauguration took place in Dublin Castle, on 25 June 1938, neither Sadleir nor Wilkinson was invited to the ceremony. Beryl Eustace later recalled that the Office staff watched the arrival and departure of dignitaries for the historic event from the balcony of the Bedford Tower.[59]

In regard to the new procedures relating to the registration of changes of name and arms, the British Government noted the 'alteration in procedure relative to exercise of functions . . . enacted by article 49 of the new constitution', and declared its willingness 'to accept any other consequences that might result from the new constitutional position', in relation to the functions of Ulster King of Arms.[60]

Concurrent changes to the procedures for granting and confirming arms were clearly expected to follow, for Wilkinson called on the Irish High Commissioner in London to assure him that 'it was his wish to work in the friendliest relations with the Éire authorities', in the context of the new Constitution.[61] Further minutes drafted by the Dominions Office, and related correspondence, show that Wilkinson actually reached an agreement with the Department of External Affairs in relation to making grants and confirmations in the context of the new Constitution. He assisted Irish parliamentary draftsmen to make 'certain alterations in the customary wording' of the patents, so as to make them 'conform with the wishes of the government of Éire', including replacing reference to 'the King' with the 'Government of

---

57 *ibid.*, p. 88–9. For interesting background about the debate on the design of the new seal, see *Dáil Debates,* 17 November 1937, 69, 992.

58 These are recorded with the Hyde family pedigree, GO, MS 263.

59 Personal communication of Beryl Eustace Phair to Dr Peter Galloway. I am grateful to Dr Galloway for providing this information.

60 Dominions Office minute, 20 April 1938, PRO, DO 35/894/9.

61 Report of meeting between Sir Nevile Wilkinson and Mr Joseph Walshe, 22 April 1938, *op. cit.*

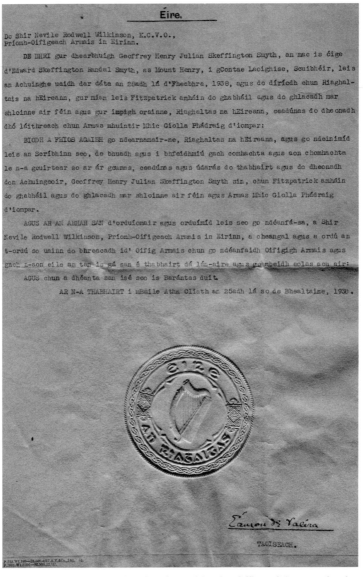

The first document issued and registered by the Office of Arms under the authority of the Government of Ireland (Éire An Rialtas) was a licence to Geoffrey Henry Julian Skeffington Smyth, permitting him to change his name. It was signed by the Taoiseach, although issued by Sir Nevile Wilkinson – described in the document in Irish for the first time, as Príomh-Oifigeach Armas in Éireann (Principal Herald in Ireland). The rusty staple that affixed the document to the register and mis-spelling perhaps indicate the internal scepticism about the new political regime. *GO, MS 154A.*

Ireland'.[62] Drafts of these documents survive in the files of the Dominions Office,[63] but they were not executed.

No alterations to the form of words used in grant and confirmation patents occurred. It appeared to be simpler to leave them the way they were, given that no changes were made to documents issued to people in Northern Ireland or elsewhere. The Office continued to issue all its patents 'by virtue of the power . . . given by His Majesty's letters patent under the Great Seal', and dated in accordance with the year of the reign of King George VI, for people domiciled within Éire, Northern Ireland, and also for Irish-Americans. That this practice was quietly allowed to continue, in spite of the constitutional changes of 1937, is confirmed by the contents of the Register of Arms for the period 1932–43.[64]

At question time in Dáil Éireann in May 1938, when asked to state whether or not the Office of Arms had been taken under the exclusive control of the Government, de Valera informed the Dáil that it was under negotiation:

> The answer is in the negative. The position of the Office of Arms is at present under examination between this Government and the Government of the United Kingdom.[65]

This did not allay concerns in Northern Ireland circles that the Office was doomed in the context of the new constitutional position in Dublin. Indeed, following the publication of one speculative press article, with the headline 'Éire may soon take over [Ulster King of Arms] duties',[66] the Northern Government raised the question of relocating it in Belfast to preserve its royal integrity. In October 1938, a memorandum circulated to all departments warned:

> The institution [Office of Arms] is now threatened with extinction and this will doubtless be its fate within the next year or two, probably unless Ulster [Northern Ireland] gives it a home'.[67]

The Belfast relocation proposal marked a radical shift of Northern Ireland policy on the matter, as the expense of such a move had previously been

---

62 Wilkinson, Office of Arms, Dublin Castle, to the Under-Secretary of State for Dominion Affairs, 21 July 1938, *op. cit.*
63 *op. cit.*
64 These are recorded in the Register of Grants, 1932–43, GO, MS 111G.
65 Question relating to the position of the Office of Arms, by Deputy Nicholas Wall, 24 May 1938, *Dáil Debates,* 71, 297.
66 *The Irish Times,* 30 September 1938.
67 Northern Ireland cabinet circular, 1 October 1938, PRONI, CAB 9R/51/22.

In Witness whereof I subscribe these Presents with my Name and Title and affix hereunto the Seal of my Office this First day of February in the Twelfth year of the Reign of Our Sovereign Lord George the Fifth by the Grace of God of the United Kingdom of Great Britain and Ireland and of the British Dominions beyond the Seas, King, Defender of the Faith and so forth, and in the year of Our Lord One Thousand nine hundred and twenty two.

After 1922, and until 1943, all grants and confirmations of arms issued by the Office of Arms were dated in accordance with the year of the reign of the British sovereign, and either sealed with the Great Seal or the Seal of Ulster King of Arms. *Detail from grant of arms registered in GO, MS 111C.*

considered too great a burden for the fledgling Northern Government.[68] However, after Wilkinson's superintendence of the early ceremonial events linked to the founding of the new Government in 1921, there is little evidence of any further prominent role in Northern Ireland for Ulster King of Arms in relation to ceremony. Events such as formal opening of the new parliamentary building at Stormont by the Prince of Wales in November 1932, for example, were handled entirely by civil servants in the Government Office at Hillsborough.[69] Later, one Northern Ireland official commented that since 1922 the role of the Office of Arms had 'gone through various vicissitudes' with the result that 'Ulster King of Arms, who is really responsible for ceremonials in Ireland, had no part in anything which occurred up here'.[70] Whilst individual clients from Northern Ireland did continue to apply for heraldic and genealogical services, the Northern Government had increasingly little recourse to refer to the Office, having secured its own heraldic identity by 1925. With the shadow of War looming in Europe, the relatively insignificant issue of Ireland's Office of Arms slipped down the political agenda in Belfast, as well as Dublin.

---

68 PRONI, CAB 9R/51/22.

69 Papers relating to the opening of the Parliamentary and Administrative Building, Stormont, November 1932, *op. cit.*

70 Oscar Henderson, Government House, Hillsborough, to R. Gransden, Cabinet Secretary, Stormont, 2 January 1941, PRONI, CAB 9R/52/1.

In the context of the Office's uncertain future and Sir Nevile Wilkinson's absence, entries in the Registers of Arms became more haphazard and rough in format. In this example, Thomas Ulick Sadleir, MA, MRIA, Barrister-at-Law, and Deputy Ulster King of Arms replaces his name on a document previously typed for Wilkinson, when issuing a grant of arms to James Corry Emerson, of Doon House, Corranny, Enniskillen, County Fermanagh, 11 July 1938. *GO, MS 111F.*

WARTIME AND UNITED IRELAND IDEALS

At some point after the outbreak of the Second World War in September 1939, Wilkinson and his wife returned to Ireland, anticipating the German bombing campaign in London. He did not take any further active part in the Office's management, however. Upset by international events and his sudden relocation, and also demoralised by Ireland's changed constitutional position, Wilkinson suffered a severe nervous breakdown in October 1939, from which he did not fully recover. He was in a nursing home in Dublin for at least five months until April 1940, and later recuperated at Shelton Abbey, Arklow, County Wicklow, the home of a family relative, the seventh Earl of Wicklow, until his death at the age of 71 in December of that year. His widow Beatrix married Wicklow two years later in Christ Church Cathedral, Dublin, on 5 March 1942.[71]

Sadleir quietly carried on the business of the Office, and it was when Wilkinson returned that the Treasury accountants became aware of the un-

---

71 *Complete Peerage*, vi, p. 625.

official financial arrangements between Wilkinson and Sadleir.[72] Having stopped Wilkinson's pay for three months as a result of his incapacity, they actually reinstated it in April 1940 to ensure that Sadleir would get a fair reward for his additional responsibilities via Wilkinson.[73] The situation was unorthodox to say the least, but the Treasury had given up trying to introduce any reforms, particularly as Sadlier was shouldering the work, faithfully calling on his senior colleague on a regular basis at the nursing home to keep him updated about business and obtain his signature for patents.[74]

Sadleir must have known that his days as a royal official paid by Whitehall were numbered. Once Wilkinson died, the additional income recouped from their agreement stopped. This had an immediate effect, forcing him to withdraw his two sons from school because he could no longer afford their fees.[75] Until the end, however, he carried on, perhaps unrealistically hopeful that the Office might retain its royal brief. He even secured a bust of Queen Victoria and other objects from the Record Tower (probably left there in 1903) for display in the Heraldic Museum, in May 1940.[76] His friend John Betjeman, the Cultural Attaché to the British Representative in Éire, promised him in August 1941 that he would try to make 'discreet propaganda about the continuation of his Office'.[77]

In the wartime context, having successfully ended the punishing 'economic war' with Britain and secured the 'Treaty ports' in April 1938, de Valera was content to delay matters relating to the transfer of the Office of Arms, especially as jurisdiction continued to include people in Northern Ireland. Whilst it might retain imperial connections, by May 1938 the Office of Arms had become the last office within the State providing services for citizens on both sides of the Border. As such it offered an attractive means of underlying the aspiration enshrined in Article 2 of his new Constitution, that 'the national territory extended to the whole island of Ireland', and he was prepared to let it be. This all Ireland dimension was clearly of great significance, the Department of External Affairs advising in November 1938:

---

72 Treasury minute, 30 March 1940, PRO, T 162/709.
73 Sadlier to Rae, 12 April 1940, and Rae to Wilkinson, 24 April 1940, PRO, T 62/709.
74 *op. cit.*
75 Interview with Randal Sadleir. See also Sadleir, *Journey to Republic*, pp. 6–13.
76 Thomas Sadleir, Office of Arms, to Mr Morrisey, PRO, requesting return of objects from the Record Tower 'to wit, a wooden spear, a wooden sword and a plaster bust, believed to represent Queen Victoria', 4 May 1940, NAI, DT S3926A.
77 John Betjeman, UK representative to Éire, 50 Upper Mount Street, Dublin, to Thomas Sadleir, 20 August 1941, SC.

it would be better to leave it as it is until we make some further progress on the unity issue. It is, after all, a good thing to have at least one office in Dublin with functions for the whole of Ireland.[78]

When Wilkinson passed away in December 1940, Irish policy was still inclined to delay the transfer, because by then the War had begun. Irish neutrality, and the controversial decision not the allow Allied forces to have access to the 'Treaty ports' were prevailing issues. Sir Winston Churchill had become Prime Minister in May 1940, and encouraged his War Cabinet to apply economic pressure on Éire to force a change of policy. The possibility of a united Ireland was even floated, although not seriously enough to encourage de Valera to give up Irish neutrality.[79] Any contemplation of reopening negotiations for the transfer of the Office of Arms was demurred by his Department of External Affairs:

We should only risk another snub if we brought up this question during the War period. Apart from not wanting to give us any concessions just now, the general British attitude with regard to outstanding anomalies is to let sleeping dogs lie. Moreover, we have so many important things to extract out of the British that . . . introduction of the Office of Arms would give a wrong view of our sense of proportion.[80]

Hopeful that the aspiration to Irish unity might be realised during or after the War, de Valera's preferred course of action, in relation to the Office, was that:

the whole question of the transfer of the Office and [its] records might be left over until after the War . . . provided that it is understood that the appointment of an officer to perform the functions of Ulster [King] of Arms can and will be left in abeyance in the meantime.[81]

An oral tradition exists that Churchill became so frustrated about de Valera's refusal to reconsider giving Allied warships access to the 'Treaty ports', that he personally involved himself in the final negotiations about the transfer of the Office of Arms, to safeguard the heraldic interests of British subjects in Northern Ireland. Whilst no documentary evidence can be found to verify the

---

78 J.P. Walshe, Department of External Affairs, to the Secretary of the Department of the Taoiseach, 4 November, 1938, NAI, DT S3926A.

79 Ward, *Constitutional Tradition*, pp. 250–1.

80 Walshe to P. Kennedy, Department of the Taoiseach, 7 May 1941, NAI, DT S3926A.

81 Opinion of Éamon de Valera, as transmitted by Moynihan to Walshe, 5 February 1942, NAI, DT S3926B.

story,[82] Churchill's direct involvement in the process, which the British chose to conclude before the end of the War, seems to suggest that it may be true. Indeed, he gave personal instructions to the Dominions Office that he was to be 'consulted . . . before any action be taken'.[83]

A DIVISION OF FUNCTIONS BUT THE RECORDS SECURED

The new Irish Constitution had moved the goal posts, as far as the British Government was concerned. A successor to Wilkinson as Ulster King of Arms could no longer be appointed as before, because there were now two jurisdictions in Ireland operating under two Great Seals, one for Northern Ireland and one for Éire. There was, simply, 'no prospect of securing agreement to the appointment of a King of Arms with jurisdiction in respect of the whole of Ireland'.[84] Whilst the functions of the Office of Arms in relation to citizens of Éire and people of Irish descent elsewhere in the world might be transferred to Dublin, those concerning people living in Northern Ireland could not be transferred.

A division of functions was unavoidable, although the Irish Government was disappointed by the prospect, believing it to be 'an acceptance of partition'.[85] To safeguard Northern Ireland interests, British policy was that 'the functions of Ulster King of Arms ought to be preserved at the College of Arms in London', where the Norroy King of Arms would be styled 'Ulster' in addition to his existing title. To facilitate this arrangement, the practical co-operation of the Irish Government was sought in relation to the records of the Office. Initially, the British Government suggested reocating the whole of the records to London.[86]

Irish officials successfully opposed this latter demand. Joseph Walshe, the chief negotiator at the Department of External Affairs, articulated the sentiments of Hugh Kennedy at the Colonial Office conferences back in 1922, by arguing that the records 'formed part of the essential documentation for the writing of Irish history', and must remain in Dublin.[87] Sir John Maffey, the

---

82 Interview with Randal Sadleir, who has a clear recollection of his father recounting this version of events.

83 Dominions Office minute, 11 January 1941, PRO, DO 35/894/9.

84 Final agreement in relation to the Office of Arms, drawn up by the Dominions Office, 6 January 1943, DO 35/894/9; Sir John Maffey to Walshe, 26 February 1943, NAI, DT S3926A.

85 Walshe to Moynihan, 16 January 1942, *op. cit.*

86 Maffey to Walshe 30 December 1941, *op. cit.*

87 Walshe to Moynihan, 8 July 1942, *op. cit.*

British Representative in Éire, respected the Irish 'sentimental attachment' to the records, and urged his Government to reconsider this aspect of the final arrangements. Thus, it was finally agreed that the records of the Office of Arms, spanning over 400 years, would remain in the Bedford Tower. In return, the Irish Government agreed to underwrite the cost of reproducing whatever records were required by Norroy and Ulster King of Arms to allow him to carry out relevant 'Irish' work, for citizens of Northern Ireland.[88]

It is remarkable, given the delicate state of international affairs during the early 1940s, that both Churchill and de Valera found time to devote to the final negotiations leading to the long-awaited transfer of the Office of Arms to the Irish Government, and the concurrent transfer of the title of Ulster King of Arms to the College of Arms in London. The final policy document produced by the Dominions Office for negotiation with the Irish Government was sent to Churchill for his approval,[89] while de Valera personally met with Maffey, to make his views on 'the thorny issue of Ulster King of Arms' known to British authorities.[90] De Valera confessed that his preference for the future of the Ulster title was simply that it would become 'abolished in toto', allowing a successor to Wilkinson to be appointed under Irish authority only. It was his view that the division of functions, creating two heraldic services for Ireland – one in London, and one in Dublin – would create public confusion. However, he agreed to the final offer, 'to get the matter wound up', paving the way for the transfer.[91]

The Irish Department of External Affairs bemoaned the transfer of the Ulster title to London as 'official acceptance of partition', severing 'one of the last links which prevent Éire from becoming a foreign country'. It also regretted that an office-holder styled "Ulster" would have heraldic jurisdiction for Northern Ireland, since the latter consisted of six counties, not the nine making up the geographical province of Ulster which transcended Partition.[92] However, in Dublin there was general relief that the original records were secured. Indeed, the record issue constituted 'the chief Irish element in the whole affair', as far as negotiating officials were concerned, one concluding 'in all the circumstances, we are lucky to get the original documents'.[93]

---

88 Maffey to Walshe, 26 February 1943, *op. cit.*
89 Draft of settlement in relation to Ulster King of Arms, approved by the Prime Minister, November 1941, PRO, DO 35/894/9.
90 'Report of interview with Mr de Valera' by Sir John Maffey, 6 January 1943, PRO, DO 130/137.
91 *op. cit.*
92 Briefing regarding Irish views on the final settlement, prepared for British Prime Minister, by Sir John Maffey, PRO, DO 35/894/9.
93 Walshe to Moynihan, 22 December 1942, NAI, DT S3926B.

Abortive plans to relocate the Office to Northern Ireland came to nothing. The Deputy Keeper of the Records at the PRO in Belfast had intimated that typescript copies of records from Ulster's Office, such as the prerogative administration records compiled by Sir William Betham, be made for his institution.[94] However, no transfer of material to Belfast occurred, either in original or copied format – the arrangement with the College of Arms satisfied the North's heraldic interests.[95] On 5 April 1943, by letters patent, Algar Henry Stafford Howard was appointed Ulster King of Arms, in addition to his existing position as Norroy King of Arms at the College of Arms. For the first time in its long history, the title of Ulster crossed the Irish Sea.[96]

CONTINUITY OF THE OFFICE OF ARMS UNDER IRISH CONTROL

An Office of Arms, however, continued to exist in Dublin, although there was a great deal of uncertainty about its nature and scope under Irish authority. However, de Valera's personal involvement in the final negotiations underlined his commitment to its preservation as a separate entity under the control of his Government. Initially there was speculation on whether it would continue 'in its present form' or become a new centre for the Irish Manuscripts Commission (founded in 1928 to survey and report on manuscript and record collections of literary, historical and genealogical interest relating to Ireland).[97] Enquiring officials were unsure what exactly was envisaged, some even referring to the concept of merging it with the PRO – as mooted by Sadleir and Kennedy back in the 1920s.[98]

A desire for continuity was emphasised by de Valera's personal efforts to secure Sadleir's employment at the Office under Irish control. He clearly respected Sadleir's unrivalled knowledge and experience of its operation, gained during his 27 years of service, and recommended 'an arrangement for the definitive transfer of Mr Sadleir to a post in the civil service of this country'

---

94 D. Chart, Deputy Keeper of the Records, PRONI, Mary Street, Belfast, to Mr Gransden, Government Office, Hillsborough, 22 March 1943, PRONI, CAB 9R/51/22.

95 I am grateful to Dr Michael Goodall of PRONI for verifying this information.

96 Combination of the heraldic offices of Norroy and Ulster Kings of Arms, and appointment of Mr Algar Henry Stafford Howard, April 1943, PRO, HO 45/25901.

97 Memorandum on procedure to take over the Office of Arms, by J. Walshe, Department of External Affairs, 22 December 1942, *op. cit.*

98 Draft report from the Taoiseach's Department to the Department of Finance, February 1943, NAI, DT S2936B.

to facilitate its smooth transfer.[99] He held two private meetings with him to persuade him to come over, in February 1943, offering him 'very generous terms' that amounted to twice his former income as Deputy Ulster. However, whilst an Irishman, Sadleir was also a royalist, whose allegiance to the Crown prevented him from making the transition, and he declined de Valera's offer on the grounds that 'only sovereigns could grant arms'.[100] His wife and children would later lament this determined stand, which put a severe strain on family finances.[101] Arrangements were initially made to absorb Sadleir in the College of Arms in London as a pursuivant, to assist the new Norroy and Ulster King of Arms in relation to Irish business, and he politely informed de Valera of his decision to accept this employment in London. He also agreed to stay on to oversee the copying of the records, and to 'clear off outstanding official business', which in the case of the 'numerous American clients w[ould] necessarily occupy many weeks'.[102] To honour his commitments in Dublin, he advised the College of Arms that he would need six months before commencing work there, the outstanding Dublin work including 'a large number of searches for arms and pedigrees, many copies of documents, and a couple of patents'.[103]

The College of Arms post never materialised for Sadleir. The heavy accumulation of arrears of work and financial deficits incurred by the Office of Arms, and subsequently investigated by the Treasury,[104] combined with Sadleir's name appearing in *Stubb's Gazette*,[105] came to the attention of the College of Arms authorities, who withdrew the offer. Indeed, poor Sadleir's financial difficulties would continue until he secured a post in the legal library of the King's Inns.[106] His faithful service to the old regime was eventually recognised by the British Government when he received a civil list pension for his outstanding contribution to genealogical scholarship.[107]

---

99 *op. cit.*

100 Sadleir, *Journey to Republic*, p. 6.

101 Interview with Randal Sadleir.

102 Thomas Sadleir, Office of Arms, to Éamon de Valera, 18 February 1943, NAI, DT S3926B.

103 Sadleir, Office of Arms, The Castle, Dublin, to Sir Gerard Wollaston, K.C.B., K.C.V.O, Garter Principal King of Arms, College of Arms, London, 15 February 1943, *op. cit.*

104 File of material relating to finances of the Office of Arms, 1943–1947, PRO, T 332/256.

105 MacLysaght, *Changing Times*, p. 183.

106 Interview with Randal Sadleir.

107 Sadleir, *Journey to Republic*, p. 6.

Many observers were skeptical of the future role of the surviving Office of Arms in Dublin under Irish control. Garter King of Arms, Sir Gerard Wollaston, intimated that he would have difficulty recognising the heraldic jurisdiction of a non-monarchial state, warning he would:

> very much protest against any proposal by Mr de Valera – or indeed the government of any dominion – to set up a local heraldic authority not appointed by the King.[108]

When questioned about the Office's future prospects under the new regime, Sadleir was not hopeful:

> When the suggestion was put forward that the grants might be made in the name of the Irish people, Mr Sadleir expressed the opinion that such grants would possess practically no attraction for the kind of persons interested in arms and pedigrees.[109]

When media stories began to circulate of the Government's proposal to link the Office of Arms with the National Library of Ireland, others believed that the Office would not survive:

> This arrangement will not secure anything like the prestige and knowledge possessed by an ancient officer like Ulster, going back centuries. ... The transformed institution will receive few enquiries and probably perish in a few years.[110]

This prediction of the fate of the transferred Office of Arms under its new authority was entirely inaccurate, as the following chapters will demonstrate.

---

108 Sir Gerald W. Wollaston, Garter, College of Arms, to C.W. Dixon Esq., Dominions Office, 6 November 1941, PRO, DO 35/894/9.

109 Interview notes with Thomas Sadleir, conducted by officials of the Northern Ireland Government, 14 March 1943, PRONI, CAB 9R/51/22.

110 D. Chart, Deputy Keeper of the Records, PRONI, Mary Street, Belfast, to Mr Gransden, Government Office, Hillsborough, 22 March 1943, *op. cit.*

SIX

'The new office will carry out the functions of the old'

Transfer and evolution of the GO, c. 1943

GOVERNMENT INDECISION

The negative speculation that preceded the transfer of the Office of Arms to the authority of the Irish Government was not completely unfounded, as the Government itself appeared uncertain about the future administrative framework. While de Valera took a personal interest in the transfer of its records and staff, there was much official indecision about the precise nature of its future administration.

At the request of the Taoiseach's Department, a conference was held in Government Buildings in February 1943 to prepare for the transfer and to 'consider to what Department supervision of the Office might most suitably be assigned'. Officials from the Departments of Justice, Finance, Education and the Taoiseach met with the Deputy Keeper of the PRO, Mr James F. Morrissey, and the Director of the NLI, Dr Richard Hayes. They agreed that initially the Office should be 'assigned to the Department of Education with a view to its being placed under the supervision of the Director of the National Library', and that any change in the nature of its supervision might 'be considered in the light of experience'.[1] To ensure a smooth transfer, it was further arranged that, apart from Sadleir who did not want to come over, the existing staff (including the heraldic artist, typist, messenger/porter, and part-time cleaner) would continue to be employed as civil servants of the Irish Government. Indeed, effecting their transfer was considered 'in the public interest',[2] and the Department of Education later went to the trouble of securing their personnel files from London, to maintain continuity of their salaries and conditions of service.[3]

---

1   Minute of Inter-Departmental Committee Relating to the Office of Arms, 19 February 1943, NAI, DT S3926B.
2   Government Order concerning staffing of the Genealogical Office, 19 April 1943, *op. cit.*
3   Tom A. Belton, Office of the High Commissioner for Ireland, London, to Norman

The transfer of the Office of Arms is announced to the public alongside international events during the Second World War. *Evening Herald*, 1 April 1943.

A temporary Government Order, issued on 24 March 1943, made provision for the creation of a new position of Genealogical Officer within the NLI. This order instructed that 'the said temporary situation' should remain in place only until 30 September 1943, after which it would be withdrawn, pending further arrangements.[4] Significantly, this temporary arrangement was the only legal instrument to cater for the transfer of the last imperial office in Éire from British to Irish control, although it was later formalised by an additional Order, which reinforced the association between GO and NLI.

The first day of April 1943 was designated as the official transfer date for the oldest Office in the State, and news of the impending change gently filtered out in the press. *The Irish Times* made the first comment about the Government's initial intentions:

> The last relic of British rule in the twenty-six counties will shortly disappear with the winding-up of the 400-year old office of the Ulster King of Arms. Within about a month the office will cease to function under its present direction.[5]

It further reported that Mr Edward McLysaght, an inspector with the Irish Manuscripts Commission (IMC), assisted by Mr John Ainsworth, an experienced record agent and the son of a Scottish baronet, would continue to deal with heraldic and genealogical enquiries under the authority of the Irish Government.[6] Continuity of function under Irish control was emphasised by the more republican *Irish Press*:

> The Office will in future be under the care of the National Library, but as a distinct body. The new Office will carry out the functions of the old – the tracing of family pedigrees and the issuing of coats of arms, except the heraldic certificates in future will not bear the signature of the King of England.[7]

Most of the patents issued by the Office of Arms had in fact been signed by the King's representative and only the occasional warrants bore the royal signature. Nevertheless, behind these headlines, the Irish Government remained cautious about continuing an Irish heraldic authority, or any association with

---

Archer Esq., Dominions Office, London, 4 May 1943, PRO, DO 35/1132.
4   Order of the Civil Service Commission, 24 March 1943, *Iris Oifigiúil*, 30 March 1943, p. 201.
5   *The Irish Times*, 24 March 1943.
6   *ibid.*
7   *Irish Press*, 25 March 1943.

the previous regime. The new title of Genealogical Office, or 'GO' as it became popularly known, indicated this caution, and suggests that at the time of the transfer official policy was to retain only the genealogical functions of the Office of Arms. However, external demands for heraldic services soon determined a more positive commitment to the traditions of the Office, and ultimately the Government preserved them, replacing the royal prerogative with its own authority) to enable this to happen.

ASSOCIATION WITH THE NATIONAL LIBRARY OF IRELAND

The decision to transfer the Office of Arms to the control of the National Library of Ireland, founded in 1877, had first been mooted by the Library's director, Dr Richard Hayes, as early as January 1941. Hayes had been appointed in November 1940, just a month before Sir Nevile Wilkinson's death, and that event in December 1940 provided Hayes with an opportunity to seek the expansion of the manuscript holdings of his institution. In contrast to many former directors, Hayes was the first to regard the acquisition of manuscript material as one of the Library's primary functions.[8] His predecessor, R.I. Best, had made a public appeal for documents in 1934, and this paved the way for the more formalised approach adopted by Hayes when he took over in 1940. Previously a record inspector with the IMC, Hayes continued to work closely with that agency after his appointment, overseeing its survey work, reporting on collections in private custody, and encouraging their deposit in the NLI.

Indeed, between his appointment in 1940 and retirement in 1967, thousands of private collections were transferred to the Library's custody and systematically catalogued, some by Hayes himself. Later the catalogue edited by him *Manuscript Sources for the History of Irish Civilisation*, published by the NLI in 1965, together with its various supplements, provided the first comprehensive index of manuscript holdings not only in NLI, but many other record repositories too, including the GO.

Hayes was also responsible for the upgrading of reprographic technology within NLI, including the introduction of microfilming equipment. This enabled the Library to borrow and microfilm considerable quantities of manuscripts from other repositories, an early example of the extensive use of this medium by a custodial organisation. A quarter of a mile of microfilm of material from French repositories alone was procured by 1947. During the 1950s and 1960s, the project was extended to include the filming of virtually

---

8   MacLysaght, *Changing Times*, p. 201.

every Catholic parish register in Ireland, an invaluable development for family historians.[9]

The availability of microfilming equipment in NLI facilitated the Government's obligation to make copies of those registers and other manuscripts in the Office of Arms required by the College of Arms as part of the transfer arrangements with the British Government. The College's Registrar visited Dublin in March 1943, and identified some 112 volumes of records (comprising over 29,000 pages of original text) as essential for the work of Norroy and Ulster King of Arms on behalf of Irish clients. These were microfilmed by Library staff in the Bedford Tower building, creating some 30,000 film exposures at a cost of £1,400, paid for by the Irish Government.[10]

Initially it was the official intention to send the microfilms made in Dublin to London, for reproduction as positive prints, because there was no equipment to output positive photographs from microfilm at the NLI. However, when this particular plan was debated in the Dáil, objections were expressed about the necessity of such work being done in England. As a result, additional equipment was provided for the Library, permitting the 'positive print-outs' to be made in Dublin.[11] The photographic prints were bound up, eventually amounting to 138 quarto volumes and two additional outsize volumes containing photostat copies of pedigrees, and conveyed directly by the Library to the College of Arms between November 1944 and November 1945.[12]

The NLI policy of securing original manuscript sources, particularly those relating to Irish families, and also its ability to make duplicates of the records, provided the context for Hayes's successful bid to secure the original records of the Office of Arms. Just a week after Wilkinson's death, he informed the Department of Education that many of the NLI's holdings (such as its extensive newspaper collections, and growing numbers of estate and family papers) would be complemented and enhanced by those created by former Ulster Kings of Arms. Given the increasing demands on his own institution for information about family history from people at home and abroad, he was convinced it represented a good arrangement:

---

9   Lyne, *Survey*, p. 69.
10 Papers relating to the reproduction of microfilm copies of the records of Ulster King of Arms, by Messrs. Kodak and Co., April 1943, NAI, S13207.
11 *Dáil Éireann, Debates,* 19 May 1943, 90, 289,
12 These 140 volumes continue to be used by the College of Arms, London, for business on behalf of Irish clients. Each volume is of high quality, and prefixed with a cover letter from an NLI official giving the details of its content and date of despatch from Dublin bound into the front.

> The unique manuscripts in the Ulster Office [*sic*] are part of the national inheritance in which every Irish citizen has a right to share. It is an anomalous position that they should be in the custody of another State . . . such national resources should be made directly available to all those who are devoting their efforts to the investigation of Irish history, and . . . they can be made available to the nation most appropriately by their transfer to the National Library of Ireland, where they can be consulted for twelve hours a day in conjunction with the Library's great collections of books and manuscripts relating to Ireland, and Irish newspapers.[13]

While the transfer of the Office was delayed for a further two years, Hayes's early anticipation of the potential value of its resources for developing genealogical research within his own institution was not forgotten when the transfer was eventually concluded in 1943.

There was nothing new in the concept of the Office of Arms becoming a genealogical service within a larger institution. Elaborate plans for just such a relationship within the PRO in Dublin had been drawn up during the 1920s. By the 1940s, the decision to merge with the NLI rather than the PRO appears to have been determined by the increasing availability of genealogical sources available in the former repository as a result of its active acquisitions policy. Indeed, no other repository appears to have shown any interest in the material – Hayes's letter of January 1941 being the only one on file.

IRISH HERALDIC JURISDICTION?

For all Hayes's interest in securing the records of the former Ulster's Office for NLI, which represented an archival triumph as far as he was concerned, initially he had no desire to continue its heraldic practices. Indeed, he informed the Department of Education a week before the transfer:

> While not questioning the right of the Government to make grants of arms to individuals inside or outside the State, I would suggest that the making of grants of arms and confirmations of grants should not be continued. No modern republican state makes grants of arms. United States citizens, for example . . . may apply to the College of Heralds in

---

13 R.J. Hayes, Director, National Library of Ireland, Kildare Street, to the Secretary, Department of Education, 8 January 1941, NAI, DT S3926B.

London. I understand that the College . . . will continue to grant arms to citizens of Éire if they apply for them.[14]

Hayes's reservations undoubtedly reflected early official policy. A memorandum circulated by the Department of Education on 30 March 1943 feared that the continuity of the practices of the old regime might be seen as unconstitutional, given that these had been so closely associated with the royal prerogative. Furthermore, they might also be perceived to elevate certain members of society by confirming a status of gentility or nobility, which would contravene Article 40 of the Constitution.[15] The Department was also unsure whether new legal instruments might be required for issuing patents of arms, and was reluctant to explore the possibility of devising them:

> It is not clear whether legislation would be necessary to regulate the position and define the authority, and the undesirability of promoting such legislation is at present obvious.[16]

Thus, on the eve of the transfer Government policy regarding heraldic jurisdiction was unduly negative. It concluded: 'it does not appear to be necessary or desirable to provide for the continuance of the issue of grants of arms. No modern state has adopted this practice'.[17]

No firm decision was made until after the transfer had taken place, but the initial caution explains the change of title from 'Office of Arms' to 'Genealogical Office'. This was intended to emphasise its then primary genealogical role, and steer the focus away from its heraldic functions. But in spite of the new working title, the words 'Formerly Office of Arms' were also retained to appear in brackets after it.[18] This format continued to be used on Office stationery, and in the entries for the GO in telephone and street directories. One of MacLysaght's first tasks on taking charge was to remove the brass sign that had been affixed to the front door of the Bedford Tower since 1903 bearing the words 'Office of Arms', and to replace them with the words 'Genealogical

---

14 R.J. Hayes, National Library, to the Secretary, Department of Education, 22 March 1943, *op. cit.*

15 Article 40.2 of the Constitution provides: 1. Titles of nobility shall not be conferred by the State. 2. No title of nobility or honour may be accepted by any citizen except with the prior approval of the Government.

16 Memorandum of the Department of Education entitled: 'Issues for Government decision in connection with the transfer of the Office of Arms, 30 March 1943, NAI, DT 3926B.

17 *ibid.*

18 *ibid.*

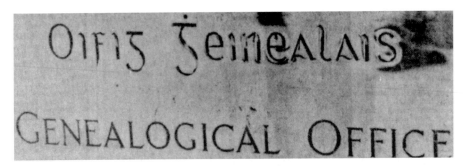

Brass plate reversed to bear the new Office title in 1943.

Office – formerly Office of Arms' engraved on the back. Whilst marking a break with the past, retention of the old title allowed continuity from the previous regime, helping also to draw public attention to the fact that the Registers of Arms and other sources created under the old regime were still available for consultation in the GO.

TRANSFER CEREMONY

On 1 April 1943 (April Fool's Day, no less), a low-key, but nevertheless significant, ceremony was held in the Office of Arms to mark its transfer from the British Crown to the Irish Government. Given the political significance of the fact that this was the very last British office to be handed over, not only did the Minister for Education, Thomás Derrig, the Director of the National Library, Dr Hayes, and the Secretary to the Taoiseach, Maurice Moynihan, accompany MacLysaght, but the Taoiseach, Éamon de Valera and the Táiniste, Seán T. O'Kelly, were present too. MacLysaght recorded the day's events in his pocket diary thus: '9.30–1.00 UO [Ulster's Office], Dev. 2.30–3.30 NL [NLI], 3.30–5.00 UO', suggesting that the Irish delegation met at the NLI, and went over to the Castle together.[19] The occasion received good press coverage; *The Irish Times*, for example, commenting:

> This event marks another stage in the extension of Irish sovereignty which previously had not covered this Office . . . [following] today's ceremonies, Mr Thomas Sadleir, who till last night was acting Ulster King of Arms, hands over charge of the office to the newly-appointed Genealogical Officer of the National Library, Mr Edward McLysaght.[20]

19 Pocket Diary of Edward MacLysaght, commencing 29 March 1943, GO, uncat.
20 *The Irish Times*, 1 April 1943.

The transfer party inspect a rolled grant similar to the one below. *Left to right, front:* Dr Edward MacLysaght, incoming Chief Genealogical Officer, and later first Chief Herald of Ireland; Thomas Derrig, Minister for Education; Thomas Sadleir, last Acting Ulster King of Arms; Éamon de Valera, Taoiseach; *back:* Richard J. Hayes, Director, NLI. From Edward MacLysaght, *Changing Times* (Gerrard's Cross, 1978).

The 'transfer party' was welcomed into the Bedford Tower by Thomas Sadleir, who was officiating for the last day at the helm. He took them on a tour of the building, including the strong room and the Heraldic Museum. A photograph of the guests poring over the documents appeared in some newspapers.[21] Several interesting manuscripts were on display, including the pedigrees of several members of the Irish nobility who had emigrated to France as a result of the Penal Laws – the "Wild Geese". Also shown were the arms of Northern Ireland, designed and issued by the office in 1924, and an example of the prescribed formula for grants of arms issued under Cromwell between 1654 and 1660. Sadleir explained to the guests that instead of the Crown, these had been issued under the Lord Protector's letters patent, when the title of 'Ulster King' was dropped and replaced by the simpler title of 'Principal Herald for the whole Dominion of Ireland'.[22] Sadleir had clearly given some thought to the selection. He may have

---

21 For example: *Evening Herald* 1 April, 1943; *The Irish Times,* 2 April 1943.
22 *The Irish Times*, 2 April 1943; *Irish Press*, 3 April 1943.

Example of a Cromwellian grant of arms issued to Dr William Petty, 'Doctor of Physick, Fellow of the College of Physicians', of Southampton, England, in recognition of his 'survey and ad-measure' of the forfeited lands in Ireland. This was granted as an 'especiall impresse of honor', by Richard Carney, Principal Herald of Arms for the whole dominion of Ireland', issued under letters patent of the Lord Protector, Oliver Cromwell, 20 March 1656. In the 1940s, the form of words used in such a grant, which contained no reference to the Crown, was used to demonstrate that the Office could function in a republic. The arms of Ireland; of Cromwell; and of Dublin are depicted along the top. Petty's arms are inset with the text of the grant. *GO Collection.*

wanted to demonstrate to the politicians how the Office had continued to function in spite of changing political circumstances. Whilst unable to engage with the new political authority himself because of his personal loyalty to the Crown, it seems that he was not averse to communicating the Office's colourful past, and the manner in which it had transcended political change through its long history, to the representatives of the new political regime.

Wilkinson's original deed of trust for the Heraldic Museum, which included a clause that in the event of the Office being abolished the contents of his Museum should be transferred to the National Museum of Ireland, was considered. However, to emphasise continuity from the past, Hayes urged the Department of Education to make alternative arrangements to preserve the integrity of the collection and maintain it *in situ*. He was anxious to secure the material for NLI. On 8 April he informed the Departmental Secretary that he took the view 'that the Office has not closed down, but is being continued under a changed title'. Sadleir and the other trustees, Captain Crawforth Smith (its curator) and also Major Guillimore O'Grady were contacted, and they agreed to transfer the objects to the NLI, provided that nothing would be added or removed without consultation with them.[23] As a further measure of co-operation and continuity, it was also arranged that MacLysaght would become an additional trustee, which Hayes believed would 'help to make relations' between the existing trustees and Library 'closer in the future'. He later secured a grant allowance of £50 from the Department of Education to purchase materials for the Museum.[24] With the compliance of the Irish Government, a number of items relating to the Order of St Patrick, including two volumes of its Register and the Seal of the Order were later removed by Sadleir to London.[25]

OFFICE POLITICS

It must have been hard for Sadleir to leave the Office that he had faithfully served for almost 30 years, but he had turned down the offer to take it over. Dr Edward MacLysaght (or 'Mac' as he was known to colleagues and friends) became the first Genealogical Officer by default. A respected Gaelic scholar and historian, MacLysaght had an impressive track record as an IMC inspector, having salvaged many records in ancestral homes and solicitors' offices throughout the country. In recommending that he take over the Office as 'our genealogical officer', Hayes considered him the 'only person' with the 'adequate experience in investigating Irish family history' or competent enough to conduct searches in the Office of Arms and other repositories. Not only had he surveyed many hundreds of collections as an inspector, he had also published a family history of his own.[26] The Chairman of the IMC, Dr Eoin Mac-Néill, was happy to release MacLysaght 'in view of the special importance of the functions hitherto allotted to the Ulster Office of Arms', and the valuable archival material in its possession.[27] Initially he went over to the GO for three

---

23 Hayes to Secretary, Department of Education, 8 April 1943, NLI File on the GO, 1943–77, uncat.
24 Hayes to Sadleir, 29 April 1943, and Sadleir's agreement to same; and Hayes to Department of Education, 5 November 1943, *op. cit.*
25 Central Chancery of the Orders of Knighthood, St James's Palace, to Sadleir, thanking him for a further batch of items, 16 July 1943, SC; see also Galloway, *Most Illustrious Order*, pp. 150–1.
26 Hayes to Secretary, Department of Education, NLI, File on the GO 1943–77, uncat. The family history was: *Short Study of a Transplanted Family in the Seventeenth Century* (Dublin, 1935).
27 Eoin MacNéill to Secretary, Department of Education, *op. cit.*

months, at a salary of £35 per month, pending a permanent appointment at a later date.[28]

A recent survey of MacLysaght's life has described him as a remarkable man,[29] and he certainly had a colourful career. Born and baptised in England as Edward Lysaght in 1887, his ancestry was closely rooted in Counties Cork and Clare. His father was the younger son of a minor gentry family, who had become 'one of the countless Irish emigrants of the nineteenth century but one who never lost touch with his own country', and aspired to return to Ireland.[30] In 1908 he did just that, purchasing a large house and 600-acre estate, including a nursery which, following two terms at Oxford, the young Edward came back to manage.[31] He used the Irish version of his name, MacLysaght, became a Catholic, and was involved in Dublin literary circles and the Gaelic League.

He joined Sinn Féin, and represented that party at the Irish Convention in 1917. His experiences in County Clare during the War of Independence coloured his political outlook. The family farm was raided several times by the Auxiliaries and Black and Tans, and MacLysaght was imprisoned for taking an active anti-military position. When he arrived to take over the Office of Arms in 1943, he confessed that his only previous visit to Dublin Castle had been 'as a prisoner in the hands of the Auxiliaries twenty-two years earlier'.[32] MacLysaght also served as an independent senator in the first Seanad Éireann, before travelling extensively, including a period as a journalist in South Africa during the later 1920s and early 1930s. He returned to Ireland in 1938, and was appointed to the IMC in 1940.[33]

By contrast, Sadleir was born in 1882 at the Curragh Camp, County Kildare, where his father was the Church of Ireland chaplain. Descended, according to his son Randal, through 'a succession of soldiers, sailors, clerics and scholars' from a Cromwellian colonel, his ancestry included several prominent clergymen. In addition to his father, Sadleir's grandfather and great-grandfather were Anglican clergy – the latter, Franc Sadleir, having been Provost of Trinity College Dublin between 1837 and 1851. He epitomised a Protestant Anglo-Irish identity, his life revolving around the 'cloistered world of the Castle, Trinity College, St Patrick's Cathedral, and the Kildare Street

---

28 Hayes to Secretary, Department of Education, *op. cit.*
29 Lyne, *Survey*, p. 68.
30 MacLysaght, *Changing Times*, p. 8.
31 *ibid.*
32 *ibid.*, p. 181.
33 For a comprehensive summary of his life, see Lysaght, *Edward MacLysaght, 1886–1986.*

The panelled sanctum of successive kings-of-arms under the old regime was occupied by Edward MacLysaght from March 1943, and was known as the Chief Herald's room from 1945. *Courtesy, Irish Architectural Archive.*

Club'.[34] Proud to his death in 1957 that he had been the last British servant to serve in the Irish Free State, Sadleir's departure from the Office was tinged with sadness, perhaps even regret, that he could not identify with the new regime that had eventually taken it over some 21 years after Independence.

The reflective memorial that his family erected after his death in Castle-knock Parish Church sums up the dilemma felt by Sadleir and many members

---

34   Sadleir, *Journey to Republic*, pp. 5–6.

of the so-called 'Ascendancy' Anglo-Irish. They were both Irish and British, loyal to the Crown, yet aware of their own distinctive Irishness:

> His life was spent during changing days in the country's administration and he, as Deputy King of Arms, was made more acutely aware of these changes on account of the nature of this work and the scope of his interests . . . he generously made available the fruits of his research to many an inquiring historian and was always ready to rescue all too easily-forgotten facts.[35]

The different backgrounds and political outlooks of the two men contributed to real tensions, both personal and political, in the Office of Arms, making the final months of transition between old and new regimes tense and difficult. For practical reasons, MacLysaght had actually commenced work at the Office of Arms on 1 March 1943, a month before it was officially transferred. This was to allow him to meet the other staff members and to learn as much as he could about the operation before taking over. Whilst MacLysaght had hoped to be coached and let loose in the strong room during this period, it transpired that Sadleir was too busy clearing outstanding work. MacLysaght was instead left alone all day in the panelled sanctum of the late Sir Nevile Wilkinson's former room, surrounded by the armorial bearings of successive kings of arms, and could only see whatever manuscripts Sadleir passed into him each day.[36] This undoubtedly soured relations between the two men.

MacLysaght would later criticise his predecessor rather unkindly as an 'unrepentant Unionist in politics, having nothing but ascendancy contempt for the new regime'.[37] By his own admission, MacLysaght regarded himself to be 'an amateur in genealogy and an ignoramus in heraldry', and this did not endear him to Sadleir.[38] Sadleir was as critical of MacLysaght as MacLysaght was of him. This became clear on one occasion when the Treasury had asked him to furnish a pedigree to a client of the old regime, outstanding for four years. Sadlier claimed the delay was MacLysaght's fault. Having visited the Office to inspect the records, he located the pedigree immediately and sent off a copy with apologies to the client. He lamented to the Treasury that he was

---

35 Sadleir died on 21 December 1957. The memorial was unveiled sometime in the spring of 1961 by the Most Revd Dr George Otto Simms, Church of Ireland Archbishop of Dublin. I am grateful to the Revd Sandra Pragnell for this information.
36 MacLysaght, *Changing Times*, p. 177.
37 *ibid.*, p. 182.
38 *ibid.*

unable to tell the client that 'the person now in charge of Ulster's records is bad-tempered and anti-British'. He added unkindly:

> When Mr MacLysaght took over he had no knowledge of the contents of the Office, in fact he was a historian not a genealogist, and I think his search was probably incomplete.[39]

Although he started from a low basic knowledge of heraldry, MacLysaght was quick to learn, and soon developed an appreciation for the subject. His early knowledge had actually started before his appointment, because he had been a client of the Office of Arms under the old regime, although he was reluctant to admit this. In February 1937, MacLysaght had been issued with a certificate of the arms of his ancestor John Lysaght, later Baron Lisle, signed by Thomas Sadleir, Deputy King of Arms, while the Lysaght family pedigree had previously been registered in the Office.[40] Unusually, Sadleir, at MacLysaght's request, had actually cancelled a confirmation of arms, issued to his father Sidney Royse Lysaght by Sir Arthur Vicars in 1904, then residing in Somerset,[41] preferring instead to identify with the heraldic heritage of his Gaelic ancestry. Knowledge of his family's own genealogy and heraldic identity, as registered in the Office of Arms before the transfer, must have made him aware of its symbolic importance and potential under Irish authority. He expressed his new found enthusiasm with a determination that as an 'Irish Government service [it] could be run in a business-like way', in all its aspects.[42]

ARREARS OF WORK

Just prior to the transfer, Sadleir had been, according to himself, inundated by telephone, telegram and letter enquiries from people all over the world 'making last-minute requests to have heraldic or genealogical work done . . .

---

39 T.U. Sadleir, Kildare Street Club, Dublin, to Mr Cook, Treasury Chambers, 7 February 1947, PRO T 21/156.
40 Certificate of arms to Edward MacLysaght, Raheen, Tuamgraney, County Clare and other descendants of his ancestor Patrick MacLysaght, alias Lysaght, of Tully-brackey, County Limerick, 6 February 1937, GO, MS 111E, p. 53. The Lysaght family pedigree had previously been registered, GO, MS 175, pp. 517–22. The certified arms were those of John Lysaght, who served under Lord Inchiquin, and who became Baron Lisle, in 1758, *Burke's Peerage and Baronetage* (1999), pp. 1732–3.
41 GO, Ms 111J, p. 159.
42 MacLysaght, *Changing Times*, p. 184.

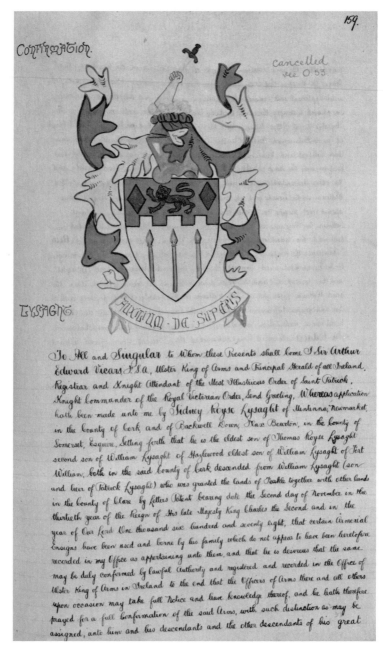

Confirmation of arms to Sidney Royse Lysaght, father of Edward MacLysaght, registered by Sir Arthur Vicars in 1904, and subsequently cancelled by Thomas Sadleir, Deputy King of Arms, at MacLysaght's request in 1937. *GO, MS 111J.*

under the old regime'. These flooded in during the run-up to 1 April, following the press announcements about the impending transfer.[43] The pressure of work appears to have been mounting for some time, resulting in some work being completed in haste. For example questioning the validity of one confirmation that had been issued back in 1938, MacLysaght later annotated it to the effect that 'the whole thing looks fishy, but being pre-1943 we can only accept it'.[44] Other applications for arms that came in during the last weeks before the transfer, and for which fees had been paid to the Treasury, were eventually completed by the GO.[45]

Whatever his political preferences, it is clear that MacLysaght soon became frustrated by the arrears of work that he inherited, and this may explain why Sadleir found him bad-tempered. He was surprised to find how poorly the Office had been run during the last six years of its existence under royal authority, and inclined initially to blame this on Sadleir's inefficiency.[46] However, Sadleir laid all the blame for the outstanding work on Wilkinson's absences and illness. He confided in Sir Arthur Wollaston, Garter King of Arms, that 'the fact that Sir Nevile was nearly two years in a mental home caused arrears, and with a small staff it has been impossible to overtake them'.[47]

MacLysaght's surprise at the administrative laxities he encountered on taking over soon turned to frustration when he realised the implications for the new regime. The Registers of Arms were in arrears by up to eight years, no copies of outgoing correspondence had been made, and accounts were 'nonexistent'.[48] The absence of any day-books (recording visitors and general business) for the entire period between 1936 and 1943 was another indication of poor administration. It appeared to MacLysaght that the official work had come to a halt in 1937, and he noted that 'no record, official or otherwise was kept of grants, confirmations etc after 1937'.[49] Significantly, MacLysaght opened new 'Post-in' and 'Post-out' Books, accounting for all correspondence; Registers of

---

43 *The Irish Times*, 1 April 1943.
44 Confirmation of arms to Charles Henry Vereker, City of Limerick, Esq, 7 February 1938, GO 111F, p. 260.
45 MacLysaght, *Changing Times*, p. 183.
46 *ibid.*
47 T.U. Sadleir, Office of Arms, to Sir Gerald Wollaston, Garter, College of Arms, 15 February 1943, NAI, DT S3926B.
48 MacLysaght, *Changing Times*, p. 183.
49 Edward MacLysaght, Genealogical Office, Dublin Castle to Sir Algar Howard, Garter King of Arms, London, 4 December 1944, GO, File Relating to Transfer, uncat.

Visitors; and Daily Registers to record the hours of staff members, several series of which remain uncatalogued in the strong room to this day.

There were some 118 pieces of outstanding work to be processed by the old regime when the Office was transferred on 1 April 1943. This total consisted of 41 pedigree searches, 22 copies of documents, 21 sketches of arms, 13 searches for arms, 9 confirmations, 8 certificates, one grant of a crest and sundry other jobs.[50] In addition, patents that had already been completed and despatched to clients as far back as 1932 had yet to be registered. MacLysaght insisted that to complete 'registration of outstanding cases . . . no where officially recorded', a new register was to be created.[51] This consisted of rough typewritten and handwritten entries, hastily put together, reflecting the pressure that Sadleir was under to bring things up to date. Its rough format also contrasted starkly with the meticulous and colourful registrations of earlier years, which until 1933 included colour reproductions of the emblazoned arms. Eventually this last register of the old regime recorded the registration of some 209 grants, confirmations and certificates, issued between 1932 and 1942. According to the fly-leaf at the front of the volume, it accounted for all the work executed 'during the last eight years before Ulster's Office was taken over by the GO, registration of which was not carried out by the late Deputy Ulster', although it actually covered the last ten years.[52]

To be fair to Sadleir, he had worked in difficult conditions for most of his career at the GO, contending with a manager who was frequently absent, inadequate staff resources, low salary, and incessant interruptions from increasing numbers of visiting enquirers. He did not want 'to hand over imperfect records' any more than MacLysaght wanted to receive them, and made arrangements to stay on for a month after the transfer to help bring them up to date as well as fulfilling outstanding orders.[53] This was, however, a totally unrealistic timeframe to cope with the scale of the outstanding work. When his promise of a post at the College of Arms fell through, the one month at the GO was extended, and in return for a lump-sum of £250 paid to him by the Treasury, he appeared content to work on.[54]

By June 1943, some 47 pieces of work had been completed, including 19 pedigree searches, but this reduced the backlog by only a third. By October,

50 List of outstanding work at the Office of Arms, March 1943, PRO, T 21/156.
51 MacLysaght to Sadleir, 20 March 1944, GO, File Relating to Transfer, uncat.
52 GO, MS 111F, p. 1.
53 Sadleir to Sir G. Wollaston, 15 February 1943, NAI, DT S3926B.
54 C.W. Dixon, Dominions Office to Mr Hankinson, Home Office, 28 September 1943, PRO, DO 130/37.

Sadleir had reduced the deficit to 63 pieces of outstanding work, but then discovered another 18 unprocessed confirmations, which, when informed about them, understandably made MacLysaght angry, as these had to be finished too.[55] To facilitate the completion of these additional confirmations, MacLysaght then arranged to 'lend the services of the heraldic artist', Miss Mary McGrane (in employment since 1929), to Sadleir to complete the outstanding artwork for the old regime, although she was now an 'Irish civil servant'. In December 1943, she was spending two thirds of her time on 'Ulster's arrears', even though the Irish Department of Finance paid her salary. MacLysaght warned that this could not continue indefinitely.[56] In March 1944, the arrangement was terminated, forcing Sadleir to employ his own external artist.[57] But the arrears continued, and in October 1944, MacLysaght told Sadleir that his patience had come to an end, being in constant receipt of complaining letters or meeting dissatisfied customers, who referred to the GO as a 'swindling office'. He even feared that 'the unsavoury odour which attached to the Office towards the end of its existence as Ulster's Office was being carried over' to the GO – in other words, the delays of completing work.[58]

Although he had departed as Acting Ulster King of Arms, Sadleir continued to be a trustee of the Heraldic Museum until his death in 1957. This lingering presence at the GO may have allowed him to keep up his private genealogical practice, which MacLysaght appears to have facilitated. MacLysaght explained to one client in December 1945, that although Sadleir's 'official connection with th[e] Office' ceased in March 1943, he continued to enjoy 'research facilities not available to the general public'.[59] As late as February 1947, Sadleir was still back and forth to the Castle from the King's Inns Library, checking queries and apparently employing an 'outside artist' to finish outstanding patents, although the artist has not been identified.[60]

Whilst MacLysaght found Sadleir's continuing presence exasperating, notwithstanding their political differences he soon came to appreciate the difficult working conditions under which his predecessor had been forced to operate in the years before the transfer, and how these had led to administrative

55 Schedule of outstanding work to be completed by Thomas Sadleir, 12 October 1943, GO, File Relating to Transfer, uncat; MacLysaght, *Changing Times*, p. 183.
56 MacLysaght to Sadleir, 9 December 1943, GO, File Relating to Transfer, uncat.
57 MacLysaght to Sadleir, 20 March 1944, *op. cit.*
58 MacLysaght, Genealogical Office, formerly Office of Arms, to Sadleir, King's Inn's Library, 23 Ocobter 1944, *op. cit.*
59 MacLysaght to Miss Henrietta Malley, Connecticut, United States, 22 December 1945, GO, *op. cit.*
60 PRO, T 21/156.

problems. Indeed, he would inherit many of them himself. The Irish Department of Education proved no more inclined to invest in Office administration than the British Treasury had been before April 1943. Limited staff resources, low pay, and curtailed finances continued as repetitive themes under the new regime, and also reflected the Irish Government's hesitancy about engaging in future heraldic practice.

STAFFING CONSTRAINTS AND OTHER DRAWBACKS

Contrary to press speculation at the time of the transfer that John Ainsworth would assist with the work of the GO, he played no official role in its work. Ainsworth actually replaced MacLysaght as an inspector with the IMC, and was given a desk in the room next to MacLysaght's, demonstrating the close links that existed between the IMC and NLI. Ainsworth's presence in the GO may, however, have been beneficial, as he was son and heir to a Scottish baronet of Irish origin, with an understanding of heraldry. Indeed, he was the first individual to receive a grant of arms under the authority of the Irish Government in 1943.[61] But he was busy on behalf of the IMC, and did not fulfil MacLysaght's need for more constant specialist support.

To compensate for the training which Sadleir had failed to give him prior to the transfer, and to cope with the demands of work that came flooding in after he took over, MacLysaght employed Beryl Eustace (later Phair), and paid her himself, in the same way as Sadleir had done since 1928. She was by then an experienced researcher, and instrumental in helping him to find his feet, as well as providing research continuity between the old and new regimes. MacLysaght later admitted that he might have had a breakdown from the strain of work without her assistance.[62] He also engaged the services of Terence Grey, an amateur but skilled genealogist, who was happy to work without remuneration. He persuaded the other trustees to make Grey a trustee of the Heraldic Museum, and this enabled Grey to hold keys to the building, allowing him to come and go as he pleased without requiring official sanction.[63]

By June 1943, MacLysaght had convinced Hayes that he needed a full-time assistant, competent enough to learn the 'highly technical' work required. Hayes agreed to create a new post to assist him, although it took over a year

---

61 Grant of arms to John Francis Ainsworth M.A., F.R.H.S, 13 August 1943, GO, MS 111Q, p. 2.
62 MacLysaght, *Changing Times*, p. 183.
63 *ibid.*, p. 189.

for the plan to be fulfilled.[64] Under the auspices of the IMC, a teacher-training lecturer and arts graduate, Gerard Slevin, was recruited from a panel of applicants for various archival posts in both the NLI and PRO in October 1944.[65] MacLysaght was grateful that the NLI decided to 'assign' Slevin to work at the GO as his assistant. He was interested in heraldry, and quick to learn, soon becoming MacLysaght's 'official coadjutor and assistant in all matters', and 'well-versed in the sciences of heraldry and genealogy'. In February 1947 he became armigerous, MacLysaght granting a coat of arms as his deputy, for the dignity and 'proper execution of the duties of his office'.[66] Slevin's assignment at the GO continued for 37 years, as MacLysaght's deputy between 1944 and 1954, and then as Chief Herald until 1981.

Staff shortages prevented the dynamic development of the GO that both MacLysaght and Slevin wanted to see, hindering the implementation of indexing projects and creating a backlog of research work for external enquirers. This was estimated to be about three years in arrears by the 1960s. As a branch of the Library, the GO was dependent on the availability of staff there who could be assigned to it. Staff numbers in the Library were low too and this had a detrimental effect on the GO. Apart from the secretarial staff inherited from the old regime, and Slevin's valuable support, MacLysaght was unhappy with his staff quota. He was only on the grade of Assistant Librarian, and argued that he needed two assistants at the same grade to work on research and general administration plus a clerical officer, in addition to the typist, artist, and man in charge of the Museum.

Although a second typist was brought in by early 1947, MacLysaght became so frustrated by pressure of incoming work that he threatened to resign, on the grounds of 'overwork and underpay' in 1949. But the Library was short of two assistant keepers at this time, and there was no opportunity to allocate extra staff to the GO. Anxious not to lose his expertise, a deal was struck whereby MacLysaght was appointed Keeper of Manuscripts at the NLI in addition to retaining the 'titular' position of Chief Herald. Thus, he continued to sign patents and other administrative documents, but had little to do with the day-to-day management of the GO. This was left to Slevin, who effectively ran the Office on the grade of library assistant between 1949 and 1954, relying on whatever occasional staffing the Library could provide from time to time. The wrangle for additional staff continued. The GO's report, contained

---

64 Hayes to Department of Education, 24 June 1943, NLI, File Relating to GO, uncat.
65 MacLysaght, *Changing Times*, p. 224; *NLI Trustees Report*, 1945–6, p. 1.
66 Grant of arms to John Gerard Slevin, MA, 28 June 1947, GO, MS 111Q, p. 38.

in the *Annual Report of the Council of Trustees of the National Library to the Department of Education* for 1954–5, reflected its difficulties:

> Since no extra staff is available to meet this continued pressure of work, it is found impossible to proceed with several projects, such as indexing large numbers of manuscripts in the collections.[67]

Whilst the specialised work at the GO did not appeal to many of the Library staff who were required to make the temporary sacrifice of working there, some were interested, such as John Barry, who was employed as an assistant during the 1950s and early 1960s. Remembered for his scholarly expertise, Barry, who went on to teach history at University College Cork, became deeply interested in the Office's heritage, and published a guide to the records in 1970, which included general information about Irish heraldry and the history of the Office of Arms.[68]

Although unsuccessful in securing an increase of full-time staff, MacLysaght did persuade the Department of Education to recruit self-employed researchers, who were paid by the hour, and directly by the Department, to complete commissioned searches. In 1944, Mary Read, a young arts graduate and also Slevin's sister-in-law, was brought in to help with the hundreds of research enquiries that flooded in, for which she was paid the princely sum of 3s. 6d. (less than 22 cents) per hour.[69] Read was instructed by Beryl Eustace Phair,[70] who took her around the main repositories, introducing her to the main sources for genealogical research and supervising her early research reports. Continuity of the GO's role as a focal point for genealogical research was preserved, because Phair had learned from Sadleir, under the old regime. A house-style was developed for the research reports commissioned by clients, which was continued by later researchers. These included Rosemary ffolliott, Eileen O'Byrne and Eilish Ellis, who are well-known figures in the world of genealogy today. Again, they were introduced to the sources in various repositories, and set to work on specific searches under instruction. Soon they became skilled in their work and would, in turn, instruct the next generation of professional genealogists.

---

67 *NLI Trustees Report*, 1954–5, p. 9.
68 Barry, 'Guide to records'.
69 Recollection of Mary Nowlan (neé Read), GO Researcher, 1944 – 57.
70 Beryl Eustace married the Rt. Revd John Percy Phair, the Church of Ireland Bishop of Ossory, 1940–62, in June 1958, RCBL, MS 345/9, p. 3.

CONTINUITY OF AN IRISH HERALDIC AUTHORITY

In spite of the difficulties, and for all his self-professed ignorance of heraldry, MacLysaght was determined to preserve the heraldic heritage passed on to him. Within a week of taking over, he received an application for the right to bear arms from Robert R. McCaffrey, living in the United States. The application – representative of the ongoing demand for heraldic and genealogical information from the Irish abroad – allowed him to make a strong case to the Government for continuing the practice of granting and confirming arms. On 8 April, Hayes informed the Department of Education that Mr McCaffrey's application raised the 'question as to whether we are to make grants of arms', and required that the matter be settled 'in order that a reply' might be sent to him. Hayes admitted that since he had by then 'a little more experience of the work of the Office' he was prepared to concede that it would be difficult to refuse the making of grants of arms and confirmations, 'most genealogical enquiries [being] connected in some way with them'.[71]

The Government reached a positive decision for continuing the heraldic practices of the old regime with 'surprising promptitude'.[72] At a meeting held on 16 April 1943, orders were given that 'the Office should continue to discharge the function of the making of grants of arms'.[73] The precise wording of future grants remained uncertain, however, and further consultation between the Department of Education and the Attorney General was advised to make provision for this. Perhaps in order to camouflage any possible association with the royal authority that had preceded it, the Government reiterated its earlier view that the Office should function as a branch of the NLI at this point, and the words 'National Library of Ireland, Genealogical Office', were ordered to appear on all future correspondence.[74] This latter instruction appears to have been unheeded, however, the words 'Office of Arms' continuing to appear as before.

The framework for the future operation of the GO, in relation to heraldic business, resulted from the Attorney General's consultative meeting with MacLysaght and other Department of Education officials on 3 June, 1943. MacLysaght came to the meeting armed with examples of documents issued under the old regime, and even the wording of the grant issued during the

---

71   Hayes to Department of Education, 8 April 1943, enclosing letter of Robert R. McCaffrey, of 7 April 1943, NLI, File Relating to GO, 1943–77, uncat.
72   MacLysaght, *Changing Times,* p. 184;
73   Department of the Taoiseach minute, circulated to other Government departments, 17 April 1943, NAI, DT S3926B.
74   *ibid.*

Cromwellian period.[75] Significantly, the forms of words prepared by Wilkinson back in 1938, in the context of the then new Irish Constitution, were also produced, and the formula agreed in 1943 was based on that 'prepared for use in the former Office in 1938'.[76] Three major revisions to the documents resulted from these deliberations, replacing the words relating to royal authority, with new forms of words.

The first revision involved modification of the rather grand form of words used by Ulster King of Arms as a greeting. Thus 'To All and Singular, as well as Noblemen and Gentlemen', was replaced with the simpler and more egalitarian 'To All Whom These Presents Shall Come'. Secondly, the formula to authenticate each document was changed. In contrast with patents issued by Ulster King of Arms under letters patent from the Crown, which were dated by the sovereign's reign and sealed with the Great Seal, the GO patents were issued simply 'by the authority of the Government of Ireland' and dated by day, month and year. The third revision was that the text of all future patents was to be issued in Irish, the first language of Ireland since the 1937 Constitution, with an English translation.[77]

In addition to the draft forms submitted by the Attorney General for the Government's approval, a new Seal of Office was designed to be affixed and authenticated, as required, by the Genealogical Officer. This enabled that officer, or his deputy, 'to prepare and execute under the Seal of the Office the appropriate instruments' for granting and confirming arms.[78] Thus, the new GO Seal replaced the Great Seal of the old regime. The Cabinet approved these recommendations at its meeting on 13 July 1943.[79] On the same day, MacLysaght received his letter of appointment as a permanent member of the NLI staff, under the title Genealogical Officer. This further granted him and his deputy the authority to prepare and execute under seal the appropriate instruments for grants and confirmations of arms in the future.[80] MacLysaght's salary was fixed

---

75 Memorandum on grants and confirmations, by Edward MacLysaght, dated 2 June 1943, GO, File Relating to Transfer, uncat.
76 Attorney General memorandum, 4 June 1943, NAI, DT 3926B.
77 Drafts of grants and confirmations, considered by meeting between the Attorney General and representatives of the Department of Education, 3 June 1943, *op. cit.*
78 Department of Education memorandum entitled: 'Issues for Government decision', 3 June 1943, *op. cit.*
79 Memorandum concerning Government decisions about the Genealogical Office, 13 July 1943, *op. cit.*
80 Letter of appointment of Edward MacLysaght as Genealogical Officer, 13 July 1943, GO, MS 527, p. 2. There was some confusion about the title itself. In some early memorandums it was termed Chief Genealogical Officer, but the 'Chief' part was deleted. By mid-1945, it was replaced by 'Chief Herald'.

Reverse of the wax seal of the GO, bearing the arms of the four provinces of Ireland, as affixed to all early GO patents with ribbon tie. *GO Collection.*

at £400 per annum. Although the post was 'whole time', like Sadleir before him, MacLysaght did not receive a pension.[81]

With the framework in place to permit the GO to continue the heraldic practices of the old regime, steps were taken to clarify the administrative status of the GO, and make provision for the continuity of its traditional functions – the designing, assigning and registering of heraldic property. By the Allocation of Administration (Genealogical Office) Order, made by the Government on 13 July 1943, the administration and business of the Office were formally allocated to the Department of Education, under the Government Seal.[82] Henceforward a new seal, bearing 'obverse [on the front] the harp of Ireland, and reverse, quartering the arms of the four provinces', was affixed to patents and other official documents issued by the GO.[83] Thus, the GO was enabled to perform the heraldic functions formerly exercised by the Crown under the authority of the Irish Government. Although its working title had changed, it continued, in effect, as Ireland's 'Office of Arms'.

In response to his initial application made in April 1943, Robert R. McCaffrey of Boston was issued with a confirmation of arms by the GO on 15 July 1943. This permitted him to bear armorial ensigns long in use by his family. A new patent was issued, and like those of the old regime, executed on vellum. This first document carried the distinguishing features under which future heraldic patents would be issued. The text of the blazon was written in Irish on the left of the patent, with an English translation on the right, and the confirmed arms in the centre. The signature of MacLysaght as Genealogical Officer, and the new seal of the GO affixed with ribbon tie appeared below.[84]

---

81 Salary arrangements for MacLysaght, NLI, File Relating to the GO, 1943–77, uncat.
82 *Allocation of Administration (Genealogical Office) Order, 1943*, S.R.O. No. 267.
83 Description of the seal of the GO in letter from MacLysaght to Maurice Moynihan, Department of the Taoiseach, 27 February 1945, NAI, DT 3926B.
84 Confirmation of arms to Robert R. McCaffrey, Boston, Massacheuetts, 15 July 1943, GO, MS 111Q, p. 1.

A second soon followed when John Ainsworth was issued with the first grant of arms by the GO, in August 1943.[85]

Unfortunately the limited staff resources available to the GO prevented a full copy being entered into a new Register of Arms that was opened for the purpose of registration. Instead, the GO availed of the photographic equipment in the NLI and simply photostated each new patent before it was sent to the client, while a typewritten copy of the blazon (the verbal description of the achievement of arms) was also made. The photostats were kept in portfolios, while the blazon typescripts were filed separately. This continued until 1982, when the practice of making a hand-painted copy of arms and blazon for the purposes of registration was reintroduced, although only until 1995, when this system was again discontinued. Only recently has a full copy been reintroduced as the form of registration. In 1997, the photostat copies made in earlier years were bound and indexed in new registers.[86]

The public response to news of MacCafrey's confirmation in July 1943, whilst low-key, was generally favourable. *The Irish Times* reported:

> When this Office was taken over from the British crown four months ago, there was some doubt as to whether the issue of coats of arms would be continued, as such grants have been made usually by kings. Now, however, this and other functions of the Ulster Office will be exercised by the new office.[87]

The report also drew attention to the cheaper rates offered by the GO in comparison to the College of Arms. Instead of paying £66, as charged in London, it advertised that a new grant of arms in Dublin, including stamp duty, emblazoning and registration, cost only £44. The report further speculated that the GO had inherited the heraldic practice of confirming arms to individuals and institutions who could prove use for at least 100 years – a practice peculiar to Ireland. In contrast to 'the British office [which could] not issue any document corresponding to the Dublin's office's confirmation grant', it presumed that this would continue to be the case in the future.[88]

---

85 Grant of arms to John Francis Ainsworth M.A., F.R.H.S, 13 August 1943, *op. cit.*, p. 2.
86 Registers of grants, 1943–2002, GO, MSS 111Q–111Y.
87 *The Irish Times*, 24 July 1943.
88 *ibid.*

One of the GO's early grants of arms was to Dublin County Council, 30 September 1944. It consisted of a raven standing on a hurdle, both black, on a gold shield background, with a flaming pile crest. The raven was symbolic of Scandinavian influence in the development of Dublin; the hurdle of the fort of hurdles, on which Dublin is said to have been built; and the flaming pile depicting the Fenian saga of the burning castles. The artwork was executed by Nellie McGrane, heraldic artist 1929–55, whose signature may be seen within the shield. *Heraldic Museum.*

A COUNTER-CHALLENGE

These developments surprised officials at the College of Arms in London, who had incorrectly assumed that a local heraldic authority for Ireland would come to nothing. Fearing a loss of revenue for his own institution, and repeating the monarchist view that it was the prerogative of the King alone (as the 'fount of all honour') to grant arms, Sir Gerald Wollaston, the Garter King of Arms accused the Irish authorities of running:

> 'a coach and four through the arrangements which have been made for the transfer of the office of Ulster, and to do all in their power to render those arrangements inoperative. The authority to grant arms emanates from the sovereign.[89]

---

89 Gerald W. Wollaston, Garter King of Arms, to C.G. Markbreiter, Home Office, 6 August 1943, PRO, DO 130/37.

With specific reference to the differences in fees alluded to in *The Irish Times* report, he clarified that the College had been obliged to raise its fees generally 'owing to War circumstances', and claimed:

> when it took Ulster's work, had had to charge considerably more than the former charges . . . with the result that applicants were discouraged from approaching [the College] and preferred to go to the Éire office'.[90]

On account of the loss of business, he continued, the College had 'decided to reduce [its] fees for Irish work, though not to the level of the former scale', in November 1944.[91] When he had been asked to re-register the confirmation issued in Dublin to Robert R. McCaffrey, he replied to this 'in the negative' and refused other similar requests. This rebuff troubled Mr McCaffrey in Boston, who enquired of the GO if his patent could be regarded as legitimate. In December 1943, MacLysaght sought to assure him there 'was no doubt that the patent already issued gave [him] a perfectly legal right to the use of the arms blazoned therein'.[92] But it was clear in Dublin that matters concerning heraldic jurisdiction would have to be resolved. Thus when Wollaston decided to visit Dublin in person, to 'look into the division of the work between the College of Arms and the local office in Dublin', in December 1944, the GO was happy to agree.[93]

Garter's principal meeting in Dublin was with Dr Richard Hayes, NLI Director, and Edward MacLysaght, the Genealogical Officer; but he also met the Taoiseach, Éamon de Valera, whose personal interest in the Office continued, along with Department of External Affairs officials. In spite of his reservations about the new Irish constitutional position, which he initially and incorrectly regarded as 'illegal' because as far as he was concerned Ireland 'remained a dominion', Wollaston found the meetings cordial and friendly. After his four-hour session with Hayes and MacLysaght, he was left in no doubt that 'Dr Hayes and Mr MacLysaght . . . [had] every intention of granting and confirming arms to residents in Éire and to other persons of Irish descent'. They went to some length to explain the new constitutional position of Éire to him, which, unlike Canada and other dominions, had removed the King from its internal politics as a result of the legislative changes since 1936.[94] Whilst unconvinced initially, Wollaston eventually accepted the Irish

---

90 Dominions Office minute relating to comparison of the fees charged by the College of Arms and 'Dublin Heraldic Authority' for Irish work, 21 November 1944, PRO, DO 35/1132.

91 *ibid.*

92 MacLysaght to McCaffrey, 22 December 1943, File of correspondence entitled 'External Affairs', GO, uncat.

93 Dominion Office minute, Sir E. Machtig, to Mr Dixon, November 1944, *op. cit.*

94 Report on Garter's visit to Dublin, PRO, 12–14 December 1944, *op. cit.*

constitutional position, admitting later that the arguments of Hayes and MacLysaght made 'it plain that I should recognise the granting and confirming ... of armorial bearings by the Éire Genealogical Office'. However, he qualified this by seeking to set 'well-defined limits', to control the future practices of both the College of Arms and GO in relation to Irish business.[95]

Regarding grants and confirmations of arms, Garter advised that the GO was authorised to issue them to corporate bodies or persons domiciled in Éire. The applicants should also be given the option of applying to the College of Arms, and advised of this in writing. The arms granted or confirmed by the GO should not clash with any previously granted either by the College or the GO itself. Contrary to *The Irish Times* report, he further advised that Norroy and Ulster King of Arms might continue to make confirmations of arms to British subjects whose paternal ancestors had been domiciled in Ireland, and whose use of arms could be proved prior to 1820. Irish citizens or other applicants (e.g. American citizens of Irish descent) who chose to deal with the Dublin office, might also re-register their Irish arms in London. To facilitate this, Garter recommended that again the GO might advise its own clients in writing that they were entitled to do this. Non-registration in London would not imply any less validity for patents issued only in Dublin.[96]

The arrangement represented a fair Anglo-Irish solution to the potential problems posed by the partition of heraldic jurisdiction between the GO and College of Arms, and appears to have been adhered to in all but one respect. Revealing the ongoing caution of the Irish Government about the whole continued practice of heraldry, which had such close associations with the British monarchy, there were objections to the notion that the GO would 'notify its applicants in writing' that they had the option of going to the College of Arms, if they so preferred. Briefed by the Irish Department of External Affairs, the United Kingdom representative in Dublin warned his Dominions Office that for the 'Éire Genealogical Office to draw attention in writing to the facilities offered by the Crown ... would be likely to lead to complaints in the Dáil or elsewhere'. To avoid such a scenario, Hayes and MacLysaght undertook to advise clients orally.[97]

---

95 Garter King of Arms, College of Arms, London, to E. MacLysaght, Genealogical Office, 14 June 1945, *op. cit.*

96 Sir Howard Algar, Garter King of Arms, to E. MacLysaght, 20 June 1945, GO, Correspondence to College of Arms, 1944–5, uncat. For comparative material in the College of Arms, the Archive of Garter King of Arms, box-file G. 31, and the College's Chapter Books, provide useful background.

97 United Kingdom representative to Éire, to Sir Charles Dixon, Dominions Office, 13 November 1945, PRO, DO 35/1132.

Relations between the GO and College of Arms remained cordial thereafter. The Grant Books of the College of Arms reveal that there was little subsequent re-registration of grants or confirmations issued by the GO in London or vice versa. Between 1945 and 1959, some 98 grants, confirmations and certificates concerning Irish clients were registered in London. Most of these clients were resident in the United Kingdom (including Northern Ireland). Only four of these commissions concerned clients who had previously been issued with patents from Dublin. The first, in 1946, was Eric Hallinan, unusually a Judge of the Supreme Court in Trinidad who, by virtue of being the son of one Edward Hallinan of Cork, was entitled to have his arms confirmed in Dublin. These arms were concurrently registered in London.[98] Two years after receipt of his confirmation from Dublin, Robert R. McCaffrey of Boston, Massachutsetts, applied for a certificate from the College of Arms. The three Kings of Arms – Garter, Norroy and Ulster, and Clarenceux – ratified and confirmed this particular application as 'recently recorded in the Genealogical Office at Dublin'.[99] Two other clients, Lieutenant-Colonel George Robert Gayrne in 1948 and Mrs Anna Sharpe in 1953, chose to have their confirmations as issued by the GO re-registered in full (including the Irish and English texts) in the College of Arms register. This was the first time in the history of that institution that official entries were registered in the Irish language.[100]

Many of the remaining 95 registrations made in London during this period were for Northern Ireland institutions. These included a grant of arms to the Church of Ireland Diocese of Connor, which geographically lies within Northern Ireland, in 1945. Several county and urban district councils were granted arms, including, for example, Antrim County Council and the City of Londonderry in 1952, and the Borough of Ballymena, County Antrim in 1953. Other grants of arms to institutions included Londonderry High School in 1957. None of these grants was re-registered in Dublin.

In contrast, the GO did issue a number of patents for clients in Northern Ireland, who opted to use its services in preference to the College of Arms. For example, Alexander Gault MacGowan, late Captain of King George's

---

98 Confirmation of arms to Eric Hallinan, GO, MS 111 G, p.23; CA, Irish Grants, 1 March 1946.
99 Confirmation of arms to Robert R. McCaffrey, Boston Massechutsetts, 3 June 1946, CA, Irish Grants Register, 3, pp. 63–5.
100 Confirmations of arms to Lieutenant-Colonel George Robert Gayrne, 30 September 1948, and Mrs Anna Sharpe, wife of the Honourable Frank Dale, 9 December 1953, CA, Irish Grants Register, 3, pp. 92, 219.

The Heraldic Museum became an important exhibition space which the NLI helped to develop from the early 1950s. *Courtesy, Irish Architectural Archive.*

Own Light Cavalry and son of Samuel Alexander MacGowan of Ballinderry, County Derry, opted to have his arms confirmed in Dublin in 1946. In 1952, Art O'Lundy resident of Lisburn, County Antrim, who was serving in the Garda Síochána in County Mayo, opted to have his arms confirmed by the GO. In contrast to the Church of Ireland Diocese of Connor, which was entirely situated within Northern Ireland, the Rt. Revd Robert McNeill Boyd, of Ballycastle, County Antrim, who was bishop of that Church's Diocese of Derry and Raphoe, opted to have his personal arms confirmed in the GO rather than the

The advertising signs for the Museum after the transfer featured the new GO arms and opening hours were given in Irish and English. *GO Collection.*

College of Arms in 1953.[101] His decision was symbolic of the fact that his diocese was located on both sides of the Border. None of these commissions were subsequently re-registered in London.

The Irish Nationality and Citizenship Act 1956 declared every citizen born on the island of Ireland to be an Irish citizen, pending the reintegration

---

101 GO, MS 111Q, p. 42; GO, MS 111R, pp. 80, 91.

of the national territory. After this development, some Northern citizens may simply have opted to go to Dublin rather than London for political reasons. Notable commissions after 1956 include a confirmation for Francis Patrick Cassidi, of Magherafelt, County Derry, son of Francis Laird Cassidi, Honorary Surgeon to King George VI, in 1957. In 1958, the Most Revd Dr William Conway, Roman Catholic Auxiliary Bishop to the Archbishop of Armagh, was certified with arms 'for the term of his life'.[102]

Later there was some controversy when the Irish Club in London applied for, and was issued with, a grant of arms by the Irish authority rather than College of Arms. However, the difficulties were overcome when the College agreed that the Irish Club, by virtue of its function and membership, was a special case. The grant was issued from Dublin, in 1960.[103]

For the entire period between 1945 and 1981, the only Northern Ireland client of the College of Arms that opted to re-register its arms in Dublin was the Ulster Transport Authority. Norroy and Ulster King of Arms had granted the company arms in December 1959.[104] However, to symbolise its cross-Border business activities, the company applied to register them at the GO too. The GO issued a certificate to that effect the following year (see Colour Section).[105]

One other example of re-registration in the GO of a grant of arms made by the College of Arms was that for the international Bank of Nova Scotia. In 1966, this company chose to re-register in Dublin, because it had opened a branch in the city. An ornate certificate was issued by the GO, symbolic of the bank's Irish link.[106] Although exceptional examples of re-registration rather than the norm, these cases emphasise that after the initial difficulties, the GO and College of Arms could recognise each other's grants. In the main, the GO catered exclusively for clients domiciled in Éire, and persons domiciled outside Éire of Irish extraction, many of whom 'preferred to come to the traditional Office in Dublin'. The College of Arms tended to cater for clients domiciled in Northern Ireland; but it was by no means a hard and fast rule, and as we have seen notable crossings of the political boundary occurred.[107]

---

102 *op. cit.*, pp. 77, 96.
103 GO, MS 111S, p. 25.
104 Grant of arms to the Ulster Transport Authority, 9 December 1959, CA, Irish Grants Register, 3, p. 251.
105 Certificate of arms to the Ulster Transport Authority, Belfast, 10 June 1960, GO, MS 111S, p. 22.
106 GO, MS 111T, pp. 16, 17.
107 MacLysaght Journal, GO, MS 527, p. 261; see also Pine, *Story of Heraldry*, pp. 111–3.

Many of the early patents issued by the GO were institutional grants and confirmations. The Dublin Stock Exchange in 1945, the Veterinary College of Ireland in 1945, Mellifont Abbey in 1947, and the Irish Medical Association in 1952, were the first institutional recipients of new grants of arms issued under the authority of the Irish Government. The Franciscan College, Multy-farnham, County Westmeath, in 1944, and the Erasmus Smith Schools and Drogheda Grammar School, both in January 1945, were the first institutions to be confirmed with arms already in use, but never previously registered.[108]

---

108 GO, MS 111Q.

SEVEN

'Republican institutions are not necessarily hostile to the practice of heraldry'

The GO as Ireland's heraldic authority, 1945–81

IDENTITY FOR THE IRISH HERALDIC AUTHORITY

By clarifying the legitimate right for the GO to continue the heraldic functions previously practiced in Ireland by succes-sions of kings of arms, the nego-tiations in 1945 guaranteed that

Early letter-head for the GO, incorporating the logo of NLI. *GO Collection.*

the armorial bearings of future GO clients would not be challenged through-out the heraldic world. This seemed to instil a new confidence, and MacLysaght became more innovative.

In 1945, he advised the Department of the Taoiseach that 'it was proper for the heraldic authority in a country to have its own arms, as Ulster's Office had done until 1943'.[1] The Government consented to the adoption of the arms of the

four provinces of Ireland quar-terly, and a portcullis between two scrolls proper, with the motto 'Patrum Memores' (mind-ful, or remembering, the fathers, or ancestors) as the arms of the GO in February 1945 (see Colour Section).[2] Soon after this, the new official armorial bear-ings were used to embellish GO

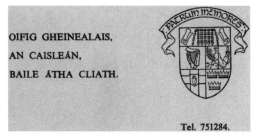

The arms of the GO embellished its stationery from 1945, helping to maintain its integrity. *GO Collection.*

---

1 MacLysaght to Maurice Moynihan, Department of the Taoiseach, 27 February 1945, NAI, DT S3926B.
2 Grant of arms for the Genealogical Office, 21 March 1945, GO, MS 111Q, p.16.

stationery, instead of the official stamp of the NLI, which had been printed on earlier letter-heads. This helped the GO to establish a distinct identity from the Library, while remaining technically part of its administration.

MacLysaght further suggested that it was time for the arms of the State to be formally recorded,[3] and eight months later, on 2 November 1945, the Department of Justice ordered official registration of the arms of Ireland, 'azure a harp or stringed argent' to be effected by the GO.[4] After securing registration of the arms of the State, MacLysaght also endeavoured to make the highest Office of State, that of the President, armigerous too.

As we have seen, the Presidential Seal had been in use since 1937, and it was MacLysaght's idea to embody the features of the Seal into a Presidential coat of arms, which he registered on 21 November 1945.[5] He envisaged that the personal arms of each successive President should be impaled (two complete coats placed side by side within a single shield) with the arms of Ireland 'azure a harp or stringed argent' on the dexter (right side), and the personal arms on the sinister (left side), with supporters, and the motto: 'Do

Arms of Ireland

The arms of Ireland, as registered by the GO in 1945. *GO, MS 111Q.*

dhum glóire Dé agus onóra Éireann'. However, it transpired that future Presidents preferred to become armigerous in their own right. Thus, after Seán T. O'Kelly was elected as the second President of Ireland, in succession to Hyde, in June 1945, he was granted personal arms which were issued on 22 November 1945.[6] O'Kelly was already familiar with the Office and its functions, having been present at its transfer when he was Tánaiste, on 1 April 1943.

Further clarification of the GO's official role was provided by the decision to change MacLysaght's title from the rather anomalous Genealogical Officer, to Principal Herald and Genealogical Officer in November 1945. The title was further modified to Chief Herald and Genealogical Officer following a decision by the

---

3   MacLysaght to Moynihan, 27 February 1945, NAI, DT S3926B.
4   Registration of the arms of Ireland, with related instructions from the Department of Justice, 2 November 1945, GO, MS 111Q, p. 20.
5   Registration of the arms of the President, 21 November 1945, *op. cit.*, p. 21.
6   Grant of arms to Tomás Ó'Ceallaigh, Uachtarán na hÉireann, 22 November 1945, *op. cit.*, p. 17.

Cabinet in February 1946, acting on the recommendation of the Lord Lyon, the principal heraldic officer in Scotland, who believed it would give the Irish office-holder greater authority.[7] The additional title of Genealogical Officer was apparently retained to emphasise the genealogical functions of the GO; but from internal correspondence it would appear that MacLysaght favoured signing himself simply as 'Chief Herald', a practice continued by his successors.[8]

The Chief Herald's seal. *GO Collection.*

The publication of *Intelligible Heraldry*, a popular guidebook about heraldry, in 1948, included illustrations of records in the GO, such as patents issued under the old and new authorities, as well as items on display in the Heraldic Museum.[9] This was the first time that the records had been used for such a purpose, and underlined the continuity between the Office of Ulster King of Arms and the GO. The book included a foreword by MacLysaght, in which he assured the public that the GO continued to 'exercise all the functions formerly carried out by Ulster except the duties [connected with] the Order of St Patrick'.[10] The book was published in the same year as the Republic of Ireland Act 1948, the latter coming into force on Easter Sunday 1949, thereby completing the separation of Éire from Britain and the Commonwealth. MacLysaght used the foreword to declare in public the position that the heraldic authority would take in the context of the new Republic:

> I happen to be the Chief Herald of that country [i.e. Ireland] . . . it is quite natural that . . . we should continue to administer heraldic affairs as part of the functions of the State. Republican institutions . . . are not necessarily hostile to the practice of heraldry. Witness the Venice of the Doges and that most ancient of existing republics, Switzerland, which may safely be described as . . . the most heraldically-minded country in the world.[11]

The book was symbolic of the manner in which Irish heraldry had the potential to transcend the political barrier created by Partition. Written by two brothers, Sir Christopher Henry Lynch Robinson, barrister, of Foxrock,

---

7   Cabinet minute, 19 February 1946, NAI, DT S3926B; also MacLysaght, *Changing Times*, p. 184.

8   NLI, File Relating to the GO, 1943–77, uncat.

9   Lynch-Robinson, *Intelligible Heraldry*, p. 112.

10 *ibid.,* p. vii.

11 *ibid.,* p. v.

County Dublin, and Adrian Lynch, Secretary at the Ministry for Home Affairs in the Northern Ireland Government, of Craigavad, County Down, its authorship was representative of an all Ireland inclusiveness. In a rather snooty review of this book published in the *Sunday Times* in January 1949, Sir Gerald Wollaston, by then Norroy and Ulster King of Arms, was dismissive of the concept of a herald for a Republic: 'I suppose a Republic can appoint an heraldic officer with jurisdiction within its territory, though I do not readily link heralds with Republics'.[12] This partly reflected his personal disdain for the new political regime in Ireland, and resulted in a flurry of letters from English and Irish correspondents, who pointed to many examples of republican heraldry, not least under Cromwell during the Confederacy, which allowed Sir Gerald's notions to be dismissed.[13]

Elsewhere MacLysaght could declare on good authority that the new constitution of the Republic 'made no difference to the heraldic position'. The functions of Ulster King of Arms had been transferred to the Chief Herald of Ireland, who now acted in the name of the Irish people in relation to heraldic matters.[14] The Republic of Ireland became, in fact, the only republic in the world with its own heraldic office. Like many countries, Switzerland, whilst protecting heraldic bearings under the law, had no heraldic officials employed by the State, and thus no heraldic authority as such. The Republic of Ireland remained in this unique position for a further 19 years until 1962, when South Africa which had a heraldic department left the Commonwealth and declared itself a republic.[15]

In Ireland, unlike Switzerland, or even Scotland, the absence of any judicial backing for the Chief Herald's activities limited his scope. The GO had been created by an order that did not confer on it any legal powers, and the Chief Herald was not given any judicial functions, even though the patents issued by him were made in the name of 'the Government of Ireland'.[16] Frustrated by this weak legal position, MacLysaght later bemoaned the fact that administration of the GO had not been assigned to the Department of Justice rather than Education in 1943. Had this happened, he believed, it might have helped to give legal credence to its procedures, such as registration of changes of surnames and arms.

---

12 Wollaston, 'Arms and the man', *Sunday Times*, 16 January 1949.
13 Pine, *Story of Heraldry*, p. 112.
14 Edward MacLysaght's notes on heralds and republics, GO, MS 527 p. 263, and GO, MS 622, p. 112.
15 Lyall, 'Irish heraldic jurisdiction' (1993), p. 134.
16 *op. cit.*, (Spring, 1994), pp. 179–80.

Heraldic illustration depicting the arms of the O'Donnells. *GO Collection.*

In the event, it transpired that a change of surname could more effectively be administered by means of a deed-poll which was processed by solicitors without any need for registration at the GO.[17] As a result, the register used for recording changes of name ceased to be maintained in the GO after 1946. The absence of any legal protection also meant that it was impossible to 'counter the ever-increasing bogus trade in commercial heraldry', or prevent the use of 'phoney arms'.[18]

Demonstrating how far he had come in recognising the importance of a heraldic authority for Ireland, and reflecting the need for its legal protection, Dr Richard Hayes actually included proposals for legal remedies to counter bogus heraldry. The context for this was his involvement in drawing up a new Record Act for submission to the Government. Hayes's ambitious proposals included merging the archive collections of the NLI, GO, PRO and SPO into a single institution, called the 'National Library and National Archives', whilst maintaining the PRO as a repository for more recent and semi-current material of a legal or administrative nature. Nothing came of the proposal, but it did

---

17 MacLysaght, *Changing Times,* pp. 194, 199.
18 *ibid.,* p. 199; Lynch-Robinson, *Intelligible Heraldry,* p. vi.

Heraldic illustration depicting the arms of the McKeons. *GO Collection.*

include an interesting clause about strengthening the legal position of the GO, to protect the grants and confirmations issued under its authority:

> The record act [*sic*] might be used to include a section giving a person who has received a grant or confirmation of arms from the Genealogical Office, or in the past from the Ulster Office [of Arms], the exclusive right to those arms, and a legal remedy against anyone infringing this right.[19]

Unfortunately, the GO was not to be empowered with any legal authority, and was unable to use the force of law to prohibit the unauthorised use of armorial bearings – a situation that continues today.

GAELIC HERALDRY

Whilst legal support did not transpire, the recognition of the GO as an established heraldic authority, and MacLysaght's heightened profile as Chief

---

19 Report on the question of altering the law and practice of the Public Record Office and other archival institutions by R. J. Hayes, Director, NLI, to the Secretary, Department of Justice, 15 February 1945, NAI, typescript copy. I am grateful to Aideen Ireland, NAI, for drawing my attention to this source.

Herald of Ireland, seem to have encouraged him to embark on a number of innovative practices aimed at reviving an interest in Gaelic heraldry.[20]

Early on, MacLysaght recognised the traditional arms used by Gaelic families of antiquity before the foundation of the Office of Ulster King of Arms in 1552. As well as wishing to re-establish this tradition, he sought to introduce heraldry to a wider audience, and to this end he introduced the somewhat controversial concept of sept or clan arms.[21] This was designed to permit individuals with a particular Gaelic surname to display 'without impropriety' the arms associated with that sept. MacLysaght was at pains to point out that such a display did not extend to bearing arms in the true heraldic sense, which continued to require research and proof of descent.[22] However, given that many individuals were unable to trace their lineage for the required three generations, especially as a result of the loss of so many records containing genealogical information in the disastrous fire in the PRO in 1922, he argued that the service of providing illustrations had its merits. It conveyed something of their ancestral identity to Irish people particularly those living abroad, allowing them at least a tentative visual link with the wider kinship group to which they belonged.

Thousands of such illustrations were executed by the heraldic artist during the later 1940s and 1950s, and purchased in large quantities by visitors to the Heraldic Museum. In 1945, following the retirement of Nellie McGrane, who had transferred with the Office in 1943, Nora Moore became heraldic artist, and worked at the Castle until 1950, when she married and moved to Athlone. Later she would return as Nora O'Shea, her artistic influence and association with the Office continuing until 1995. After O'Shea's relocation, McGrane returned in 1950, then aged 76, employed on a piece-work basis, as there were few other artists skilled enough to undertake the specialist demands of herald painting. By 1955, however, Myra Maguire a young graduate of the National College of Art fulfilled these demands, and she replaced McGrane, working for the GO until the early 1970s. Between them, the three artists were responsible for the execution of hundreds of patents, and thousands of heraldic illustrations – the demand for the latter becoming particularly heavy during summer months, coinciding with the influx of tourists.[23] Indeed, the revenue from the sale of

---

20 MacLysaght, *Irish Families. Their Names, Arms and Origins* (Dublin, 1957), p. 11.
21 The term sept may be defined as a kinship group, the members of which bear a common surname and descend from a common ancestor.
22 MacLysaght Journal, GO, MS 527, p. 509.
23 Biography of Nellie McGrane in *Sunday Express*, 2 April 1950; interviews with Nora O'Shea and Myra Maguire.

Myra Maguire and Edward MacLysaght at the launch of *Irish Families. Courtesy, Myra Maguire.*

illustrations represented a considerable proportion of the annual income of the Office. For example, in 1951 some 172 heraldic illustrations were sold, realising an income of £306 out of the total of £1,121 raised that year.[24] Some 243 sept arms copied 'from the archives of the Irish Office of Arms (Genealogical Office)' were later reproduced in the book for which MacLysaght is still best remembered, *Irish Families: Their Names, Arms and Origins*, published in 1957. Many in fact were copied from Betham's transcript of *Linea Antiqua*, the Office's most extensive source for the arms of Gaelic families.[25]

Whilst this publication promoted Irish genealogy and sept arms and became a best seller throughout the world, it actually contributed to the sale of bogus arms. The first printing sold out quickly, the publisher Allen Figgis having taken it on a promotional tour of Canada and the United States in 1957,[26] and it has subsequently been re-published and revised. Neither Figgis nor MacLysaght were able to control the unsolicited reproduction of the coloured illustrations of arms that the book contained. This happened soon after the book went into

---

24 *NLI Trustees Report*, 1951–2, p. 7.
25 GO, MSS 145–7.
26 Promotional flier for *Irish Families*, in the possession of Myra Maguire.

circulation. In 1964, when Myra Maguire, the heraldic artist who executed the artwork for the book, visited the New York World Fair, she was surprised on entering the Irish Pavilion to find the walls in the entrance hall were decorated by enlarged copies of arms from MacLysaght's book – her own work. The concept of reproduction filtered into Irish souvenir shops, and on shopping visits she was overwhelmed to find duplication of her work on a variety of Irish merchandise – from tea towels to crockery – displayed in many of the larger department stores.[27] Whilst the concept of Irish heraldry had truly been delivered to America, it was not perhaps achieved in the manner envisaged by MacLysaght.

A further example of MacLysaght's innovative approach to promoting Gaelic heraldic culture was seen in the way he tackled the 'vexed question of the Irish chieftainships', and those who claimed to be the direct descendants of the chiefs of each kinship group, or 'chiefs of the name'. He recorded in his journal in 1945:

> Now that the Office of Arms has come under the authority of the Irish Government, I submit that the time is opportune to consider the question of the use of certain ancient Irish titles by persons claiming to be the chiefs of the clans.[28]

This practice had been ignored by Ulster's Office because Gaelic titles did not emanate from the Crown, and no proper register was kept, with the result that anyone might appoint himself as a chieftain, and appear in the list of 'Ancient Irish Chieftains' as published in *Thom's Directory* and other official lists. Whilst chiefs had been appointed by members of their extended kin group by 'tanistry' under the old Gaelic order, MacLysaght introduced a system of courtesy recognition whereby a person would only be recognised if he could prove decent by primogeniture from the last inaugurated or *de facto* chieftain known by the GO.[29] Claimants submitted evidence, and after further research conducted by Terence Grey (working for the GO without remuneration) MacLysaght either accepted or rejected the claims.[30] Grey's work established some 15 chiefs of the name, whose genealogical details were duly accepted and recorded in a new Register of Chiefs,[31] and proclaimed in the official Government publication, *Iris Oifigiuíl*.[32] The process was controversial, because a

---

27 Recollection of Myra Maguire.
28 GO, MS 527, p. 210
29 *Iris Oifigiuíl*, 22 December 1944.
30 MacLysaght, *Changing Times*, pp. 189–90.
31 GO, MS 627.
32 *Iris Oifigiuíl*, 22 December 1944.

number of claimants were demoted through lack of genealogical evidence. Some took it well, but others such as Raymond Moulton Sean O'Brien, who claimed to be 'The O'Brien' – a chieftainship which carried with it the courtesy title of Prince of Thomond – were incredulous and threatened legal action. O'Brien claimed that he was directly descended from BrianBorú, although there was not a shred of evidence to prove it. He actually appeared as 'His Highness, Prince of Thomond' in the 1950 edition of *Thom's Directory*, but was then demoted, and after the GO's investigations appeared simply as R.M.S. O'Brien in the 1951 edition. His fanciful claims did not end there, however, as he later tried to claim the right to a seat at Westminster Abbey for the coronation of Queen Elizabeth II in 1952. Having been advised by the GO, via the College of Arms, that his claims were unfounded, officials in the Court of Claims in London refused his right to admission.[33]

Chiefs-of-the-name controversies have arisen again in recent years as a result of the well-publicised bogus claims of Terence McCarthy. In the 1980s, he presented a pedigree without genealogical integrity to gain recognition as the MacCarthy Mór, Chief of the Name, and to support his claim to be Prince of Desmond and Lord of Kerslawny. Extensive genealogical research, commissioned by the current Chief Herald, Brendan O Donoghue, subsequently established that McCarthy's claims were false, and the courtesy recognition was declared to be 'null and void' in 1999.[34] The MacCarthy Mór hoax has brought into question the validity of other courtesy recognitions, which the GO, with expert assistance from leading genealogists, is currently endeavouring to resolve.

MacLysaght was also keen to introduce an Order of Merit for Ireland, not as a means of elevating a member of society one above another, which would have contravened Article 40 of the Constitution, but rather to honour citizens or visiting dignitaries. Drawing on international examples, he cited the Legion d'Honneur in France – the highest French distinction – and presented a dossier for the Government on a proposed Irish equivalent, which he called the Rolla Onóra, suggesting that it might be administered by the GO.[35] The Government chose not to endorse this innovation, much to MacLysaght's disappointment. He was also disappointed that legal procedures to authorise changes of surname did not become part of the business of the GO, resulting in the register

---

33 MacLysaght, *Changing Times*, pp. 211–20; *The People Newspaper*, 13 July 1952, 2 November 1952 and 25 January 1953.

34 GO, MS 627, p. 52; Statement of Chief Herald, dated 6 August 1999; and see also 'The MacCarthy Mór affair', in Berresford Ellis, *Erin's Blood Royal*, chapter 12.

35 Notes on the Rolla Onóra, GO, MS 622, pp. 112–29.

for that purpose being closed.[36] It was partly his frustration that such creative ideas were ignored, as well as the ongoing staff shortages, that led to his effective departure from the GO in 1949, after only six years in the new post.[37]

Beginning in MacLysaght's time, and continuing under his successors, the GO has conducted valuable work on behalf of various Government departments and agencies. This included such matters as designing naval and military flags and badges, commissioned by the Department of Defence for various army corps, and advising the same department about dress instructions for army personnel.[38] Having registered the arms of Ireland under the authority of the Irish Government in 1945, MacLysaght standardised the format of presentation. He advised that it would be impossible to reproduce all 30 strings, as depicted on the Brian Ború harp, and that at least 15 of them vertically should be shown (later this was reduced to nine strings).[39]

SPLENDID ISOLATION?

Although it had been the ambition of Dr Richard Hayes, when he sought the transfer of the former Office of Arms in 1941, that it might be subsumed into the NLI, where its manuscripts would be made available 'twelve hours a day' for public inspection,[40] this did not happen for practical reasons. Lack of space in the main Library buildings prevented immediate relocation to Kildare Street.[41] The physical isolation of the Office was to continue for nearly 20 years, thus enabling it to maintain an independent profile from its parent institution.

In its original plan for the GO, drawn up in July 1943, the Government had made it clear that the words 'Office of Arms' might be dropped from its title eventually. This happened much more slowly than envisaged, and the words still appeared on office stationery well into the 1970s. Indeed, the introduction of the GO arms to its stationery after 1946 helped to maintain its separate and specific identity. Believing that the term 'Genealogical Office' actually created 'a misnomer' once its heraldic functions were retained,

---

36 MacLysaght, *Changing Times*, pp. 194, 199.
37 *ibid.,* p. 194
38 GO, MS '111 I or S', includes examples of army badges and other insignia, and instructions for army dress, post-1943.
39 MacLysaght to Department of Education, regulating use of the arms of Ireland, May 1947, NLI, File Relating to the GO, uncat.
40 R.J. Hayes, Director, National Library of Ireland, Kildare Street, to the Secretary, Department of Education, 8 January 1941, NAI, DT S3926B.
41 *NLI Trustees Report*, 1945–6, p. 8.

MacLysaght even tried to have the title 'Office of Arms' reintroduced, as early as 1947:

> Our experience has been that the adoption of the name Genealogical Office has led to the erroneous belief that the Office of Arms had been abolished or transferred to London. . . . The phrase "Office of Arms" connotes an office which deals not only with heraldic matters . . . but also with all questions of genealogy and kindred subjects. . . . For those reasons it would seem advisable to revert to the former name "Office of Arms" which . . . always in fact appeared on our stationery in conjunction with the Genealogical Office.[42]

The authorities remained unreceptive to this idea, and no alteration in the official title was made, but in the public mind it was difficult to erase the traditions of the past. For many people, the Bedford Tower building remained 'the Office of Arms'. For example, in 1952 a *Sunday Express* promotional feature stated that 'the Office of Arms is also known as the genealogical office [*sic*]',[43] whilst in 1953, an *Irish Press* article referred to the building as maintaining the 'headquarters of Hibernian heraldry'. It explained that whereas formerly the building had been home to Ulster King of Arms, by the early 1950s it had become:

> labelled, somewhat more tersely . . . the Genealogical Office, but that is the only real change. For the GO deals in the immutable, in pedigrees of the past, in coats of arms, in blazonry and the gilded wizardry that is the age-old craft of heraldry.[44]

In 1960 an *Irish Times* article stated that the 'GO contains the Office of Arms'.[45] By the 1970s the word 'formerly' and brackets were dropped from around the 'Office of Arms' on stationery so that the address read: Genealogical Office, Office of Arms, Dublin Castle, making it appear that the GO was actually operating as a branch of the Office of Arms.

---

42 Edward MacLysaght, Chief Herald, Genealogical Office, formerly Office of Arms, Dublin Castle, to the Secretary, Department of Education, 20 February 1947, NLI, File Relating to the GO, uncat.
43 *Sunday Express,* 7 December 1952.
44 *Irish Press*, 15 September 1953.
45 *The Irish Times*, 5 November 1960.

GENEALOGICAL RESEARCH

Whilst the title of the GO remained an issue for discussion, the main focus of its work did continue to be genealogical rather than heraldic. A certain amount of genealogical research was required for most grants and confirmations of arms, particularly for people domiciled in other countries, to prove their descent from a known Irish ancestor. This required research in the main record repositories, particularly the General Register Office, to obtain certificates of birth, marriage and death, and perhaps also parish records for additional certificates of baptism, marriage and burial. In addition to this work, the number of general genealogical enquiries received by the GO that were unrelated to heraldry continued to increase. By 1953 one newspaper article noted that people had become 'more pedigree conscious than ever they were under the old regime'.[46]

Some requests involved research from manuscripts available in the GO itself. Classed as in-house 'pedigree searches', the number of these enquiries grew from the 1940s. In 1947, for example, 146 pedigree searches were received; in 1960 this rose to 222; by 1967, to 554 and in 1976, to 753 searches.[47] In addition to these in-house search requests, many thousands more were received from people who were not descended from the wealthy élite covered by the registers of arms, pedigrees and other genealogies, and who required research using resources in other repositories.

A significant factor in the increase of business was the fact that Government Departments were able to forward communications about family research directly to the GO after April 1943. Before that date, no governmental agency had existed to deal with such enquiries because, technically at least, the Office of Arms functioned as a British service. After the transfer, enquirers were informed that 'the GO undertakes as part of its normal functions to trace and compile histories and pedigrees of individuals and families'.[48] By the 1960s, the record collection in the GO was recognised by the Minister for Education, Dr Patrick Hillery, as one of the most important basic sources for Irish biographical information.[49]

During the 1950s, the revolution in international communication made possible by cheaper air travel opened up Ireland to mass tourism. Third and

---

46 *Irish Press*, 15 September 1953.
47 *NLI Trustees Reports*, 1947–81.
48 Department of the Taoiseach memorandums relating to the official reply to enquiries about procedure for ancestral research, 19 February 1937, and 6 June 1945, NAI, DT S9621.
49 *Dáil Debates*, 13 June 1961, 190, 34.

fourth generations descended from Irish emigrants who were making good in the new world began to return to the old country in great numbers. Many were curious to establish where their ancestors had come from, and when and why they had left. Reflecting this development, the GO became the first point of contact for many such enquirers.

Research for these clients involved extensive trawling through records in various repositories in Dublin and Belfast, as well as surviving parish records in local custody (then including many Church of Ireland records),[50] or on microfilm in the NLI (Catholic records only). This was conducted by a corps of external researchers employed by the GO on a freelance basis. By the mid-1960s, the GO was said to be in constant demand by researchers and the general public, and employing between five and eight external researchers to work on commissioned searches.[51] In 1972, the GO received some 4,000 postal enquiries alone, over half of them from the United States, in addition to hundreds of telephone calls and personal visits.[52] By 1976, the proportion of staff time taken up by commissioned genealogical searches was simply 'undreamt of in early years of its operation'.[53]

It was Gerard Slevin who initiated a formal advisory service for personal callers to the Office during the 1960s. The clients were interviewed by staff, and filled out their details on printed forms (modelled on the *pro forma* forms first designed by Burtchaell prior to 1921) which facilitated the researchers in producing reports on their ancestry. The heraldic and genealogical reference books were relocated from the Heraldic Museum to a room on the first floor at the rear of the building – Burtchaell's old office, in fact, where shelving was installed, and reading facilities provided to accommodate researchers and members of the public.[54] This room became known in-house as the 'library'.

When the GO finally discontinued its research service in 1985, the collective endeavours of these researchers had created a specific archive, amounting to over 20,000 research files. Given their personal content, and the fact that the work had been privately commissioned and paid for, these files remain unavailable for public inspection for the time being. Confidentiality was always taken seriously by the GO, and even the in-house researchers did not usually know the names of the clients for whom they conducted research. This confidentiality

---

50 In recent years many Church of Ireland registers have been transferred to the safe custody of the RCBL, Dublin.
51 *NLI Trustees Report,* 1964–5, p. 7.
52 *ibid.,* 1972–3, p. 11.
53 *ibid.,* 1976, p. 9.
54 *ibid.,* 1957–8, p.7.

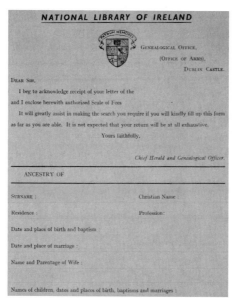

GO ancestral research form. *GO Collection.*

has been protected by a special order under the National Archives Act 1986 (to which both the NLI and GO have been subject since 1996).[55]

GENERAL WORKING CONDITIONS

The physical distance between Kildare Street and Dublin Castle may have led to the GO being treated as an outpost, and working conditions there were rather antiquated and unsuitable. Incredible as it may seem by today's standards, the building remained heated by open turf fires in all the main receptions rooms until the early 1950s. This resulted in an unbearable smoky atmosphere during the winter – conditions that were, of course, completely unsuitable for the storage of manuscripts. On at least one occasion, the prolonged use of turf fires and the absence of a fire detection system almost resulted in catastrophe.

One night in February 1947 – one of the coldest winters of the twentieth century – a piece of live turf fell out of the fireplace in the typists' room on the

---

55 National Archives Act 1986 (Description of Classes of Records Amendment) Order, 2000, relating to the Genealogical Office client files, signed by Bertie Ahern, An Taoiseach, 21 December 2000. The Order will be reviewed after five years from that date.

The cantilevered staircase gave the Office a distinctive charm, but internal working conditions were far from satisfactory. *Courtesy, Bestick Williams.*

top floor after they had finished work. Unnoticed by the porter when he came to lock up the room in the evening, a fire took hold, and the entire room was gutted, including all the then current research files.[56] Fortunately, a passer-by in Castle Street raised the alarm, and the fire brigade managed to contain the fire, although considerable damage resulted from fire and water.[57]

The follow-up investigation revealed that fire places in the building were never raked out in the evenings, but left for the cleaner the following day. The porter's final check of the building took place about 7pm each evening, after which there were no further inspections, because the GO was not included on the watchman's rounds for other Castle buildings. This omission was apparently a legacy of the 'imperial status' of a building 'considered to be part of the British civil service', which could not be entered by Castle police. After the transfer in 1943, this particular aspect of administration was simply over-

---

56 Report on outbreak of a fire at the Herald's Office, to the Office of Public Works, 1 March 1947, NAI, OPW 9/A6/4/6/47.

57 T.U. Sadleir, Newcastle Lyons, County Dublin, to Mr Cook, Treasury Chambers, London, 7 February 1947, PRO, T 21/156.

looked, with the result that the building remained in 'splendid isolation', from a fire-detection and security point of view. The near-disaster in 1947 served as a warning, and the procedure was changed so that the building was included on the night-watchman's rounds thereafter.[58]

Even after the reforms occasioned by the the fire, however, the GO remained well below the 'standards required for other repositories of valuable documents and irreplaceable material', such as the NLI or the National Museum, as Slevin was quick to point out to the OPW.[59] It transpired that turf fires continued to heat the Bedford Tower until 1951. 'Emphatic protests' by MacLysaght resulted in the installation of an electrical heating system in February of that year. Other public offices, including the Land Commission, had turf fires until the 1970s.

The new heating system was not very satisfactory. The in-house researchers recalled that that the strong room and Heraldic Museum remained 'deadly cold', encouraging them to work fast at all times, while in contrast the heat was stifling on the attic floor, where the typists' and artist's rooms were located. The artist spent most of her GO career with the windows wide open to allow heat to escape.[60] Complaints about irregular temperatures continued; indeed the problem was never properly rectified.[61] In other respects, the atmosphere on the top floor was cold – several researchers continue to refer to a 'shifty' feeling along the corridors, some having experienced ghostly encounters from time to time. In the basement, where the tea-room was installed for the convenience of staff during the 1950s, mice, and occasionally rats, were an ongoing working hazard.[62]

The structural safety of the Bedford Tower building became a growing concern. Its main feature – the magnificent cantilevered staircase – required strengthening by the mid-1960s, while its façade was described as 'beyond repair' in 1971.[63] After heavy rain, pools of water seeped through the roof onto the top-floor rooms, necessitating repairs to keep the roof waterproof in 1973.[64] By 1977 the incline on the top steps and the landing on the attic or top floor had

---

58 Report on outbreak of a fire at the Herald's Office, to the Office of Public Works, 1 March 1947, NAI, OPW 9/A6/4/6/47.
59 Report of Gerard Slevin, on behalf of the Chief Herald, concerning conditions in the GO, *op. cit.*
60 Recollection of Miss Rosemary ffolliott, GO Researcher 1957–early 1970s, and Myra Maguire, heraldic artist, 1950–70s.
61 Slevin to the Architect-in-Charge, OPW, 6 November 1974, OPW, A6/14/4.
62 Recollection of Rosemary ffolliott.
63 Structural report, OPW, A6/14/4.
64 *op. cit.*

The weight of the tower put structural pressure on the façade which eventually forced the closure of the building. *Courtesy, Klaus Unger, OPW.*

increased so much that for safety staff and equipment were withdrawn temporarily to allow repair work. As a result, the Heraldic Museum became an office for the typists, artist, and in-house researchers. Public access was restricted and working conditions were cramped.[65] In 1978, the building completely closed to enable further structural repairs to be made to the pediment. This time, staff members were accommodated elsewhere in the Castle, although the books and manuscripts remained *in situ*, which was a great inconvenience. Special arrangements had to be made with the site builder to gain access to the building even to check a reference.[66] Although repairs were made, and the GO returned to normal later in the year, these structural difficulties were ominous

---

65 *op. cit.*
66 *NLI Trustees Reports*, 1977, p. 15; 1978, p. 12.

warnings of more serious problems which eventually closed the Bedford Tower building, and resulted in the relocation of the GO in 1981.

TOURISM AND SUSTAINED GROWTH

After MacLysaght's departure to Kildare Street in 1949 to take up the new post of Keeper of Manuscripts, the demand for the Office's services continued to rise steadily. Slevin promoted a greater public awareness of heraldry, genealogy and family history, on an international scale, and there was a corresponding growth in heraldic work during his tenure. The net income of £896 in 1946 (the first year for which figures are available), had increased by 1956 to £2,096, by 1966 to £2,792, and by 1976 to £9,019.[67] A major factor was tourism, and a related brisk business in municipal arms during the 1950s and 1960s, when many urban district councils, borough corporations and town commissioners had the armorial bearings of the areas for which they were responsible registered for the first time.

The launch of An Tóstal (meaning pageant) an annual festival devised to encourage emigrants and their descendants to visit Ireland by the Irish Tourist Board (later Bord Fáilte), during the 1950s,[68] had significant repercussions for the GO and its workload, because it led to a 'stirring of the heraldic conscience'.[69] The festival included programmes of cultural and social events in cities, towns and villages throughout Ireland, but most festivities centered on the capital. For the first events, held in April 1953, Dublin Corporation commissioned the GO to produce outsize shields bearing the arms of some 96 Irish towns and cities, which were affixed to lamp standards throughout the city. This work kept the artist Myra Maguire, along with three colleagues from the National College of Art and Design, busy for several months. Before some of these shields could be displayed, several towns were required to register their arms for the first time, including Tullamore, Sligo, Bantry, Cavan, Castlebar and Birr (whose arms had long been in use), whilst the Urban District Council of Ballinasloe was granted new arms to mark the celebrations.[70]

Tourism had a positive impact, resulting in improvements being made to the Heraldic Museum during the 1950s. Dr Hayes had been well aware of the Museum's potential for public outreach when he secured the Library's link

---

67 *ibid.*, 1947–8, p. 6; 1955–6, p. 9,1966–7, p. 8; 1976, p. 15.
68 'An Tóstal', 'Ireland at Home, 1953', NAI, DT S15297.
69 *Sunday Express*, 7 December 1952.
70 *NLI, Trustees* Report, 1954–5, p. 9.

Outsize heraldic shields were produced by the GO heraldic artist for the An Tóstal festival during the 1950s. *Courtesy, Myra Maguire.*

with it back in 1943.[71] He observed then the large numbers of Americans and other visitors to Dublin Castle who included the Office of Arms on their tours of the Museum,[72] and the number of visitors continued to increase into the 1950s. New display cases were provided for the display of heraldic material as part of a 'quadracentennial' exhibition, held in 1952 to celebrate the 400th anniversary of the Office of Arms. Significantly, the theme was continuity,

71 Dr Richard Hayes to Department of Education, 5 November 1943, NLI, File Relating to the GO, uncat.
72 *NLI Trustees Report*, 1954–5, p. 9.

featuring artefacts and manuscripts illustrating the work of the Office over four centuries. The importance of the Museum on the tourist trail was recognised when a request for improved lighting to show off the material in the cases was given by the OPW in 1957, the approving engineer commenting: 'this Museum is unique and represents one of the show-places of the Castle'.[73] When the new lighting was installed, it showed up defects in the linoleum floor of the Museum, and this was replaced in the autumn of 1958, following 'the crush of summer visitors' that year. Again, the improvement was justified because the Heraldic Museum was 'much in the public eye'.[74] At the same time a new carpet was laid in the Chief Herald's room. Although it was commented that 'Mr Slevin would not ordinarily qualify for supply of a carpet', given his rank within the civil service, it was acknowledged that 'since

The Heraldic Museum at Dublin Castle provided much interest for passing tourists. *Courtesy, Irish Architectural Archive.*

---

73 Report of site engineer, 6 March 1957, OPW, A6/14/4.
74 Report of site engineer, 22 October 1958, *op. cit.*

his predecessors . . . had a carpet', and more significantly because he received 'important visitors frequently', the expense of a replacement carpet could be allowed.[75]

The GO promoted its activities through tourist literature, most notably *Ireland of the Welcomes*, published six times a year by the Tourist Board since 1952. An illustrated article on heraldry by Gerard Slevin appeared in 1957, explaining the visual symbolism of the coats of arms of several Irish families, and encouraged people to visit the Museum.[76] This was followed by a series of feature articles about the arms of various Gaelic families and chiefs-of-the-name during the 1960s. The Aer Lingus in-flight magazine *Cara* also helped to promote GO services and encouraged more visitors.[77]

The GO conducted a significant level of business with various banks and banking institutions. Arms were granted to the Institute of Bankers in 1951, and both the Institute of Chartered Accountants and Hibernian Bank received arms in 1960. Further grants were made to the Provincial Bank of Ireland and the Munster and Leinster Bank Ltd in 1961, and to the National Bank of Ireland in 1966.[78]

In spite of the constraints imposed by low staff levels and generally poor working conditions, the link with the NLI benefited the GO's efficiency in various respects. Hayes's multi-volume catalogue provided the first systematic indexing and listing of many of the manuscripts holdings of the GO.[79] For this, a new numbering system was introduced for some 822 manuscripts in the GO, each prefixed with the letters 'GO'. However, the system broke down in the upper numbers, and has never included a large quantity of loose material that remains uncatalogued in the strong room to this day. Another positive development in the NLI that benefited the GO was compilation of the *Index of Surnames*, a massive index based on two nineteenth-century primary sources, *Griffith's Primary Valuation of Property* and the *Tithe Applotment Books*, completed during the late 1950s. Thousands of surnames were extracted from these sources for each county in Ireland, and listed in alphabetical order.[80] The index

---

75 Memorandum of inspection of the GO, 19 June 1958, *op. cit.*
76 Slevin, 'Irish Heraldry', *Ireland of the Welcomes*, 61 (1957), pp. 19–22.
77 See for example, Ida Grehan, 'Arms of a gentler kind', *Cara Magazine 5.4* (1972), pp. 29–31.
78 GO, MS 111R, p. 51; GO, MS 111S, pp. 23, 27, 40, 56.
79 Richard Hayes (ed.), *Manuscript Sources for the History of Irish Civilisation* (Dublin 1965).
80 The index was largely the work of Edward (Ned) Keane, a special research assistant employed by the Library, and assisted by a member of the full-time Library staff, Willie Buckley.

THE CHIEF HERALD, Dr. Gerard Slevin, beside (left) the robes of a Knight of the Order of St. Patrick, with an Earl's coronet, and, right, the Cork Herald's uniform.

Heraldry, and all that...

Gerard Slevin, Ireland's longest-serving Chief Herald to date, in the Heraldic Museum, shortly before retirement. *Evening Herald*, 17 August 1981.

revolutionised the approach to genealogical research, making it possible to identify surnames with places, and became an invaluable working tool for the GO researchers conducting research on behalf of clients. It remains one of the most valuable sources for genealogical research today.

The microfilming of Catholic parish registers at NLI, begun under Hayes's direction in the early 1940s, was continued by MacLysaght when he became Keeper of Manuscripts, in addition to his role as Chief Herald, after 1949. This had significant benefits for the research work conducted by GO researchers. MacLysaght formulated a policy 'to permanently preserve the genealogical information continued in parish registers', which was accepted by the Catholic bishops in October 1949. They agreed to 'co-operate with the Genealogical Office' in the copying of parish registers. Individual bishops advised their parish priests to co-operate with Library staff who were despatched to collect registers from local custody and take them to Dublin, where they were microfilmed by the NLI and then returned.

Permission to access the information contained on the films was granted to 'responsible GO officials' by individual bishops. This greatly facilitated the processing of the GO's commissioned searches, the majority of which involved Catholic families. The initial phase of microfilming work was completed in the early 1960s, and additional registers from parishes in Dublin were filmed on new equipment in 1976. Since the late 1990s, the Library has continued to fill in gaps in the original filming programme, and some registers are now available on film up to 1905.[81] The NLI also facilitated the work of the Church of the Latter-Day Saints, the Mormons, who were given permission to microfilm many of the records of the GO, and worked *in situ* in a room in the basement of the Bedford Tower during the 1950s. This made the GO records accessible to researchers using the Mormon History Centres throughout the United States, generating further interest in the Office from abroad.

HIGH-PROFILE CASES GENERATE MORE BUSINESS

Under Slevin's direction, the GO was successful in confirming the Irish connections of several high-profile figures, some of which resulted in heraldic commissions. These cases generated additional publicity, and increased the demand for its services. For example, the inauguration of John Fitzgerald Kennedy as President of the United States in 1961 presented an important opportunity for the Irish Government to promote Irish links with the United States.

Kennedy was not the first American president of Irish descent (Andrew Jackson, son of emigrants from Ulster, had been inaugurated in 1829), but he was the first of Catholic origin. In his first State of the Union speech, in January 1961, Kennedy made reference to the heraldic symbolism in the Presidential arms of the United States.[82] Slevin picked this up, and following

---

81 Typescript notes on microfilming of parish registers by Brendan O Donoghue, Chief Herald; also NLI, *Trustees Report,* 1976, p. 14; MacLysaght, *Changing Times*, pp. 205–8.

82 Kennedy's State of the Union speech was made on 20 January 1961, in which he made the following heraldic references: 'On the presidential coat of arms, the American eagle holds in his right talon the olive branch, while in his left is held a bundle of arrows. We intend to give equal attention to both'. *The Irish Times*, 23 March 1961.

President Kennedy was genuinely impressed by his heraldic gift from the people of Ireland, presented to him by the Irish ambassador, T.J. Kiernan, at the White House, St Patrick's Day, 1961. *Courtesy, Myra Maguire.*

some informal discussions the GO was commissioned by the Government to design a personal coat of arms for the President symbolic of his Irish ancestry. The design was based on the traditional sept arms of the O'Kennedys of Ormonde, with a recollection of the Fitzgerald of Desmond arms – Kennedy belonging to the Fitzgerald sept by virtue of his mother's ancestry – and with a play on the olive branch in the Presidential arms.

Drafts of various designs were submitted to the White House, via the American Embassy in Dublin for Kennedy's approval, before the final design was executed. The patent bearing the arms was executed on a vellum scroll, accompanied by a genealogical chart showing the immediate decent of the President's family, and general information about the O'Kennedy clan. Both were presented to Kennedy in a magnificent mahogany case, lined in Irish poplin, with the harp emblem woven in gold thread inside the cover, at the White House on St Patrick's Day 1961 by the Irish ambassador in Washington,

T.J. Kiernan.[83] The ambassador later gave television interviews giving 'an account of the presentation and details of the grant'.[84]

Extensive genealogical research had been carried out by the GO to verify Kennedy's Irish descent. The limited availability of sources meant that it could only be established that Kennedy's grandfather had emigrated to Boston from County Wexford at some point during the 1840s, and that a possible place of origin was Dunganstown, but it was impossible to prove this with certainty. Thus in the grant itself, he is described as the grandson of Patrick Kennedy, who emigrated to the United States from County Wexford during the 1840s. Some newspapers sensationalised the story by stating as fact that the Kennedys originated in Dunganstown; while the accurate interpretation of the evidence, as found by the GO, was more speculative about this connection.[85] Whilst some media reports were far-fetched, the publicity did an enormous amount to publicise Ireland and the rewards of genealogical research. A flood of enquiries received 'by the Irish embassy at Washington' was transmitted to the GO, via the Department of External Affairs, in the months after March 1961. By September these represented 'a marked increase in the work' of the Office, causing considerable delays to other work. They were directly attributable to the publicity following Kennedy's grant.[86] When Kennedy visited Ireland two years later, the GO provided 'what information may be regarded as proven fact' about the President's ancestral links with Ireland for distribution to the press.[87] After Kennedy's assassination later that year, his heraldic links with Ireland were maintained when a banner of his arms was carried to the top of Mount Kennedy in the Yukon Territory, Canada, the mountain having been named in his memory by the Canadian Government.[88]

---

83 Grant of arms to President J.F. Kennedy, 8 March 1961, GO, MS 111S, p. 30.

84 Copy of letter from T.J. Kiernan, Embassy of Ireland, Washington, to the Secretary, Department of External Affairs, 21 March 1961, recounting in detail the presentation of armorial ensigns to President Kennedy, GO, Material relating to grant of arms for President Kennedy, uncat.

85 For example, the New York magazine *Look* published an eight-page spread entitled '*Look* finds Kennedys and Fitzgeralds in the counties of Ireland where JFK's ancestors were born', which inferred that the president's maternal and paternal grandfathers had sailed on the same ship together to America. It also claimed to have interviewed his cousins, *Look*, 14 March 1961, pp. 24–32.

86 GO, File of correspondence entitled 'External Affairs', uncat.

87 Kennedy visited Ireland in June 1963. A press release based on information provided by the GO was circularised on 30 May 1963.

88 Lyall, 'Irish heraldic jurisdiction' (Spring, 1994), p. 180.

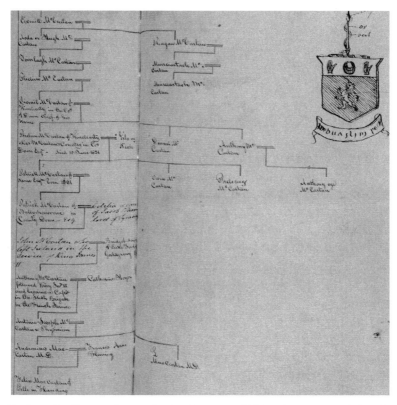

Registered pedigree and arms of Felix Maccartan of Lille, France, as recorded by Sir William Betham, Ulster King of Arms, in 1836. Emphasising the continuity of the Office of Arms, this evidence was used by GO researchers when compiling the genealogy of Maccartan's great-nephew, Charles de Gaulle, in the 1960s. *GO, MS 145.*

Other high-profile cases investigated under the auspices of the GO did much to promote genealogical research. As early as 1945, the Irish links of the French statesman General Charles de Gaulle had been the subject of some speculation in the Irish press.[89] In 1964, research completed by a GO researcher, Eilish Ellis, in conjunction with French genealogists, established that his grandmother's family, the Maccartans of Lille, in Flanders, were direct descendants of Captain John McCartan, 'who left Ireland in the service of King James', and that he was a member of 'the ancient princely family of McCartane, Lords of Kinnelartie or MaCartane's County in the County of

---

89 A biographical feature about de Gaulle appeared in *The Irish Times*, 10 October 1945.

Down'. In fact, de Gaulle's maternal great-uncle, Felix Maccartan of Lille, had applied to Sir William Betham for arms in 1836. As a result, Betham compiled a pedigree showing links between the chiefs of the Clan Maccartan and the family in Lille, which was registered in the Office of Arms in January 1836.[90] A certificate of arms of the clan was then issued to him on 16 February 1836.[91] Headlines such as 'de Gaulle's Irish ties established by genealogists: definite County Down link', generated public interest, and included details of the information derived from the former Ulster King of Arms records in the GO archives.[92] Unlike Kennedy, who visited his 'homeland' in County Wexford, de Gaulle turned down the opportunity to visit County Down, because it was under British control. Following his resignation from French politics in 1969, however, he spent several months in Cork, Kerry, Connemara and Dublin, and President de Valera entertained him, along with 30 other members of the MacCartan clan, at a reception at Áras an Uachtaráin on 19 June 1969.[93]

The GO also conducted research to establish the Irish descent of Grace Kelly, Princess of Monaco, prior to her visit to Ireland in 1963, and of President Richard Nixon, prior to his visit in 1970, although this work did not result in heraldic commissions. The interest in genealogical history was not of course confined to world leaders. In the mid-1970s, the most dramatic impact on GO business resulted from publication of Alex Haley's biographical novel *Roots: The Saga of an American Family* (New York, 1976), in which he traced his ancestors from America to Africa through seven generations. The book sold one million copies within a year, and its subsequent adaptation for television brought the story to over 130 million viewers worldwide. The impact on GO business was described as 'startling' and income more than doubled the following year, jumping from £9,020 in 1976 to £14,835 in 1977.[94] Directly attributed to the *Roots* phenomenon, this interest was sustained in the following years – income peaking at £15,530 in 1981.[95]

---

90 Registered pedigree of Felix Maccartan, Lille, France, from the Clan Macartan, GO, MS 145, pp. 297–9.
91 Annotation to pedigree, *op. cit.*, p. 299.
92 *The Irish Times*, 25 February 1965.
93 Joannon, *De Gaulle and Ireland*, pp. 115–6.
94 *NLI Trustees Report*, 1978, p. 15.
95 *op. cit.*, 1981, pp. 13–4.

Europe's symbol *par excellence* was the design concept of Gerard Slevin, Chief Herald of Ireland, 1954-81. *Courtesy, Photo European Parliament.*

DESIGN OF THE EUROPEAN EMBLEM

One final heraldic development during this period that is still of interest today and symbolic of the Office's evolving influence, is the role played by Gerard Slevin (Ireland's longest-serving Chief Herald to date) in the design of what is now the EU flag. During the 1950s, the emerging Council of Europe, founded in 1949, decided that it needed a visible mark of its corporate identity, and that a common flag for use in all its member states would be the best means of providing this. In September 1954, a vexillogical committee was established, consisting of three representatives of the Council and three heraldic experts from the Netherlands, Italy and Ireland (the latter represented by Slevin), to advise on the matter and prepare designs.[96] At the first meeting, held in Strasbourg on 12 November 1954, when design concepts were submitted by each of the representatives, it was Slevin's concept that found favour with the committee. Showing both foresight and ecumenical sensitivity, Slevin

---

96   Lager, 'L'Europe en quête de ses symbols', p. 47.

persuaded them that a competing design, proposing to incorporate the Christian cross in the new emblem would be inadvisable, because it was potentially 'offensive to non-Christian states', who might join the Council in the future.[97]

Featuring a clock-like circle of 12 gold stars or mullets on a blue background, Slevin's design aimed to encapsulate graphically the ideal of an evolving Europe over the course of time. In heraldry, the circle is symbolic of perfection and entirety, capturing the European ideal of unity and harmony, while the clock symbolises the passage of time. Thus, the use of twelve stars relates to the clock, and *does not*, as is often assumed, have anything to do with the number of member States. The design was adopted by the Parliamentary Assembly of the Council as its emblem in October 1955, and became the European flag following a unanimous decision of the Committee of Ministers in

Symbolic of Ireland's integral role in European affairs, Pat Cox MEP was elected President of the European Parliament in 2002, the first Irishman to hold this position. *Courtesy, Photo European Parliament.*

---

97 GO, File marked 'Council of Europe', uncat. See also obituary to Gerard Slevin, *Daily Telegraph*, 15 May 1997.

December 1955. The significant Irish input to its design during the 1950s is evidence of the international recognition given to Ireland's heraldic authority at this time. Slevin was later honoured with membership of the prestigious Académie Internationale d'Héraldique – the only Irishman ever to gain such recognition – for his role in designing Europe's symbol of identity.[98]

After much negotiation, the emblem was secured by the European Economic Community as its symbol during the early 1980s. Since 1985, it has been the emblem of the European Parliament, and its institutions. It is now the symbol *par excellence* of a united Europe with a common identity, all who use it obliged to follow the strict graphical specifications for its correct reproduction.[99] With the introduction of the Euro as Europe's common currency in 2002, which carries the emblem of the stars on all its notes and coins, the symbol is part of everyday life throughout the states of the EU, in the pockets of millions of Europeans. That it originated in the mind of Ireland's longest-serving Chief Herald is a powerful symbol not only of the significance of the Irish heraldic authority internationally, but also Ireland's integral role in European affairs.

---

98 Personal file for Gerard Slevin, Archives of the Académie Internationale d'Héraldique, in the possession of M. Michael Popoff, Secretary General, Paris.
99 Graphical specifications for the European emblem, issued by the European Parliament, http://www.europa.eu.int/abc/symbols/emblem.graphics/.

EIGHT

Postscript: Return to an Office of Arms?

RELOCATION TO KILDARE STREET

In 1981 the GO moved from Dublin Castle, its base since 1831. The structural problems that had forced temporary closure of the Bedford Tower building during the 1970s had been a matter of continuing concern to the OPW, and following an inspection on 6 November 1981, architects discovered that the supporting beams over the balcony had become unstable. The weight from the attic floor added during the nineteenth-century restoration of the tower was putting so much pressure on the foundation pile beneath the building and the pediment at the front that there was a risk of the building collapsing.[1] The architects declared the building to be 'officially condemned'. The Chief Herald, Gerard Slevin, had retired the previous month, and Donal Begley, his Deputy, was abroad, with the result that Fergus Gillespie, the Assistant Keeper temporarily assigned to the GO, was consulted by the OPW, and had no option but to close the Bedford Tower immediately.

The decision had some dramatic side-effects. On returning from their lunch, the two typists found their place of work 'condemned', and were promptly despatched, by taxi, to the main Library buildings with typewriters on their knees, surrounded by administrative papers.[2] Initially, correspondence files, administrative records and accounts were removed from filing cabinets, and sent over to the Library during the next few days. Whilst the Library had a long-term plan to integrate the GO within the main Library complex in Kildare Street, such a sudden arrival was not anticipated.

Initially temporary accommodation was provided in a room at the rear of the main Library building, which was dreary and over-crowded by comparison with the spacious charm of the Castle, antiquated though it was. During the spring of 1983, when arrangements in the Library became unworkable,

---

1   *NLI Trustees Report*, 1981, p. 5. I am grateful to Klaus Unger, Assistant Principal Architect, OPW, for the technical information.
2   Recollection of Kay Maher, GO typist.

In 1981, the Office was forced out of the Bedford Tower at Dublin Castle, its home since 1903, because of structural problems. *Courtesy, Klaus Unger, OPW.*

accommodation at 65A Earl Court, off Earlsfort Terrace, was provided.[3] This proved more satisfactory, and continued as the GO headquarters until 1987. Before the OPW could undertake restoration work at the Bedford Tower building, when the tower was saved and the attic floor removed – resulting in its subsequent restoration and enhancement as a focal point in Upper Castle Yard – the building had to be completely cleared.[4] This did not happen until 1984, when the entire contents of the GO were packed into tea chests and moved to a storage room in Lower Castle Yard. It was painstaking work to wrap and box up all the records representing over 400 years of history from the strong room, the reference works from the library, and the contents of the Heraldic Museum.[5] The work was supervised by Donal Begley, who succeeded Slevin as Chief Herald, in March 1983, and who was also present when OPW contractors lifted the floorboards throughout the building, just in case the missing

3   Donal Begley, typescript notes about temporary accommodation.
4   Unger and Rolfe, *Dublin Castle Architectural Report* (1983).
5   Recollection of Donal Begley, Chief Herald, 1982–95.

'Crown Jewels' might have been hidden somewhere. It was an ongoing part of the folklore amongst staff that this might be a possibility, but they did not turn up.

One 'lost' piece of insignia that was recovered during the move was the badge of the Order of St Michael and St George issued to Roger Casement when he was knighted as a Commander of that Order for his diplomatic and humanitarian services in 1911, together with the earlier warrant issued when he became a Companion of the same Order in 1905. Casement's family handed these items back to the British Government after his execution for treason in 1916. At some stage after this, they were transferred to the Office of Arms for safekeeping, presumably because the Government of the day regarded the Office as the most appropriate location for such a deposit. Given the political sensitivities surrounding Casement's case, however, they were carefully concealed behind a panel in one of the display cases in the Heraldic Museum, and only uncovered as a result of the relocation in 1981. The badge and warrant are now on display in the Heraldic Museum in Kildare Street (see Colour Section). Another item that was found during the relocation process was a pike 'left behind by the rebels in No. 5 Castle Street' during the 1916 Rising, when the Castle was surrounded. Presumably someone gave it to Sir Nevile Wilkinson, who engraved the details of its provenance onto it, and then buried it beneath the floorboards of his room. In 1982, the pike was transferred to the National Museum, where it now forms part of the permanent 1916 Rising exhibition.[6]

Closure of the Bedford Tower and relocation of the GO compounded the National Library's own accommodation and storage problems at this time.[7] Back in 1976, when the greater part of the former Kildare Street Club, located at 2–3 Kildare Street, came on the market, it was acquired by the State on behalf of the Library, to facilitate extension of its storage facilities and general development of its infrastructure.[8] In 1977, the Library Trustees had decided that these elegant premises would be a suitable place to accommodate both the GO and the Manuscripts Department, allowing for the overall improvement and expansion of the Library service whilst also integrating the GO alongside its parent organisation.[9] This, it was envisaged, would fulfil Dr Richard Hayes's long-term aspiration when he had sought to secure the records of the

---

6   *ibid.*

7   *NLI Trustees Report*, 1982, p. 4.

8   *ibid.*, 1976, p. 6; 1977, p. 5; McDowell, *Land and Learning: Two Dublin Clubs*, p. 115.

9   *NLI Trustees Report*, 1977, p. 5.

In 1986, the Office re-opened in the former Kildare Street Club, 2–3 Kildare Street. *NLI.*

Office of Arms for the NLI in the early 1940s. However, the transfer process was slow.

Part of the Kildare Street Club at 1 Kildare Street had previously been sold, first in the 1950s to an insurance company, and later to a property developer, who destroyed much of its fine interior, including its magnificent staircase, during the 1960s.[10] After the Club vacated the building in 1975, fire damaged several reception rooms and corridors, and poor reconstruction work hindered conversion of the premises at 2–3 Kildare Street to Library use.[11]

---

10   O'Dwyer, *Lost Dublin*, p. 41
11   I am grateful to Kevin Wollohan, OPW, for this information.

Indeed, the general working conditions of the building did not 'give any promise of the early availability of a functional Library', to quote one Library report.[12] Three changes of Government in rapid succession between 1979 and 1982 slowed the bureaucratic wheels, and authorisation to commence the work was delayed. It was not until February 1982, some six years after the building had been purchased, that conversion of the Kildare Street Club began.

The OPW undertook the work as a conservation project, preserving as much of its original fabric as possible, including the red-brick external façade, one of Dublin's finest examples of Victorian architecture. An arresting feature of the exterior decoration is the animal, bird and reptile sculpture on the stonework at the base of the great double windows, whilst some interior cornices and architrave supports have also been salvaged.[13] The refurbishment and redecoration of the building as office accommodation, and fitting out the basement for archival storage, took about 18 months to complete. The entire ground floor was set aside for the Heraldic Museum, while a room off this was fitted out for genealogical consultancy. Offices on the first mezzanine and second floor of the building were devoted to GO accommodation. Storage facilities were provided in the basement for the collections of the Manuscripts Department and GO, a separate GO strong room replicating the one constructed by Vicars at the Castle.[14]

Although the building was ready for occupation early in 1984, the Department of Education was slow to recruit the additional staff required to service it,[15] and it was not until March 1987 that the GO reopened officially to the public at Kildare Street.[16] In the interim, there was some 'unofficial' occupation of the building. The consultancy room on the ground floor was fitted out as a priority to facilitate lectures to groups of overseas visitors, and the record collections were gradually moved from the Castle and re-shelved in the GO strong room in the basement during 1986.

LOSS OF PROFILE?

The enforced early departure from the Bedford Tower in 1981 left the GO in temporary accommodation for the best part of six years.[17] The loss of the prestigious Castle address had a detrimental effect on the public profile of the

---

12 *NLI Trustees Report*, 1976, p. 6.
13 Donal Begley, *Our House*, information leaflet.
14 I am grateful to Gerry Browner, Dúchas, for technical information.
15 *NLI Trustees Report*, 1986, pp. 6–7.
16 GO, Visitors' Book, 1985–9.
17 *ibid.*

Office, which had benefited from being part of the tourist trail to Dublin Castle. Thus the GO slipped into relative anonymity until 1987. Ironically, the GO's last years at the Castle had been its busiest and most lucrative, with income in 1980 and 1981 reaching recorded levels of about £15,000 each year.[18] Following the transfer, however, heraldic services and genealogical research were initially completely curtailed, with income dropping to just £9,120 in 1982, in spite of a revision of heraldic fees, which included an increase in the charge for a grant of arms from £300 to £400. However, general enquiries from people seeking basic information about genealogical research continued, and there was 'unremitting pressure from the public at home and abroad', both by letter and telephone. But even genealogical enquiries could not be answered as effectively as before, because the bulk of the general reference stock remained out of commission at the Castle.[19]

In 1981, no less than eight freelance researchers were working at the GO, some of them having been taken on following the six-month postal strike in 1979 specifically to clear the backlog of work that had accumulated to that point. When this was work was completed, the individual researchers were anxious to continue genealogical research, and there was plenty of demand to allow them to extend their work beyond the remit of the GO. They formed their own company called Hibernian Research – the first devoted to genealogical research in Ireland – in 1981.[20] The GO retained the services of some of the researchers on a contract basis, as before, to carry out pedigree searches, genealogical research connected with heraldic matters, or general postal enquiries. However, after the relocation, it made more sense to allow the private sector to take over these services completely. By 1985, the GO research service was scaled down.[21]

CONSOLIDATION AND OUTREACH

During the period of temporary accommodation between 1982 and 1987, the heraldic work continued, when no less than 79 patents were registered.[22] Many of these were a spin-off from the increased genealogical business of previous

---

18 *NLI Trustees Report*, 1980, p.5; 1981, p. 14.
19 *NLI Trustees Report*, 1982, p. 6.
20 The self-employed researchers were: Anne Brennan, Anita Dušck, Eilish Ellis, Paul Gorry, Tom Lindert, Tom McNally, Anne Neary, and Eileen O'Byrne. Information from Paul Gorry.
21 *NLI Trustees Report*, 1984, p.12.
22 GO, MS 111W+X.

The arms of the Faculty of Notaries Public in Ireland, as registered 16 March 1982, with emblazon details and hand-painted copy of the arms. *GO, MS 111W+X.*

237

years, some clients choosing to complete their genealogical researches with a grant of arms, whilst a significant number of institutional grants were also made. For example, the Faculty of Notaries Public, the Medical Council of Ireland, and the College of the Garda Síochána were issued in the first two months of Begley's term of office as Chief Herald.[23] Rather than the earlier practice of photocopying or photographing outgoing patents as the means of registration, the new Chief Herald had register entries of the emblazon and arms hand-painted by the heraldic artist Nora O'Shea, who was responsible not only for the high quality of the colour registrations but also much of the design-work on the issued patents. O'Shea had taught herself the art of heraldry, having studied the registers and work of previous artists. For a time following her retirement in 1995, the constraints of under-staffing and growing pressure of work prevented continuance of the practise of colour registration. More recently, however, colour registration has been restored, and O'Shea's skill and expertise has influenced the current generation of heraldic artists employed by the GO.

In the absence of accommodation to facilitate the public, the GO began to focus on outreach projects aimed at encouraging and facilitating people to conduct their own research. Publication of promotional literature and general information about genealogical research were major features of this process. Tourist brochures were prepared in co-operation with Bord Fáilte, for distribution worldwide through embassies, consulates, and Bord Fáilte offices. The concept of ancestral-research holidays was promoted in publications of the Department of Foreign Affairs.[24] Three guidebooks written by Donal Begley were published and republished during the 1970s and early 1980s, aimed at assisting people to do their own research, and thus disseminating elementary information to a much wider audience. The basic information they provided and the widespread demand for them reflected the growth of amateur genealogical research, and their concise style was popular with amateurs.

The first impression of the *Handbook on Irish Genealogy*, published in 1970, was based on an in-house guide that had been as a source of reference by GO staff since the 1960s. It was the first detailed guide to conducting genealogical research since Wallace Clare's *Simple Guide to Irish Genealogy* – first published in 1930 – and updated and reprinted in 1966. By the mid-1970s, this no longer contained up-to-date repository information.[25] The sequel to the *Handbook* was *Irish Genealogy: A Record Finder*, first published

---

23   *ibid.*
24   See for example, *Ireland Today. Bulletin of the Department of Foreign Affairs, 986*, March 1986, pp. 8–10.
25   Clare, *Simple Guide to Irish Genealogy*. Revised edition (Dublin, 1966).

in 1981. This included a foreword by the first Chief Herald, Edward MacLysaght, and specialist essays by several of the country's most experienced genealogical researchers, all of whom had been trained at the GO.[26]

Reflecting public demand, and the general global "Roots-mania" that had followed the publication of Haley's book in 1977, the *Handbook* was reprinted no less than six times before 1984. Some 60,000 copies of it were sold, while the *Record Finder* was reprinted three times. The third publication, *The Ancestor Trail in Ireland: A Companion Guide*, which first appeared in 1982, summarised the information contained in the earlier books and included repository addresses, maps, and useful starting tips. It was printed again in 1984.

The GO co-operated with tourist-related projects in Ireland aimed at encouraging genealogical research and the Chief Herald undertook promotional visits to the United States and Canada. This led to a good deal of media coverage of the GO's work, including two documentaries made for American and Japanese networks.[27] The visit of President Ronald Reagan to Ireland in June 1984 gave the genealogical industry an unprecedented boost, generating considerable media attention at home and throughout the United States, continuing to promote Irish links with its diaspora. On arrival at Shannon Airport on 1 June 1984, Reagan declared himself a 'great-grandson of Ireland', and his entire four-day visit was focused on his ancestral links – one whole day being devoted to the 'journey home' to Ballyporeen.[28] Several American newspapers made reference to the visit of President Kennedy 21 years before, while Reagan's visit was also given considerable air-time on American television networks.[29] This encouraged further interest from the American public at large, and the concept of ancestor-hunting holidays was developed by several American organisations in the wake of the President's visit.

One Irish-American travel company, Irish Heritage, based in Bath, Ohio, developed the Irish Heritage Programme in 1984, which specifically aimed at bringing Americans with Irish roots to Ireland for a cultural heritage experi-

---

26 Rosemary ffolliott demonstrated the value of directories, newspapers, and resources of the Registry of Deeds for genealogical research, in three separate essays, whilst she and Eileen O'Byrne examined the value of surviving wills and administrations. Beryl Phair produced an essay on genealogical sources for attorneys and barristers. In addition to these in-house contributions, based on years of experience, general essays by Begley and the historical geographer William Nolan introduced general themes, and also emphasised the value of local research.

27 *NLI Trustees Report*, 1983, p. 12.

28 The headline in *The Irish Times*, 4 June 1984, read simply 'Back home in Ballyporeen'.

29 *New York Times*, 4 June 1984.

Donal Begley, Chief Herald of Ireland, 1982–95, with staff and researchers in the consultancy room at the GO, 1989. *Courtesy, The Irish Times.*

ence including ancestral research. Entitled the 'Grand Reunion in Ireland', the programme had a sensational impact, and as a result over 3,500 people visited Ireland between 1984 and 1986 (usually in groups of about 40 people, often of the same family name – Sullivans, Butlers and Moores coming together, for example). These holidays lasted a few weeks, included visits to the country, tours of several cultural institutions, and also allowed time for genealogical research in Dublin, facilitated by the GO. An induction session with the Chief Herald was also included, which many visitors remember as entertaining, as well as informative about the main sources of information available for their research. The economic spin-off for the national exchequer from this particular programme was estimated to be in the region of £1 million during the three-year period 1984–6.[30] By 1988, a report commissioned by the Department of Tourism and Transport found that over one third of visitors from abroad chose Ireland as a holiday destination because of either a primary or secondary

---

30 Promotional literature relating to Heritage Travel's 'Ireland Heritage Tours', 1984–6.

interest in pursuing such research.[31] Visitor interest in genealogy thus contributed significantly to Irish tourism.

CULTURAL TOURISM AND THE IMPORTANCE OF GENEALOGY

In 1986, responsibility for the NLI and GO was transferred to the Department of the Taoiseach and placed directly under the Minister for State responsible for Arts and Culture within that Department. Both institutions fared better here than under the wider umbrella of Education, where they had been well down the pecking order behind universities, schools and other training schemes. This was not unrelated to the fact that Charles J. Haughey, who became Taoiseach again in March 1987, was also personally interested in genealogy and heraldry, having himself been granted armorial bearings when Minister for Agriculture and Fisheries in 1966.[32]

The shift in accountability to the Taoiseach's Department coincided with completion of the refurbishment programme at Kildare Street. At an informal ceremony held on 6 March 1987, Mr Ted Nealon TD, Minister of State for Arts and Culture, officially installed the GO in its new premises.[33] Entries in the Office Visitors' Books thereafter attest to the busy activity that centred on it. It hosted lectures on behalf of the Irish Genealogical Research Society; book launches; meetings of the Irish Heraldry Society; and a host of other promotional events, raising the profile of genealogical and heraldic research. It also provided a base, for an interim period, for the Association of Professional Genealogists of Ireland (APGI), the regulated and accredited body established in 1986 in the context of the growing number of private businesses and individuals offering genealogical services.[34]

The former dining room on the ground floor of the Kildare Street Club provided an ideal space for a permanent heraldic exhibition, and the re-opening of the Heraldic Museum in Kildare Street. This was designed by Donal Begley and his predecessor Gerald Slevin, in conjunction with architects from the OPW, aiming to introduce heraldry 'as a highly organised form of symbolism', and show how it had developed in Ireland and other European countries as a means of proclaiming identity.[35] Whilst many materials from the former display

---

31 Buckley and Smith, 'Ireland, land of your ancestors', p. 20.
32 Grant of arms to Charles J. Haughey, Government Minister, of Raheny, County Dublin, 21 February 1966, GO, MS 111T, p. 88.
33 GO, Visitors' Book, 1985–9. uncat.
34 APGI, *Tracing Your Ancestors in Ireland*. See also the APGI website: http://indigo.ie/~apgi.
35 *State Heraldic Museum: A Guided Tour*, information leaflet.

The former dining room of the Kildare Street Club provided an ideal heraldic exhibition space. *NLI.*

at the Castle (including book-plates, china, coins and seals) were included in the new exhibition, many additional objects were also introduced. The shields, crests and mottoes of the Presidents of Ireland; provincial, county and urban municipality arms; as well as the banners representing the chiefs of several Gaelic families were hung from the walls. Purpose-built display cases in the main body of the room were filled with a variety of heraldic objects, demonstrating the widespread application of heraldry in everyday life. Continuity from Ulster's Office was emphasised in the exhibits. The tabards and uniforms of former Ulster Kings of Arms were displayed in one cabinet, while the police reward notice for information about the stolen 'Crown Jewels', and the empty box that once contained the regalia of the Order of St Patrick, formed the centrepiece of another case. The bust of Sir William Betham, formerly located in the hallway of Bedford Tower building, was also prominently displayed,[36] as was the heraldic shield of the arms of Ireland that formerly had hung over the Speaker's Chair in the Irish House of Commons at College Green.[37]

---

36 *ibid.*
37 Donal Begley, *Armas na hÉireann*, information leaflet.

Postscript: Return to an Office of Arms?

Guided tours of the exhibits were organised during the summer months, and these attracted large numbers of visitors. John Wilson, the Minister for Tourism and Transport, had singled out these tours for commendation in the Dáil as a valuable aspect of cultural tourism, by 1988.[38] In 1991, statistics presented to the Dáil estimated that 8,000 visitors had passed through the Museum the previous year.[39] Previously, in May 1988, during a debate about the national cultural institutions, Taoiseach Charles Haughey focused on the potential of 'genealogy-roots'. He announced that he was establishing a Task Force on Genealogy and Tourism whose terms of reference required it, *inter alia*, 'to identify a positive role for the Genealogical Office'.[40]

The report of the Task Force resulted in the establishment of a fee-paying consultancy service at the GO, the main aim of which was to enable visitors to undertake their own research during their stay in Ireland. The service was formally inaugurated by Mr Noel Tracey, Minister of State for Arts and Culture, on 15 March 1989.[41] It was manned by APGI members, in association with trained staff of the Library, who gave direction and charted appropriate courses of research for clients.[42] Visitors also received the *Genealogical Office Ancestry Research Pack* published by the GO, which outlined the principal sources for genealogical research in Ireland, and contained reference sheets, maps and addresses. The scheme basically formalised the work that the GO had been conducting for years in an *ad hoc* way at the Castle, and which had ceased after 1981.

The public demand for the GO's genealogical information services from clients at home and abroad probably reached a highpoint in 1991, when its success and statistics were reported in the Dáil. A total of 1,400 fee-paying clients availed of the consultancy service, generating an income of £7,730. In addition, an estimated 4,500 general enquiries, and 6,000 telephone queries were dealt with by the GO. Heraldic business was secondary to the genealogical activity. Although a potential 150 clients were personally received by the Chief Herald or his Deputy in 1991, only 32 of these resulted in grants of arms being issued, realising a further £10,270.[43]

The profile of the GO further increased as a result of its association with the First Irish Genealogical Congress, held at Trinity College Dublin in 1991,

---

38 *Dáil Debates,* 380, 1574.
39 *Dáil Debates,* Genealogical Office Statistics, 20 February 1991, 405, 923.
40 *Dáil Debates,* Charles J. Haughey, An Taoiseach, contributing to debate specifically about the 'National Genealogical Office', 18 May 1988, 380, 1782.
41 GO, Visitors' Book, 1985–9, uncat.
42 'Forebears galore: how to trace an ancestor', *The Irish Times,* 4 August 1989.
43 Genealogical Office Statistics, *Dáil Debates,* 20 February 1991, 405, 923.

an event which attracted over 350 delegates from 14 countries and four continents, and which was held again in 1994, 1997 and 2001. The theme of the first congress was the diaspora, symbolised by the Wild Geese in flight. The Chief Herald acted as the congress president, and President Mary Robinson, who attended the closing banquet as guest of honour, articulated the flourishing of cultural tourism and in particular the significance of genealogical research, to which both the NLI and GO had contributed.

Well known for her interest in symbolism, she emphasised how Irishness, in its broadest sense, was fostered by genealogy, providing a means for the return for their descendants, 'embracing Irish people from every era who left these shores, whatever their class, creed or reason for leaving', to find their roots. She commended the Congress for bringing people of Irish descent together, and providing them with the means of finding a unique identity in Ireland.[44] Later she became the first President to receive her arms in person, at a private reception held in Kildare Street in January 1997.[45]

There was an expectation in the early 1990s that the GO would develop as the central focal point for people conducting ancestor research, or as Gerard Slevin had anticipated in the late 1970s:

> Our business is not to examine our own records only and say whether or not any information relevant to the enquiry is to be found in them . . . The Genealogical Office has not inherited a sort of amalgam of every Irish vital statistic. It is rather a consulting room where a need may be ascertained and defined, and the needy advised, directed and offered assistance.[46]

The GO could no longer be seen as catering only for a small élite interested in registering their pedigrees or arms. By the early 1990s, it was at the forefront of genealogical and heraldic research, with a potential 60 million clients to target throughout the world. It was actively promoting its services, with tangible success, through publications, tourist literature, promotional lectures and international visits, making a valuable contribution to Ireland's cultural tourism. But the initial success of its genealogical consultancy service was not maintained. It proved to be less popular than the free consultations of the past, and by the mid-1990s the numbers availing of it fell to very low levels.

---

44 President Mary Robinson, 'Address to delegates at the dinner of the First Genealogical Congress', 1 September 1991, in O'Duill and Evans (eds.), *Aspects of Irish Genealogy,* I, pp. 7–8.
45 GO, Visitors' Book, 1997, uncat.
46 Slevin, 'The Irish Genealogical Office', p. 54.

Postscript: Return to an Office of Arms?

The genealogical research mania that followed publication of Alex Haley's *Roots* in 1977 and President Reagan's visit in 1984 had radically changed both the demand for and the supply of genealogical information. Whilst the GO had played a significant role in the early developments, other factors affected its position as the central focus for genealogical research in Ireland. A proliferation of private businesses and individuals began to offer a range of genealogical services, while the development of the World Wide Web and access to information via the Internet increased the level of client expectation and offered new opportunities to conduct research from home. The controversial Irish Genealogical Project, supported by Government funding, set up 35 centres operating throughout the island of Ireland to computerise genealogical records and conduct searches for those willing to pay the appropriate fees. The combined effect of these factors was to bring into question the need for a significant GO role in the provision of genealogical research services and to focus more attention on the Office's traditional role as the heraldic authority for Ireland – the reason for its creation in 1552.

THE LAST TEN YEARS

In January 1993, a new Department of Arts, Culture and the Gaeltacht was created, bringing together responsibility for the main cultural institutions, including the NLI and the GO, under one department. In 1994, the GO submitted proposals for the establishment of a Heraldic Council, to be composed of members knowledgeable in the practice of heraldry, history and related disciplines. It represented an innovative approach, recognising that the heraldic authority was in the process of transition and that there were issues to be addressed.[47] Also in 1994, the NLI publication *Treasures From the NLI*, included an article by the Chief Herald on the history the Office illustrated by several colour plates of it most important heraldic treasures.[48]

Following Donal Begley's retirement as Chief Herald in June 1995, the Minister for Arts, Culture and the Gaeltacht, Michael D. Higgins, appointed the Director of the NLI, Dr Patricia Donlon, to the additional position of Chief Herald in September 1995.[49] Dr Donlon had been appointed NLI director in 1989, and had proved an effective and dynamic manager. Her additional

---

47 Donal Begley, 'Proposed Heraldic Council', typescript.
48 Kissane (ed.), *Treasures*, pp. 202–33.
49 Appointment of Dr Patricia Donlon to act as Chief Herald and Genealogical Officer in pursuance of the Allocation of Administration (Genealogical Office) Order, 1943, 15 September 1995, NLI.

Dr Patricia Donlon who became the first woman to hold the position of Chief Herald in 1995 signing a heraldic patent, accompanied by Fergus Gillespie, Deputy Chief Herald. *NLI Trustees Report, 1995.*

appointment as Chief Herald was a unique development, as she became Ireland's first woman principal herald, following in the steps of no less than 26 male predecessors. But the appointment led to an outcry in heraldic and genealogical circles that the post of Chief Herald of Ireland was to be linked with that of Director of the Library. This decision, it was widely felt, had the potential of subsuming the former and historically much older position under the latter and of diminishing its status.

A flurry of letters to *The Irish Times* followed between October and December 1995, and several articles on the subject were published in the *Sunday Tribune*, *Irish Roots*, and *Phoenix Magazine*. These drew attention to the specialist functions of the GO, emphasising its long history and continuity from the former Office of Arms, and argued that it should be given independent status as an office in its own right, as had been the case until 1943. Some correspondents also raised the important symbolic role that the Office played in post-modern Ireland, transcending traditional political barriers because it provided genealogical and heraldic services for all people of Ireland descent, North and South of the Border. A strong case was made that the Office should be strengthened as an institution of common interest.[50]

The GO, it was argued, deserved 'a full-time administrator *au fait* with the subjects' and with 'more resources in order to cope with the increased demands'.[51] Even the Clarenceux King of Arms in London, John Brooke-Little, entered the fray, following publication of an article in the *Daily Telegraph*.[52] He urged that the most important aspect was to make provision for expertise in the laws of arms and Irish genealogy, whatever administrative framework was adopted for its day-to-day management.[53] The Chairman of the Heraldry Society of Ireland, Daithi Hanly, summed up the case for greater autonomy, urging that 'to lessen the dignity of this internationally important office would be a pathetic denunciation of almost four and a half centuries of Irish history.'[54]

Arguably, these voices represented a small lobby of heraldry enthusiasts, professional genealogists, and other interested parties but the unanimity of expression was palpable, opening up a public debate, and forcing the Minister to make a response. He gave a well-reasoned reply in the press, and went

---

50 Letters to the editor, *The Irish Times*, 10 October 1995.
51 *ibid.*, 25 October 1995.
52 'Hark, the Irish heralds whinge', *Daily Telegraph*, 23 October 1995.
53 John Brooke-Little, College of Arms, to the editor, *Daily Telegraph*, 25 October 1995.
54 Letters to the editor, *The Irish Times*, 19 October 1995.

to some lengths to assure critics that the GO would be neither abolished nor diminished, but that its interests were best served by placing it under the super-vision of the executive authority of the Director of NLI.[55] In both the Senate and the Dáil, he explained that forthcoming legislation – the National Cultural Institutions Bill (which amongst other things proposed establishing the Library as an autonomous body) – would make explicit provision in statute for the GO 'within the framework being provided for the National Library'.[56] He pointed out that:

> In the period since 1943, the administrative arrangements underpinning the overall structure have gradually proved detrimental to both the Genealogical Office and the National Library, with the former regularly feeling obliged to assert its independence and the latter its jurisdiction. It became manifestly clear that it was not in anyone's interests that there should be ongoing difficulties of this nature.[57]

When the National Cultural Institutions Bill received its second reading in the Senate a year later, there was further controversy, opponents again spec-ulating that it was the Minister's intention 'to close down the oldest Office of State'.[58] A particular area of grievance was the first subsection of Section 13 (dealing with the GO). Some legal doubt had arisen about whether or not the Statutory Instrument made in 1943, the Allocation of Administration (Genealogical Office) Order, had technically established the GO or merely allocated its administration and business to the Department of Education.[59] Thus, the Minister explained, it had to be abolished before the 'pre-existing functions c[ould] be formally reconstructed and assigned to the National Library'. The Minister assured the Senate that this technical "abolition" would not 'make any substantial change to the operation of genealogy or heraldry within the Library as an institution', the intention merely being to clarify 'the authority in charge of the operation of those functions'.[60] Nevertheless, the public debate continued, the Opposition members in the Senate taking up the external lobby's campaign for greater autonomy for the GO.

For example, Pascal Mooney, the Fianna Fáil Senator and Spokesman on Arts, Culture and the Gaeltacht, called for the Government to consider

---

55 Michael D. Higgins, Minister for Arts, Culture and the Gaeltacht, to the editor, *The Irish Times*, 19 October 1995.
56 *Dáil Debates*, 26 October 1995, 457, 1680.
57 *Seanad Debates*, 25 October 1995, 144, 1942.
58 *Sunday Tribune*, 13 October 1996.
59 *Allocation of Administration (Genealogical Office) Order, 1943, 267.*
60 *Seanad Debates*, 17 October 1996, 148, 1842.

establishing 'an independent and autonomous organisation of the Chief Herald'. Rather than tying it legislatively to another national institution, he argued that it should be allowed to sit on its own, on account 'of its history and place in the cultural diversity of this island'. He cited the examples of the Republic of Zimbabwe, where a new Chief Herald's Office had recently been established, directly accountable to its Prime Minister's Office,[61] and also Canada, where an independent heraldic authority was established on 4 June 1988, directly accountable to the Governor-General,[62] and made a strong case that the Irish authority should be 'retained separately . . . and not incorporated into anything else'.[63]

The issue was further discussed when the Bill came to Committee Stage in November 1996. The offending Section 13 was modified, so that the GO was declared 'for the avoidance of any doubt to be a branch of the Library', although this remained a disappointment to those who had campaigned for its separate identity. At the final stages of the debates, the Minister admitted that 'in the light of representations from those with a close interest in those subjects' he had striven to achieve a balance, which he believed strengthened the position of the GO. For the first time 'the executive function of granting and confirming of coats of arms by the Chief Herald of Ireland' would be recognised 'in primary statute'.[64]

Whilst the debates of 1995–6 did not secure the independent status that many enthusiasts had hoped for, they did focus considerable public attention on the GO and its functions. In contrast to the absence of any public debate preceding the formal transfer and allocation of the functions of the former Office of Arms to the NLI in 1943, the Senate debates and external published comment of the 1990s raised public awareness about the issues. At the conclusion of the debates in the Senate, it was acknowledged at parliamentary level that there was 'a greater and deeper understanding' of the GO's work than ever before.[65]

RETURN TO AN OFFICE OF ARMS?

Although the Bill, which became the National Cultural Institutions Act when it was formally enacted on 2 April 1997, generated a good deal of controversy,

---

61 *op. cit.*, 148, 1865.
62 *The Canadian Heraldic Authority*, p. 11.
63 *Seanad Debates*, 17 October 1996, 148, 1859–64.
64 *Seanad Debates*, 12 December 1996, 149, 1627.
65 *Seanad Debates*, 17 October 1996, 148, 1861–2.

Artistic creativity at work: the Herald Painter, Katy Lumsden, puts the finishing touches to a new heraldic piece.

it has yet to be brought into operation in relation to the NLI. Section 13 states that the GO is a branch of the Library, and thus makes provision for the Library Board to appoint future Chief Heralds:

> the Board may from time to time as occasion requires designate a member of its staff to perform the duty of researching, granting and confirming coats of arms, and such member shall be called the Chief Herald or in Irish, Príomh-Aralt na hÉireann, whilst performing such duties.

Section 13 also provides that the Board of the Library may establish a Committee on Genealogy and Heraldry, to perform such functions of the Board in relation to those fields, as in its opinion, 'may be better or more conveniently performed by it and are assigned to it by the Board'.[66] But a Library Board has yet to be appointed, as has the Committee on Heraldry and Genealogy. In the meantime, both the NLI, and by virtue of its administrative association with

---

66 *National Cultural Institutions Act, 1997* (Dublin, 1997).

that institution, the GO, have benefited from increased Government funding and administrative support in recent years. The specifics of organisation have attracted less attention.

As matters stand, both institutions are functioning well, and if the 1997 Act is ever to come into operation in relation to the Library, the clause allowing for the appointment of the Chief Herald by the Library Board might be reconsidered. Given that the authority to grant and confirm arms is exercised by the Chief Herald and/or his deputy 'on behalf of the Government', it would be more appropriate for the Government to continue to appoint the office-holder as has been the case since 1943. If the appointment were to be delegated to a semi-state Board, the status and dignity of the Office of Chief Herald would be reduced. Again, in the event that the Committee on Heraldry and Genealogy is to be appointed, heraldic experts should be included, and attention should be given to its regional composition. Given that the Office remains the heraldic authority for the island of Ireland, representatives from Northern Ireland might also be included. This would be particularly appropriate in the spirit of inclusiveness and cross-Border co-operation enshrined by the Good Friday Agreement.

When Dr Patricia Donlon's tenure of office was cut short by ill-health, forcing her to retire in February 1997, her successor as Director, Brendan O Donoghue, was appointed to the position of Chief Herald in September 1997. He, like his predecessors, was empowered to execute 'the appropriate instruments for the grant and confirmation of arms', and to appoint a deputy to assist in these functions. In practice, the Deputy Chief Herald, Fergus Gillespie, is responsible for the day-to-day operation of the GO, and much of the interface with the public. He has the grade of Keeper within the Library's staffing framework, and as such participates fully in the management arrangements for the organisation as a whole.

Brendan O Donoghue's tenure of office has seen dynamic growth of the Library and the establishment of a clear chain of command and administrative structure both between central Government and the institution, and within the NLI, between its constituent parts. Commitment to maintaining the professional staff of the Office has been underlined by recent developments. In addition to the Deputy Chief Herald, a second professional herald has been engaged on a contract basis to process applications from private individuals and corporate bodies for the right to bear arms, and to design new coats of arms.[67] The resident heraldic artist enjoys civil servant status at the level of

---

67 *ibid.*, p. 35; *NLI Trustees Report*, 2000, pp. 13–4.

Assistant Keeper. Four additional artists are also employed on a contract basis to assist with commissions, as and when required, an indication that the volume of work is increasing. Their work has helped to bring the Registers of Arms up to date, with a hand-painted emblazonment of each coat of arms, together with its related blazon. In addition, an archivist from within the ranks of the Library has been assigned to take responsibility for GO manuscript and record collections, and to ensure more effective cataloguing.

The transfer of genealogical consultancy services to the main Library now allows the GO to concentrate on the more specialist demands of heraldry. In the summer of 1998, the NLI set up a free genealogical service to provide advice for visitors in a dedicated genealogy room in the main Library building. This operation is most successful, manned by accredited professional researchers and trained Library staff, and deals with up to 15,000 visitors each year. It has proved more popular than the fee-paying consultancy service of the early 1990s, based at the GO, and is appreciated by foreign visitors in particular. Significantly, from the perspective of the GO, it has freed up the time and resources there to concentrate on the specific remit of heraldic work.

Heraldic output has continued at a steady pace in the past few years. In 2000, the GO issued 28 patents, and received a total of £55,691 in fees for grants of arms and associated heraldic services.[68] In 2002, 22 patents were issued, slightly down on the previous year, but with total fees of €66,248 (£52,175).[69] The launch of a new Library website in 2000 has allowed worldwide promotion of the Irish heraldic authority on the Internet. Concise information about the procedures involved in applying for arms, together with illustrations of recent grants and their recipients, are available online, and this has increased the number of heraldic enquiries.[70]

In the light of these developments, it may be argued that the Office has, in effect, returned to the original function for which it was established in 1552: the granting and confirmation of arms. But grants and confirmations are no longer exclusively granted only to 'illustrious persons' and 'men of rank', as envisaged by King Edward VI in 1552. Today, all Irish citizens, male and female, as well as other persons living outside Ireland with significant Irish ancestral links, public and corporate bodies, and organisations with Irish connections, may petition to bear arms. The provision of heraldic services for the Irish abroad has been a recurrent function of the Office since the trend in mass emigration began in the seventeenth century, and, as we have seen, has played

---

68   *ibid.*, p. 14
69   *NLI Trustees Report*, 2001.
70   http://www.nli.ie, visited 18 May 2002.

a significant role in its survival during the twentieth century. This connection with Irish people on a global scale has recently been embodied in the spirit of the Irish Constitution, as amended in 1998, which 'cherishes its special affinity with people who share its cultural identity and heritage living abroad'.[71]

In post-modern Ireland, the concept of a vibrant, confident and active heraldic authority sits more easily than it did after Independence, and indeed after the transfer of control in 1943. Given the reversion to heraldry as its principal activity, and the fact that the Office no longer undertakes genealogical research (except when specifically linked to its heraldic work), the time may now be opportune to consider reverting to the historic title of Office of Arms. In the minds of many enthusiasts and friends of the Office, it has never ceased to be anything else. As early as 1947, MacLysaght declared that the title of 'Genealogical Office' had become a misnomer. Today, it remains confusing for the public, who approach it as a first point of contact for genealogical information, rather than the genealogical consultancy focused on the NLI, or the genealogical information and resources available in many other record repositories and family history centres around the country. Re-adoption of the title Office of Arms would end this confusion. It would also raise the status of the Office, allowing it to outwardly project its principal function and separate identity, whilst operating within the Library framework from an administrative point of view.

It might also provide the context for the formal introduction of a national honours system, along the lines of the Rolla Onóra, as envisaged by MacLysaght in the 1940s, which the Office could administer on behalf of the Government. Thus, rather than the controversial system of honouring sporting personalities with university doctorates, something might be offered from the people of Ireland, and the Office might more appropriately be given responsibility for the design, issue and registration of honours and achievements. Three separate Taosigh – Charles Haughey, Albert Reynolds and John Bruton – directly requested the Chief Herald to provide the means of honouring three important visitors to Ireland in recent years. As a result, the Canadian Premier, Brian Mulroney, and the Prime Minister of Australia, the Honourable Paul Keating, were each presented with illuminated family trees on vellum that had been created in the Office, during their State visits, in 1991 and 1993; while the President of the United States, Bill Clinton was granted arms, and presented with a leather-bound manuscript containing information about the arms and the work of the Office, during his historic visit to Ireland in 1995. This is the kind

---

71   The 19th amendment of Irish Constitution altered Articles 2 and 3, on 3 June 1998.

The tradition of heraldry and the Office of Arms honoured by the Head of State. On 1 February 2000, the staff of the Office was invited to Áras an Uachtaráin to present the grant of arms designed for, and issued to, the eighth President of Ireland, Mary McAleese. *Left to right:* Fergus Gillespie, Deputy Chief Herald; Katy Lumsden, Herald Painter; An tUachtarán; Brendan O Donoghue, Chief Herald; Mícheál Ó Comáin, Consultant Herald. *Courtesy, Lensmen, Dublin.*

of high profile work that the Office might be encouraged to develop in the future.[72]

Specifically excluded by Sir Bernard Burke from the Public Records Act 1867, the records of the Office of Arms remained *in situ* in the Record Tower in Dublin Castle until the Office of Arms was transferred to Bedford Tower in 1903. At this point, Sir Arthur Vicars went to great lengths to ensure that fire-proof storage was provided for them and that they were properly looked after. In 1922 their future was specifically discussed during the Treaty negotiations, when Hugh Kennedy and other Free State representatives were deeply concerned about their welfare. Their survival to the present day is nothing short of a miracle, because in April 1922 they were close to being transferred to the PRO, just before its contents were reduced to ashes in June of that year, during the Civil War. During the early 1940s they might also have been transferred to London, as was the initial intention of the British officials who negotiated the transfer of the Office to the Irish Government. Only the concerned determination of the Irish officials to keep the records in Ireland, and the availability of microfilming technology at NLI, prevented this unhappy scenario.

Given the efforts that were made to safeguard them in the past, and the fact that they contain so much genealogical detail, a comprehensive single catalogue would be an ideal means of preservation for the future. The lack of such a catalogue is still the biggest obstacle to research.[73] Notwithstanding the valiant attempts of Dr Richard Hayes to catalogue them for inclusion in his *Manuscript Sources for the History of Irish Civilisation*, and the several in-house indexes and finding aids that have been attempted over the years, a substantial quantity of papers remains uncatalogued, including a large collection of rolled pedigrees, as well as boxes of loose papers relating to the administration of the Office itself. In the last few years an independent catalogue was commenced by Mrs Virginia Wade McAnlis, an American genealogist, using the microfilms of GO material made by the Mormon Church in the 1950s. Her catalogue is based on the principal indexes to the collections. Whilst it accounts for thousands of surnames, it is by no means complete.[74]

Randal Sadleir, the son of Thomas Sadleir, the last Acting Ulster King of Arms, recently presented his father's papers to the Chief Herald of Ireland. Before being transferred to the GO, these papers provided an important

---

72 Interview with Donal Begley, Chief Herald of Ireland 1981–95.
73 Grenham, 'The GO and its records', p. 9.
74 McAnlis, *Consolidated Index*.

primary source for this book and they will be available to the public as soon as they are catalogued. Unlike his father whose perception of the Office of Arms was unrelentingly royalist, Randal, now in his seventies, sees the development of the Office in a natural evolutionary context that is as relevant today under the Government of Ireland as it was in his father's time under the British Crown. Randal's experience was quite different to his father. He spent the greatest part of career in the British Colonial Service in Africa and was the last expatriate District Officer to leave the service of the independent Republic of Tanzania, having been invited by its first President, Julius Nyrere, to remain as an adviser during the first period of independence. Both in his autobiography, *Tanzania: Journey To Republic*, and the lecture he delivered to the NLI Society in 2002, Sadleir spoke approvingly of the Irish Government's retention of the Office of Arms after the transfer to the NLI in 1943.[75] These were developments that his father simply could not have foreseen in the 1940s nor did he believe were possible.

The wheel has thus turned full circle in a generation. The presentation of Thomas Sadleir's papers at this time is symbolic, in true heraldic tradition, of the continuity of the Office of Arms. Moreover, it is a recognition that the new regime continues to serve the heraldic needs of the people of Ireland, at home and abroad. The Sadleir Correspondence will contribute to a better understanding of the Office's diverse and colourful history. It adds one more strand to the rich tapestry of heritage and heraldic tradition that the Office of Arms, the oldest Office of State, has to offer future generations.

---

75 Randal Sadleir, 'Memories of the Office of Arms, Dublin, 1933–43, was delivered at Dublin Castle, 21 February 2002.

BIBLIOGRAPHY

PRIMARY SOURCES

L'Académie Internationale d'Héraldique, in the possession of M. Michael Popoff, Secretary General, Paris.

Personal File for Gerard Slevin (1919–97), Chief Herald of Ireland 1954–81.

College of Arms, London

Archive of Garter King of Arms, Box File G. 31.
Chapter Book 20, 1935–45.
Chapter Book 21, 1945–49.
Grants Register, 94.
Irish Grants Register, 3.

Genealogical Office, Dublin

MS 22	Memorials & Extracts From the Rolls, compiled by John Lodge, 18th century.
MS 77	Funeral Entries, xv, 1861–93.
MS 93–9	Chaos Volumes, comprising miscellaneous material bound and organised by Sir William Betham, 16th–18th centuries.
MS 101	Register of Knights, iv, 1853–92.
MS 102	Register of Knights, v, 1893.
MS 109	[Vicars's Series 'G'] Register of Arms, 1863–80.
MS 110	['H'] Register of Arms, 1880–97.
MS 111J	Register of Arms 1898–1909.
MS 111A	['K'] Register of Arms, 1909–14.
MS 111B	['L'] Register of Arms, 1914–19.
MS 111C	['M'] Register of Arms, 1920–29.
MS 111D	['N'] Register of Arms, 1929–37.
MS 111E	['O'] Register of Arms, 1934–40.
MS 111F	['P'] Register of Arms, accounting for 'particulars supplied by Mr T.U. Sadleir, of grants and confirmations made during the last eight years before Ulster's Office was taken over by the GO, the registrations of which were not carried out…', compiled in 1943 [actually covers the ten-year period 1932–42].
MS 111Q	[continues Vicars's series format] Register of Arms, 1943–52.
MS 111R	Register of Arms, 1955–59.
MS 111S	Register of Arms, 1959–66.

MS 111T	Register of Arms, 1966–72.
MS 111U	Register of Arms, 1973–78.
MS 111V	Register of Arms, 1978–81.
MS 111W+X	Register of Arms, 1982–95.
MS 111Y	Register of Arms, 1996–99.
MS 111Z	Register of Arms, 1999–2002.
MS '111 I or S'	Grants to army corps, and examples of army badges and other insignia, post–1943.
MSS 145–7	*Linea Antiqua*, compilations of pedigrees and alliances of Gaelic families, with details of their arms and genealogies, by Sir William Betham.
MS 150	King's Letters & Other Entries, 1789–1909.
MS 152	Royal Warrants, iv, 1845–68.
MS 153	Royal Warrants, v, 1868–88.
MS 154	Royal Warrants, vi, 1889–1910.
MS 154A	Royal Warrants & Changes of Name, including those issued under the authority of the Irish Government, for the period 1910–45.
MS 175	Pedigrees, I-xxvii.
MSS 189–93	Plea and Patent Roll Excerpts, compiled by Sir William Betham.
MS 202	Gazette Notices, with index to changes of name recorded therein, 1864–76.
MSS 203–14	Miscellaneous Pedigrees, compiled by Sir William Betham.
MSS 215–19	Ancient Anglo-Irish Families, compiled by Sir William Betham.
MSS 220–22	Milesian Families, compiled by Sir William Betham.
MSS 223–6	Prerogative Will Pedigrees, compiled by Sir William Betham, pre-1700.
MSS 227–54	Prerogative Will Pedigrees, compiled by Sir William Betham, 1700–1800.
MSS 255–6	Prerogative Wills Marriage Alliances, extracted and compiled by Sir William Betham.
MSS 261–76	Sketch Pedigrees, compiled by Sir William Betham.
MSS 292–8	Sketch Pedigrees, compiled by Sir William Betham.
MS 319	Collection of *pro-forma* applications forms, as devised by George Dames Burtchaell, pre–1921.
MS 322	Official Entries & Letters, 1854–69.
MS 323	Official Entries & Letters, 1869–78.
MS 324	Official Entries & Letters, 1879–85.

MS 325	Official Entries & Letters, 1885–91.
MS 326	Official Entries & Letters, 1891–92
MS 327	Official Entries & Letters, 1896–1905.
MS 328	Official Entries & Letters, 1905–08.
MS 336	Ceremonial Book, including orders for processions, 1805–1911.
MS 337	The Viceregal Court, i, compiled by Sir Bernard Burke, including orders, processional lists, press cuttings and related correspondence, 1876–85.
MS 348	The Viceregal Court, ii, 1853–85. [This volume appears to overlap with the previous one].
MS 349	The Viceregal Court, iii, commenced in Burke's time, and completed by Sir Arthur Vicars, 1882–1903.
MS 355	Letter Book of Sir William Betham, 1814–16.
MS 362–77	Letter Books of Sir William Betham, 1810–49.
MS 388	Miscellaneous papers of Ulster's Office, 1610–1820.
MS 412	The 'Barry' Volume, containing miscellaneous pedigrees and extracts, commencing with the pedigree of the Barry family of Fryarstown, Rockstown and Sandhill, County Limerick.
MS 424	Will Abstracts, compiled by Thomas U. Sadleir, from 17 March 1903.
MS 429	Index to Will Abstracts, compiled by Miss Beryl Eustace.
MS 469	Registered Pedigree Index.
MS 470	Unregistered Pedigree Index.
MS 507	'Loss of the Irish Crown Jewels', scrapbook compiled by Mr J.C. Hodgson, 1907–25.
MS 527	Journal of Dr Edward MacLysaght, compiled as a 'repository of material' gathered by him relating to heraldry, genealogy and various aspects of GO administration, including drafts of lectures, papers, and other anecdotal material, 1943–49.
MS 557	'Irish genealogical notes', notebook compiled by Thomas U. Sadleir, from 27 February 1903.
MS 622	Volume entitled the 'Ainsworth Miscellany', containing some genealogical material compiled by Sir John Ainsworth, but largely consists of additional notes compiled by Dr Edward MacLysaght, post–1943.

Official Correspondence, consisting of six volumes of press bound copies of outgoing letters, as follows: I, December 1901-May 1902; II, May 1893-February 1909; III, February 1909-November 1910; IV, November 1911-March 1912; V, March 1912-February 1914; VI, February 1914-January 1923.

National Archives of Ireland, Dublin

Census Returns	Dublin City and County, 1911.
CSORP 1890/11178	Papers relating to appointments at the Office of Arms, 1890–91.
CSORP 1913/18119	Papers relating to the larceny of the State Jewels, 1907–13.
CSORP	Index to the papers of the Chief Secretary's Office, 1908.
DT 1587A	Papers concerning seals for the State and Government Ministers, 1922–37.
DT S3926A	File of correspondence and memorandums relating to the Office of Arms, Dublin Castle, 1922–40.
DT S3926B	File of correspondence and memorandums relating to the Office of Arms, Dublin Castle, transfer to State, 1940–43.
DT S3926C	File of correspondence and memorandums relating to the Office of Arms, Dublin Castle, transfer to State, 1943–63.
DT S4618A	File of correspondence concerning the official procedure for answering applications for coats of arms, and other related queries, including the design of a State flag, 1923–55.
DT S5708	Papers relating to the Order of St Patrick, 1927–69.
DT 9621	Papers concerning the official procedure for answering requests for information about family histories and pedigrees, 1937–53.
DT S13207	Papers relating to the reproduction of microfilm copies of the records of Ulster King of Arms, with Messrs Kodak and Co., April 1943.
DT S15297A-C	File relating to 'An Tóstal' (pageant), the national festival sponsored by the Irish Tourist Board (Bord Fáilte), 1952–8.
	Principal Registry, Dublin, will of Sir Arthur Vicars, probate granted 20 March 1922.
OPW 9/A6/4/6/47	File of reports and correspondence relating to the outbreak of fire in the 'Herald's Office', formerly the Office of Arms, and subsequent improvements for the building, 1947–52.
OPW 9/A6/14/2	File of reports and correspondence relating to defects in the Bedford Tower building, as occupied by the 'Heraldic Office' (Office of Arms), 1938–40.

999/664 Address from the Corporation of Cork to the Earl of Aberdeen, Lord Lieutenant, May 1909, by Gilbert, Cork, transferred by Sir Nevile Wilkinson, December 1921.

SPO Search Book, Vol. 3 (Record Tower), 1898–1905.

National Library of Ireland, Dublin

Maps and Drawings, 1208 Four drawing of the Office of Arms at the Bedford Tower, Dublin Castle, including details of cornices, architraves and mantelpiece details in the Heraldic Museum, by C. F. Quinlan, School of Architecture, University College Dublin, October 1938.

P. 4944 Correspondence between Sir Arthur Vicars and Mr James Fuller, F.S.A., mainly concerning genealogical matters, but also containing references to the theft of the Irish 'Crown Jewels', 1904–15. [Microfilm copy of originals, in possession of Mr Basil O'Connell].

Uncatalogued / current material File of correspondence and memorandums relating to the administration and business of the GO, 1943–77.

Papers of (William) Dermod O'Brien (185–1945) in the process of being listed. Collection List 64.

National Archives Act, 1986, Description of Classes of Records Amendment Order, 2000, relating to the Genealogical Office client files, signed by Bertie Ahern, An Taoiseach, 21 December 2000.

Statement of the Chief Herald, Brendan O Donoghue, 'Recognition of Mr Terence McCarthy as MacCarthy Mór, 6 August 1999.

Typewritten notes on microfilming of Catholic parish registers, by Brendan O Donoghue, undated.

Office of Public Works, Dublin

A6/14/4 File concerning the upkeep of the Bedford Tower, as occupied by the Genealogical Office, 1955–81.

A6/14/5/43   File concerning certain improvements and furnishings for the Genealogical Office, Dublin Castle, 1958.

A6/14/7/48   File relating to the accommodation of the Office of Arms, 1900–03.

A136/1/1   File relating to the reconstruction of Dublin Castle, 1946–53.

Public Record Office, Kew

BS 22/7   Crown Jewels Commission (Ireland), the Shaw Commission: Reports and Papers, 1907–11.

C 195/5/11   Petitions for places to be assigned to Sir Nevile Wilkinson and Captain Guillimore O'Grady, at the coronation of George VI, submitted on their behalf by T.U. Sadleir, Registrar and Deputy King of Arms, 27 October 1936.

Cabinet, Dominions Office, Home Office, Prime Minister's, and Treasury files concerning the Office of Arms, Dublin, 1871–1943, as follows:
CAB 27/68; CAB 9R/51/22; CO 904/221; DO 35/14; DO 35/1132; DO 35/894/9; DO 35/359/6; DO 130/137; HO 45/9860/B2823; HO 45/109512/3; HO 45/25901; HO 144/1648; HO 267/46; PREM 2/75; T 11744; T 4/24/1; T 21/156; T 60/192/7335; T 62/709; T 160/190; T 160/192; T 162/709; T 162/316; T 164/24/1; T 332/256; T 15880

Public Records Office of Northern Ireland

CAB 9R/12/2A   Correspondence relating to the use of royal arms, 1921–31.

CAB 9R/51/22   Papers relating to the visit of the Prince of Wales to Northern Ireland, November 1932.

CAB 9R/52/1   Papers relating to the Office of the Ulster King of Arms, and the passing of that Office from the control of the Crown to the Irish Government, with subsequent material concerning the Office of Norroy and Ulster, at the College of Arms, London, 1923–66.

Representative Church Body Library, Dublin

MS 209   B.J. Burke, Dublin Castle, 'Opinion on the Precedence of the [Church of Ireland] Bishop of Meath', 18 December 1876.

MS 14   Papers of John Ribton Garstin, President Royal Society of Antiquaries (1903–05), 1863–77.

MS 345/9   Supplement to the Clerical Succession Lists of the Church of Ireland Diocese of Ossory, compiled by Geraldine Willis.

Bibliography

University College Dublin

Kennedy Papers.

PRINTED PRIMARY SOURCES

An Act For Keeping Safely the Public Records of Ireland, 1867, 30 & 31, Vict. c.lxx.
An Bhratach Náisiúnta (The National Flag), Government publication leaflet (latest edition, 2002).
Allocation of Administration (Genealogical Office) Order, *S.R.O. No. 267 of 1943.*
Annual Reports of the Council of Trustees of the National Library of Ireland, 1945–2002.
Bunreacht na hÉireann (Constitution of Ireland).
Crown Jewels (Ireland) Commission, *Report of the Vice-Regal Commission, Appointed to Investigate the Circumstances of the Loss of the Regalia of the Order of Saint Patrick and to Inquire if Sir Arthur Vicars Exercised Due Vigilance and Proper Care as the Custodian Thereof, Presented to Both Houses of Parliament*, Cd. 3906 (London, HMSO, 1908).
Dáil Debates, 1922–95.
Free State Constitution, Irish Free State (Saorstát Éireann) Act, 1922.
Hansard, Debates of the House of Commons, Third Series, 1886–1908.
National Cultural Institutions Act, 1997 (Dublin, 1997).
Seanad Debates, 1922–96.

NEWSPAPERS, JOURNALS AND PERIODICALS

Belfast Newsletter
Ireland Today, Bulletin of the Department of Foreign Affairs
The Daily News
The Daily Telegraph
Dublin Evening Mail
Dublin Express
Dublin Gazette
Dublin University Magazine
Freeman's Journal
Iris Oifigiúil
Irish Press
Look Magazine
The Irish Times
New York Times

Preservation of the Memorials of the Dead Ireland Journal
The Times
The Star Newspaper
Sunday Express
Sunday Times
Sunday Tribune

WEBSITES

APGI: http://indigo.ie/~apgi, last visited 1 May 2002.
European Parliament: http://www.europa.eu.int/abc/symbols/emblem.graphics/graphics_en.htm, last visited 18 May 2002.
National Library of Ireland: http://www.nli.ie/, last visited 18 May 2002.

SECONDARY SOURCES

Isbel Aberdeen and Temair and Aberdeen and Temair, *More Cracks With We Twa'* (London, 1929).
L'Académie Internationale d'Héraldique, *Mémorial du Jubilé, 1944–99* (Brussels, 2000).
Anon. 'The last days of Dublin Castle', in *Blackwood's Magazine, ccxii* (August 1922), pp. 137–90.
APGI, *Tracing Your Ancestors in Ireland*, information leaflet and membership list, 1996–7.
Francis Bamford and Viola Bankes, *Vicious Circle. The Case of the Missing Irish Crown Jewels* (London, 1965).
John Barry, 'Guide to records of the Genealogical Office, Dublin, with a commentary on heraldry in Ireland, and on the history of the Office', in *Analecta Hibernica, 26* (1970), pp. 3–43.
Audrey Bateman, *The Magpie Tendency* (Canterbury, 1999).
William J. Bayly, *Historical Sketch and Description of Dublin Castle* (Dublin, undated).
Donal Begley, *Armas na hÉireann, Arms of Ireland*. Government information leaflet (undated).
—— *Handbook on Irish Genealogy* (Dublin, 1970).
—— *The Ancestor Trail in Ireland: A Companion Guide* (Dublin, 1982).
—— *Our House*, GO information leaflet (undated).
—— *Some Manuscript Treasures of the Genealogical Office* (Dublin, 1994).
—— *State Heraldic Museum*. GO information leaflet (undated).
Peter Berresford Ellis, *Erin's Blood Royal* (New York, 2002).
Frederic Boase, *Modern English Biography* (Truro, 1892).

Bibliography

Bord Fáilte, *Tracing Your Ancestors*. Information leaflet MB28 (Dublin, 1989).

Nicola Gordon Bowe and Elizabeth Cumming, *The Arts and Crafts Movements in Dublin and Edinburgh 1885–1925* (Dublin, 1998).

William Buckley and Sandra Smith, 'Ireland, land of your ancestors', in *Inside Ireland* (Spring 1990), pp. 20–1.

J. Bernard Burke, *The Book of Precedence* (London, 1887).

—— *The General Armory of England, Scotland, Ireland and Wales* (London, 1878).

—— *The Rise of Great Families* (London, 1873).

—— *The Romance of the Aristocracy,* 3 vols. (London, 1855).

—— *Vicissitudes of Families* (London 1859).

—— *Burke's Peerage and Baronetage* (London, 1999).

George Dames Burtchaell and Thomas Ulick Sadleir (eds.), *Alumni Dublinenses* (London, 1924); and new edition (Dublin, 1935).

T. Blake Butler, 'The officers of arms of Ireland' in *Irish Genealogist, 2,1* (1943), pp. 2–12; and *2,2* (1944), pp. 40–7.

John Cafferky and Kevin Hannafin, *Scandal and Betrayal. Shackleton and the Irish Crown Jewels* (Dublin, 2002).

The Canadian Heraldic Authority (Rideau Hall, 1990).

Wallace Clare, *A Simple Guide to Irish Genealogy*, revised edition, edited by Rosemary ffolliott (Dublin, 1966).

—— 'Irish genealogy', in *Genealogists' Magazine*, v, i, (1932), pp. 43–9.

Gerard Crotty, 'Chiefs of the name' in M. D. Evans, *Aspects of Irish Genealogy, 3,* (Dublin, 1996), pp. 20–32.

William F. Dennehy, *Record: The Irish International Exhibition 1907* (Dublin, 1909).

Dictionary of National Biography from earliest times to 1900 (Oxford, 1917–).

Eilish Ellis and P. Beryl Eustace (eds.), *Registry of Deeds, Dublin, Abstracts of Wills, 1785–1832* (Dublin, 1984).

P. Beryl Eustace, 'Index of will abstracts in the Genealogical Office, Dublin', in *Analecta Hibernica, xvii* (1947).

Countess of Fingall, *Seventy Years Young. Memoirs of Elizabeth, Countess of Fingall* (London, 1937).

Percy Fitzgerald, *Recollections of Dublin Castle and of Dublin Society by a Native* (London, 1902).

Frances-Jane French, *'Nepotists and sinecurists: a history of Ulster's Office, 1552–1943'*, in *Irish Genealogist, 10, 3,* (2000), pp. 333–71.

—— *Heralds in Ireland: A History of Ulster's Office, 1552–1943*, forthcoming.

Peter Galloway, *The Most Illustrious Order. The Order of Saint Patrick and its Knights* (London, 1999).

J. Anthony Gaughan, *Listowel and its Vicinity* (Cork, 1973).

Genealogical Office, *Ancestry Research Pack* (Dublin, 1989).

Fergus Gillespie, 'Heraldry in Ireland'. The St Andrew Lecture, 1999, in *Journal of the Heraldry Society of Scotland, 23* (2000), pp. 7–25.

Ida Grehan, 'Arms of a gentler kind', in *Cara Magazine 5.4* (1972), pp. 29–31.

John Grenham, 'The GO and its records', in *Irish Manuscripts Commission Guide to the Genealogical Office, Dublin* (Dublin, 1998), pp. 3–33.

Philip Guedalla, *The Duke* (London, 1931).

Alex Haley, *Roots. The Saga of an American Family* (New York).

David Harkness, *The Restless Dominion. The Irish Free State and the British Commonwealth of Nations, 1921–31* (New York, 1970).

Richard Hayes (ed.), *Manuscript Sources for the History of Irish Civilisation* (Dublin 1965).

G.A. Hayes-McCoy, *A History of Irish Flags From Earliest Times* (Dublin, 1979).

Heritage Travel, Ohio, *Ireland Heritage Tours*. Information leaflets, 1984–6.

Bulmer Hobson, *Ireland Yesterday and Tomorrow* (Tralee, 1968).

Pierre Joannon (ed.), *De Gaulle and Ireland* (Dublin, 1991).

Edward Keane, P. Beryl Phair and Thomas U. Sadleir (eds.), *King's Inns Admission Papers, 1607–1867* (Dublin, 1982).

N. Kissane (ed.), *Treasures from the National Library of Ireland* [(Drogheda, 1994]).

Carole Lager, 'L'Europe en quête de ses symbols', in P. Lang (ed.), *Euroclio Etudes et Documents* (Bern, 1995).

H.G. Leask, 'House at Old Bawn, County Dublin', in *Royal Society of Antiquaries of Ireland Journal, 6th series, iii* (1913), pp. 314–25.

J.J. Lee, *Ireland 1912–1985. Politics and Society* (Cambridge, 1989).

Sidney Lee, *King Edward VII: A Biography*, 2 vols. (London, 1927).

John Lodge, *The Peerage of Ireland*, 4 vols. (Dublin, 1754).

Andrew Lyall, 'Irish heraldic jurisdiction', in *The Coat of Arms, NS, x, no. 164* (Winter, 1993); pp.134–42; *x, no. 165* (Spring, 1994), pp. 178–87; *x, no. 166* (Summer, 1994) pp. 238–44; *x, no. 167* (Autumn, 1994), pp. 266–75.

Christopher and Adrian Lynch-Robinson, *Intelligible Heraldry* (London, 1948).

Charles Lysaght, *Edward MacLysaght, 1886–1986* (Dublin, 1988).

Virginia Wade McAnlis, *The Consolidated Index to the Records of the Genealogical Office, Dublin* (Issaguah, Washington, 1994).

Terence Francis McCarthy, *Ulster's Office, 1552–1800. A History of the Irish Office of Arms From the Tudor Plantations to the Act of Union* (Arkansas, 1996).

John McColgan, *British Policy and Irish Administration* (Dublin, 1983).

R.B. McDowell, *Land and Learning: Two Dublin Clubs* (Dublin, 1993).

—— *The Irish Administration 1801–1914* (London, 1964).

Bibliography

Michael McDunphy, *The President of Ireland. His Powers, Functions and Duties* (Dublin, 1945).

Edward MacLysaght, *Changing Times. Ireland Since 1898* (Gerard's Cross, 1978).

—— *Irish Families. Their Names, Arms and Origins* (Dublin, 1957).

—— *Short Study of a Transplanted Family in the Seventeenth Century* (Dublin, 1935).

Edward McParland, *Public Architecture in Ireland, 1680–1760* (Yale, 2001).

James H. Murphy, *Abject Loyalty. Nationalism and Monarchy in Ireland During the Reign of Queen Victoria* (Cork, 2001).

David Neligan, *The Spy in the Castle* (Dublin, 1968).

Mark Noble, *History of the College of Arms* (London, 1805).

Leon O'Brion, *Dublin Castle and the 1916 Rising* (London, 1970).

Séamus Ó Brógáin, *The Wolfhound Guide to the Irish Emblem* (Dublin, 1998).

Micheál Ó Comáin, *The Poolbeg Book of Irish Heraldry* (Dublin, 1991).

Gréagór Ó Dúill, 'Gilbert and the Public Record Office', in Mary Clark, Yvonne Desmond and Nodlaig Hardiman (eds.), *Sir John T. Gilbert 1829–1898, Historian, Archivist and Librarian* (Dublin, 1999), pp. 25–44.

Frederick O'Dwyer, *Lost Dublin* (Dublin, 1988).

Charles O'Mahony, *The Viceroys of Ireland* (Dublin, 1912).

Robert Perrin, *Jewels* (London, 1977).

P.B. Phair, 'Sir William Betham's manuscripts', in *Analecta Hibernica, 27* (1972), pp. 3–99.

L.G. Pine, *The Story of Heraldry* (London, 1963).

John M. Regan, *The Irish Counter-Revolution, 1921–1936* (Dublin, 1999).

Joseph Robins, *Champagne and Silver Buckles. The Viceregal Court at Dublin Castle, 1700–1922* (Dublin, 2001).

Sir Henry Robinson, *Memories: Wise and Otherwise* (London, 1923).

Mary Robinson, An tUachtarán, 'Address to the First Irish Genealogical Congress', 21 September 1991, in Eileen Ó Dúill and Mihail Evans (eds.), *Aspects of Irish Genealogy, I* (Dublin, 1991), pp. 7–8.

J. Ross of Bladensburg and Nevile Wilkinson, *A History of the Coldstream Guards 1815–1895* (London, 1896).

Randal Sadleir, *Tanzania. Journey to Republic* (London, 1999).

Thomas U. Sadleir (ed.,) *An Irish Peer on the Continent* (London, 1920).

Thomas U. Sadleir and Page L. Dickinson, *Georgian Mansions in Ireland with Some Account of the Evolution of Georgian Architecture and Decoration* (Dublin, 1915).

T.U. Sadleir, 'The romance of Dublin Castle: personalities and pomp in the famous citadel of British rule', in William G. Fitzgerald, *The Voice of Ireland* (Dublin, 1924), pp. 57–61.

T.U. Sadleir and Charles W. Seagrave, *The Seagrave Family, 1066–1935* (London, 1936).

T.U. Sadleir, 'Ulster's Office records', in *Genealogists' Magazine, vi, xi* (1934), pp. 434–8.

Brendan Sexton, *Ireland and the Crown, 1922–1936. The Governor-Generalship of the Irish Free State* (Dublin, 1989).

Gerard Slevin, 'George Dames Burtchaell', in *Carloviana, 1, NS, 18,* (December 1969), pp. 19–22.

—— 'Irish Heraldry', in *Ireland of the Welcomes*, 61 (1957), pp. 19–22.

—— 'The Irish Genealogical Office', in Hugh Montgomery-Massingberd, *Burke's Introduction to Irish Ancestry* (London, 1976), pp. 51–5.

Theo Snoddy, *Dictionary of Irish Artists. Twentieth Century* (Dublin, 1996).

A.T.Q. Stewart, *The Ulster Crisis. Resistance to Home Rule, 1912–14* (Reprint, London, 1969).

Walter G. Strickland, *A Dictionary of Irish Artists* (Dublin, 1913).

Daisy Lawrenson Swanton, *Emerging From the Shadow* (Dublin, 1994).

The Complete Peerage or a History of the House of Lords and all its Members From the Earliest Times (London, 1959).

Thom's Directory (Dublin, 1922–).

Klaus Unger and Angela Rolfe, *Dublin Castle Architectural Report* (Dublin, OPW, 1983).

Anthony Wagner, *A Herald's World* (London, 1988).

—— *The Records and Collections of the College of Arms* (London, 1952).

Alan J. Ward, *The Irish Constitutional Tradition* (Dublin, 1994).

Nevile Rodwell Wilkinson, 'Heraldry in relation to archaeology', in *Royal Society of Antiquaries of Ireland Journal, 5th series, xx* (1910), pp. 52–5.

—— *Titania's Palace. Illustrated Guide,* (21st ed., London, 1926).

—— *To All and Singular* (London, [1925]).

—— *Yvette in Italy and Titania's Palace* (London, 1922).

—— *Yvette in Switzerland and Titania's Palace* (Oxford, 1926).

—— *Yvette in Venice and Titania's Palace* (Oxford, 1927).

—— *Yvette in the USA with Titania's Palace* (London [1930]).

Nicholas Williams, *Armas* (Coiscéim, 2001).

Arthur Vicars, *An Account of the Antiseptic Vaults Beneath St Michan's Church, Dublin* (Dublin, 1888).

—— 'Heraldic notes on the monuments in St Audoen's Church, Dublin', in *Irish Builder*, xxix, (1887), p. 205.

—— *Index to the Prerogative Wills of Ireland 1536–1810* (Dublin, 1897).

—— 'Old Bawn, County Dublin', in *Journal of the Kildare Archaeological Society, v* (1906–8), pp. 52–5.

Who Was Who, 1916–28 (London, 1929).

Who's Who, 1929 (London, 1929).

Index

Index

Index

Canada, Prime Minister of, 253
Canterbury, 59
Captain John McCartan, 225
Casement, Roger, 233
Cassidi, Francis Laird, Honorary Surgeon to
  King George VI, 197
Cassidi, Francis Patrick, 197
Castle Season, 12, 46, 49, 70, 73, 76
Castle Street, Dublin, 49, 95, 214, 233
Castlebar, County Mayo, 217
Castleknock, County Dublin, parish church
  of, 177
Castletown, Lord, 53, 55, 76, 90, 152
Catholic, 18, 169, 176, 212, 221, 222
Catholic Church, 197
  archbishop of Armagh, 197
  bishops, 221
  families, 222
  parish registers of, 221
Cavan, County of, 217
Celtic art, 79, 152
Central Chancery of the Orders of
  Knighthood, 142
ceremonial events, xiii, xx, 1, 6, 16, 17, 18,
  19, 23, 27, 39, 39, 41, 59, 61, 65, 89,
  92, 94, 99, 105, 107, 156, 172
ceremonial books, xviii, 6
ceremonial dress, 29, 101
certificates of arms, 167, 182, 197, 211
Ceylon, 69
Chamberlain, office of the, 46, 61, 110, 135
Chamney, William, 33
Chancellor of the Exchequer, 146
Chandos, John, xiv
changes of name, 142, 203, 208
Chapel Royal, Dublin Castle, 45
Carney, Richard, Principal Herald for the
Dominion of Ireland, xix
Chart, David Alfred, 51, 162, 164
Chelsea, 2
Chief Genealogical Officer, 173, 188
Chief Herald and Genealogical Officer, 188,
  200
Chief Herald of Ireland, xxiv, xxv, 79, 148,
  173, 185, 200, 201, 202, 204, 205, 208,
  219, 221, 227, 229, 231, 232, 238, 239,
  240, 243, 244, 245, 246, 247, 249, 250,
  251, 253, 254, 255

link with directorship of the National
  Library of Ireland, 245, 247
proposed separation from the National
  Library of Ireland, 249
seal of, 201
title of, 201
Chief Justice of the Irish Free State, 137
Chief Secretary for Ireland, 22, 28, 72
Chief Secretary's Office, 13, 63, 97
chiefs of the name, 207
China, 72
Christ Church Cathedral, Dublin, 157
Christian cross, 228
Christianity, xiv
  non-Christian, 228
Church of Ireland, 6, 17, 76, 97, 123, 176,
  177, 178, 186, 194, 195, 212
  Archbishop of Dublin, 76, 178
  archbishops of, 18
  Bishop of Meath, 17
  bishops of, 17
  records of, 212
Church of the Latter-Day Saints, 222, 255
Churchill, John Winston Spencer, seventh
  Duke of Marlborough, 15, 18, 19
Churchill, Winston, 112, 138, 159, 160, 161
Civil War, xxi, xxiii, 113, 118, 125, 255
clan arms, 205
Clancy, John Joseph, MP, 22
Clare, County of, 72, 176, 179
Clare, Wallace, 238
Clarenceux King of Arms, xvi, 194, 247
Clerk of the Crown and Hanaper, 109, 116
Clinton, President Bill, 253
Clonskeagh, County Dublin, 39
Clyde Road, Donnybrook, County Dublin, 39
Coldstream Guards, 67, 69
Collectanea Genealogica, 7
College Green, Dublin, xix, 36, 242
College of Arms, London, xiv, xvi, xvii, 12, 23,
  27, 34, 40, 83, 130, 141, 142, 145, 146,
  149, 160, 161, 162, 163, 169, 170, 182,
  190, 191, 192, 193, 194, 196, 197, 208
  heraldic commissions, 194
  negotiations about Irish heraldic
    jurisdiction, 193
  registers of, 194
  re-registration of grants in, 197

Index

Index

Elizabeth II, Queen, 141, 208
Ellis, Eilish, 186, 225, 236
Emerson, James Corry, 157
England, xiv, 6, 25, 40, 62, 69, 110, 115, 117, 129, 133, 144, 145, 167, 169, 174, 176
Enniskillen, County Fermanagh, 157
Erasmus Smith Schools, 198
Euro, 229
Europe, xiv, xv, 78, 92, 96, 228, 229, 241
European Economic Community, 229
European emblem, 227
European flag, xxv, 228
European Union, 227, 229
Eustace, P. Beryl, 148, 153, 184, 186 *see also* Phair
Eustace Street, Dublin, xxi
Evening Herald, 166, 221
Exchequer, British, 141, 146
Exchequer, Irish Free State, 137, 240
Executive Authority (External Relations) Act 1936, 151
exemplification of arms, 8
External Affairs, Department of, 150, 151,153, 158, 159, 160, 161, 192, 193, 224

Faculty of Notaries Public in Ireland, 237, 238
Farnham Papers, 34
Farrell, Mary, 70
Farrell, Mr, coal carrier, 96
fees of honour, 9, 10
Fenian, 191
Fermanagh, County of, 157
ffolliott, Rosemary, 186, 215, 239
Fianna Fáil, 139, 143, 149, 150, 248
Figgis, Allen, 206
Finance, Department of, 135, 165
Finance, Minister for, 135, 138
Fintona, County Tyrone, 131
First World War, xxiii, 72, 73, 77, 78, 89, 92, 94, 96, 105, 122, 126, 127, 145, 160
Fisheries, Inspectors of, 45
FitzAlan, Viscount of Derwent, 99, 105, 106
Fitzgerald, Lord Walter, 31, 57, 107
Fitzgerald, of Desmond, 223
Fortescue, Sir Chichester, xx

Four Courts, Dublin, xxiii, 8, 14, 112, 114, 115, 116, 138
Foxrock, County Dublin, 201
France, 128, 173, 208, 225
Franciscan College, Multyfarnham, 198
Free State Government, 65, 103, 105, 107, 118, 120, 121, 122, 134, 136, 138, 139, 140, 141, 142
French genealogists, 225
French record system, 13
French repositories, xx, 168
Froissart, *Chronicles* of, xiv
Fuller, James, 64
Funeral Entries, 5, 6, 9, 19, 25, 57, 107
Gaelic ancestry, 179
Gaelic heraldry, xv, 7, 204, 207
Gaelic mottoes, 41
Gaelic nobility, xix
Gaelic titles, 207
Galway, 131
Garda Síochána, 195, 238
Garter King of Arms, xvi, 34, 42, 164, 181, 193, 194
Gas, Weights and Measures Commission, 135
Gayrne, Lieutenant-Colonel George Robert,194
genealogical consultancy service, 244, 252
genealogical enquiries, rate of, 94, 118, 167, 187, 211, 236
genealogical functions, 168, 201
Genealogical Office, xiii, xiv, xxiv, xxv, 19, 165, 167, 168, 172, 175, 187, 188, 192, 193, 194, 200, 201, 204, 206, 209, 210, 221, 243, 244, 248
all Ireland status, 251
arms of, 189, 199, 209
arrears of work, 185
fees of, 190, 236, 243, 252
heraldic commissions, 194, 236, 243, 252
introduction of title, xiii, 168, 171
legal position of, 202, 204
misnomer of title, 253
recruitment of staff, 184, 185, 205, 235
registers of, 203
re-registration of grants in, 197
reversion to title of Office of Arms, 210
seal of, 106, 188, 189

Index

Herlihy, Sergeant Daniel, 71, 98
Hibernian Bank, 220
Hibernian Research Ltd, 236
Hibernian School, 19
Hicks-Beach, Sir Michael, Chief Secretary for Ireland, 22
Higgins, Michael D., 245, 248
Hillery, Dr Patrick, 211
Hillsborough Castle, County Down, 111
His Majesty's Stationery Office, 33, 111
historical research, 170
Hobson, Bulmer, 54, 56
Hodgson, J.C., antiquary, 50, 63
Holyhead, 19
Home Affairs, Minister of, 138
Home Office, 58, 62, 108, 112, 120, 123, 125, 134, 141
Home Rule, 22, 41, 80, 82, 86, 96, 135
    anti-Home Rule movement, 80
Home Rule Bill, 80
Honan Hostel, Cork, 79
honorary degrees, 253
honours, creation of, 9
Horlock, Sydney, 59, 60
Houghton, Lord, 30
House of Commons, 4, 11, 40, 72
House of Lords, Dublin, xviii, xix
Howard, Algar Henry Stafford, first Norroy and Ulster King of Arms, 162, 181
Huband, Revd Hugo, 77
Hughes, Séamus, 135
Hyde, Douglas, 153, 200

Illinois, 132
Imperial Government, 109
Inchiquin, Lord, 179
Index of Surnames, created by the National Library of Ireland, 220
Inland Revenue Department, 125
Inspectors of Fisheries, 45, 46
Institute of Bankers, 220
Institute of Chartered Accountants, 220
Intelligible Heraldry, 201
Internet, and genealogical research, 245, 252
Ireland, 2, 40, 127, 149, 227
    arms of, xv, 77, 80, 110, 120, 121, 125, 143, 144, 145, 152, 174, 189, 200, 209, 223, 242

Government of, xiii, xiv, xxiv, 55, 64, 79, 81, 119, 133, 137, 141, 143, 146, 148, 151, 152, 153, 160, 161, 162, 165, 167, 169, 170, 172, 175, 179, 184, 189, 193, 198, 207, 209, 222, 248, 251, 255, 256
    Government Seal of, 152, 189
    Lordship of, xv
Ireland of the Welcomes, 220
Ireland, flag of, 143
Iris Oifigiuíl, 207
Irish Bar, 91
Irish Border, xxiv, 119, 158, 161, 196, 197, 201, 247, 251
Irish Builder, 25
Irish Cabinet, 201
Irish Chieftains, 207
Irish Club, London, 197
Irish Convention, 176
Irish Crown Jewels, xxii, 17, 31, 36, 45, 50, 60, 62, 63, 64, 75, 77, 106, 233, 242
    speculated recovery of, 65
    theft of, 52, 53
Irish Families: Their Names, Arms and Origins, 206
Irish Free State, xiii, xxiii, 103, 106, 108, 109, 113, 119, 120, 137, 140, 142, 146, 150, 151, 177
    cabinet of, 140
    Constitution of, 105, 106, 132, 151
    Executive Council of, 139
    fiscal and postage stamps, 122
    flag of, 120, 121, 139
    Government of, 65, 103, 105, 107, 118, 120, 121, 122, 134, 135, 136, 138, 139, 140, 141, 142
    Governor-General of, 103, 106, 119, 122, 140, 141, 151
    Seal of, 121, 122
    stamp-duty in, 125
    telephone charges, 129
Irish Genealogical Congress, 243, 244
Irish Genealogical Project, 245
Irish Genealogical Research Society, 241
Irish Genealogy: A Record Finder, 238
Irish Guards, 71
Irish heraldic authority, 2, 22, 24, 27, 28, 149, 167, 187, 199, 229, 252

Index

Index

Index

Index

Index